Lovin' That

LONE STAR FLAG

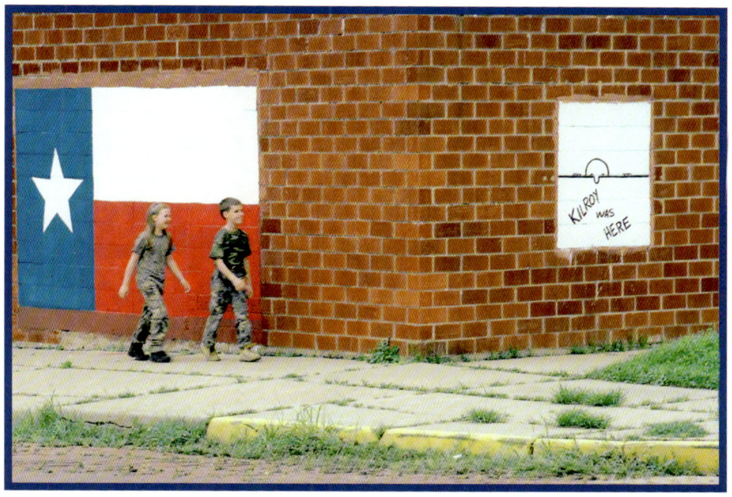

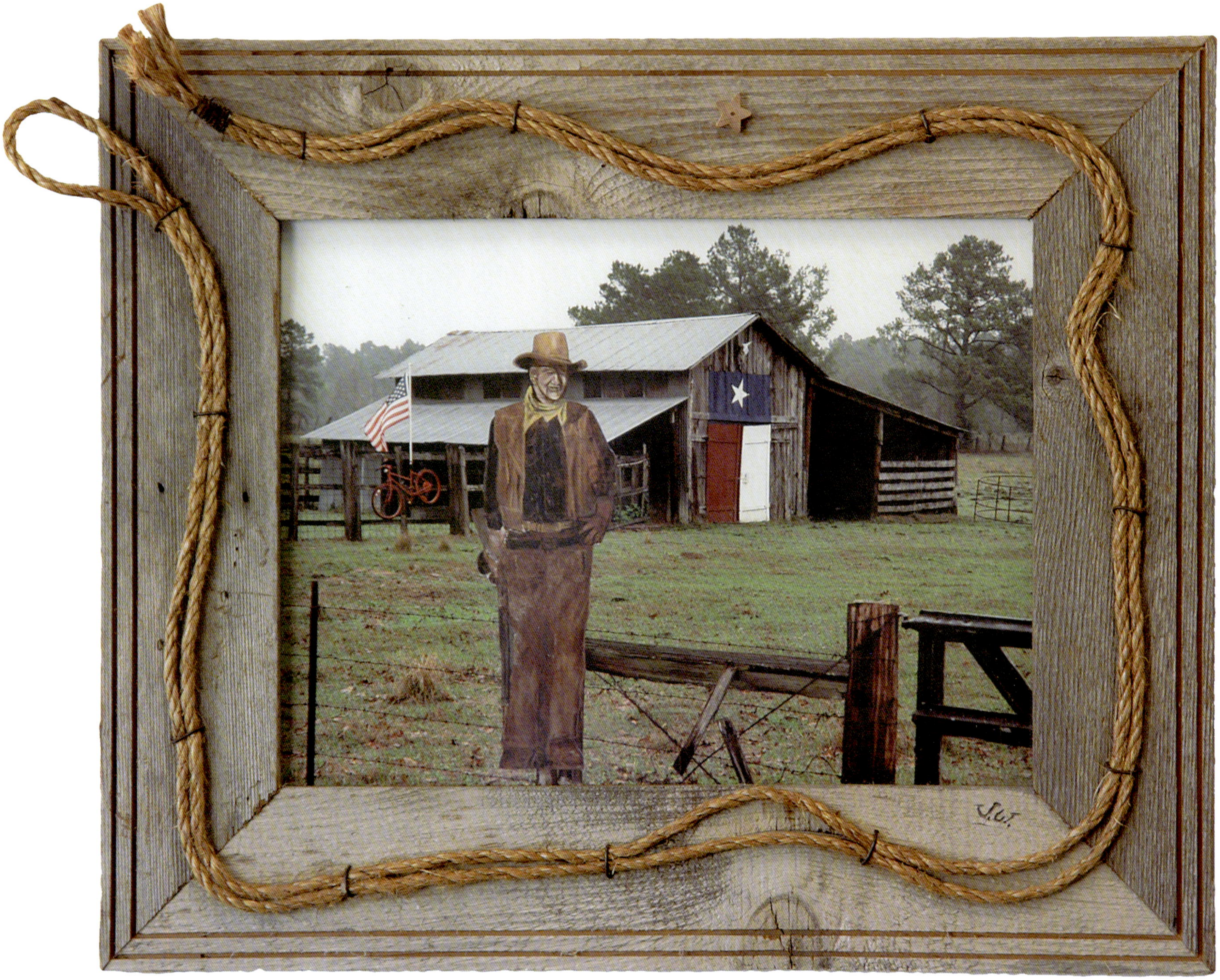

Lovin' That
LONE STAR FLAG

E. Joe Deering

With an introduction & afterword by Ruth Rendon

TEXAS A&M UNIVERSITY PRESS
COLLEGE STATION

Manufactured in China
by Everbest Printing Co. through
Four Colour Printing Group

First edition

This paper meets the requirements
of ANSI/NISO Z39.48-1992
(Permanence of Paper).
Binding materials have been chosen
for durability.
∞

LIBRARY OF CONGRESS CATALOGING-IN-PUBLICATION DATA

Deering, E. Joe, 1943–
Lovin' that Lone Star flag / E. Joe Deering ; with an
introduction and afterword by Ruth Rendon. — 1st ed.
p. cm.
Includes index.
ISBN-13: 978-1-60344-148-3 (cloth : alk. paper)
ISBN-10: 1-60344-148-4 (cloth : alk. paper)
1. Flags—Social aspects—Texas—Pictorial works.
2. Photography of flags—Texas—Pictorial works.
3. Photography of flags—Texas—Exhibitions.
4. Flags in art—Pictorial works. 5. Flags in art—
Exhibitions. 6. Emblems, State—Social aspects—Texas—
Pictorial works. I. Rendon, Ruth. II. Title.
CR114.T4D44 2009
779'.99299209764—dc22
2009008255

Dedicated to the memory of my buddy,

Bill Arnold.

★

In his lifetime,

he was always there for me.

Contents

Acknowledgments

No book is ever a singular effort, especially one such as this that includes the creativity of so many people. First, I wish to acknowledge the proud Texans pictured herein who lovingly display the Lone Star flag—on barns, water tanks, boats, trains, planes, automobiles, and plenty more—proudly for all to see, and who invited me into their homes and lives with open and friendly arms.

I also want to thank the following people who helped with this project: Mark Burns, friend and photographer. Without him this project, exhibit, and book would not be complete. Thanks, Mark.

The editors and photo staff of the *Houston Chronicle* for their continued support and help—especially John Janik and Bruno Torres. Thanks go also to the five photo chiefs—Bob Maxwell, George Honeycutt, Dave Einsel, John Davidson, and Steve Gonzales––who directed my career.

Mary Lenn Dixon, Editor-in-Chief at Texas A&M University Press, who could inspire a turtle to break the speed limit; Patricia Burchfield, deputy director of the George Bush Presidential Library and Museum, and her staff, who started the project rolling; Skye Alexander: without her guidance and intelligence I surely would have been lost.

Jeff Hood of Hood Real Estate, for all his solid support. And finally, my six sisters: Lucy, Annabella, Mari Magooshie, Cora, Roza, and Nyda Joy. I hope they can take a little pride in their only brother.

Lovin' That
LONE STAR FLAG

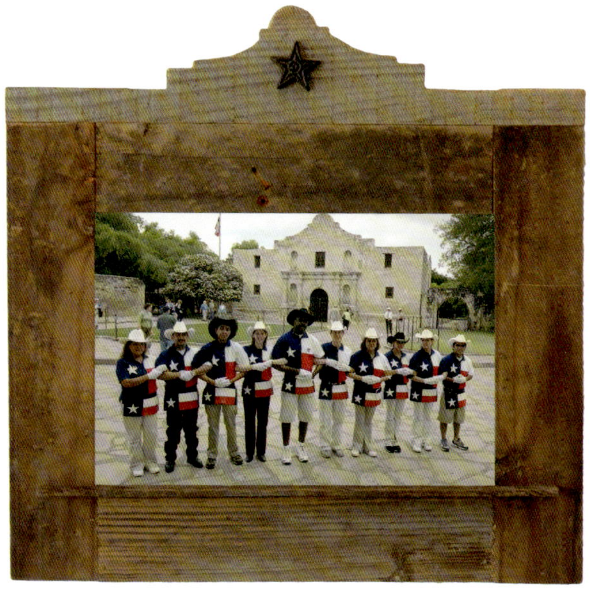

Introduction

THE LONE STAR FLAG flies boldly from poles around the state—it waves in front of state office buildings and the capitol in Austin. It flutters over sports stadiums and businesses. It hangs in schoolrooms and flies in front of rural and urban homes alike. Historian Robert Maberry Jr. rightly says in his book *Texas Flags* that "the design, brilliant in its simplicity and visually unforgettable, remains one of the best-known symbols in the world."

But not all the flags are on flagpoles. Texans love that Lone Star flag, and they use its likeness to adorn restaurants and outbuildings, mailboxes and bird feeders, shirts, hats and ties, cars, airplanes, and hot air balloons. (Hot air? Texans?)

Drive along the interstates or travel the back roads, ride through small towns or big cities. Wherever you go in Texas, you are likely to spot some creative use of the state flag that celebrates a history and identity famous far beyond the state lines. That is what E. Joe Deering, then a photographer for the *Houston Chronicle,* discovered as he toured the state following story leads. Starting in 2000, his camera snapped the colorful images wherever he found them, and he spent hours talking to the folk artists who had honored the Texas flag. In 2005 the George Bush Presidential Museum in College Station exhibited a selection of 137 of his photographs, framed in his own imaginative creations from scrap lumber and "do-dads."

This volume showcases some 124 of those photographs, demonstrating the range of uses Texans make of their banner and the spirit that motivates them to do it.

Texas Pride and the Decorative Urge

Every story of using the Texas flag is different, but they all have one thing in common: Texas pride. Don Jones, whose flag-painted water tank is shown on page 100, tells the story of his flag art. "All my adult life I've flown the Texas flag," he says. "You could say I've got the passion of Texas." After retiring as business manager for the Hamilton Independent School District in 2000, he was ready for some new challenges. That June he went to the Texas Music Nation's first annual Texas Music Fest in Glen Rose. "There were Texas flags on everything there: RVs, barbecue grills, shirts, hats, chairs . . . everything. I saw how much others liked the Texas flag, and I could imagine it on the 7,000-gallon water tank on my land. It needed some cleaning up and a good paint job, and I could suddenly see this pattern for it."

Jones came home and started planning. He turned to the Internet for the flag's dimensions and with his wife, Pam, drew up a plan that came as close as possible to the prescribed ratios for the long, lean water tank on his family's place near Lanham. Pam drew the star to scale on a piece of stiff cardboard, and Don found implement paint that came close to the shades of the flag. On the three-day Labor Day weekend, Don put his plan in action. He marked off the lines, taped the star in place, and used a paint roller to reproduce the Lone Star flag.

"Even while I was still painting," he remembers, "as soon as you could see what it was going to be, people started slowing down as they drove past. They'd wave and honk and holler. I could tell it was going to be a hit." In those three days, he finished the paint job, creating an instant landmark along Highway 22 between Cranfill's Gap and Hamilton. The art work was not cheap, at $22.00 a gallon for the paint, but the response to his flag has given Jones great satisfaction. "I had a sense of accomplishment. People in the community seem to be proud of it, and it helps us share our pride in being Texans."

Indeed, the community does appear to share Don's attachment to the flag. When the exhibition of Deering's flag photographs opened at the Bush Museum in July 2005, Don's local newspaper, the *Hamilton Herald-News,* ran a front-page story with a picture of Don standing beside his water tank and wearing a Texas-flag-design shirt.

In 2007, as the shine on the water tank's flag had started to dim, Don began planning a new paint job to bring the colors back to life. "I'd never fly a Texas flag at night without a light on it, just like the rules for the U.S. flag, and I don't want the daytime flag to look dim, either." The sixty-year-old Jones hopes someone will keep the flag painted after he is gone. "It's something I'm proud of, something I can leave behind."

Don Jones is a fourth-generation Texan, but even transplants to the state come to honor the Texas flag. Bruce Lavorgna moved to Texas in the 1970s. "I wasn't born in Texas but I've been in the state for almost thirty years and I'm proud about where I live," he explains. Lavorgna features the Lone Star banner on the hot air balloon he flies. He had it custom-made in England in 1993. A few weeks after he sent his design for the hot air balloon, Lavorgna received a fax from the company saying they were having a difficult time putting a five-pointed star on the balloon. "We can do a lovely six-pointed star. Please let us know what you want us to do," the fax said.

"We sent them a fax back and said, 'Hey guys, I want a five-pointed star and if it's a little distorted I'll understand. Now let's deal,'" Lavorgna remembers. The balloon finally arrived, and the price came down from $2,000 to $700 for the star. "They actually built the top of the balloon twice before they were happy with it. They did a beautiful job."

Lavorgna's balloon (p. 81) gets a lot of looks. "Everybody loves it. There is no mistaking what it is. We get a lot of attention even from people who aren't from Texas," he says.

Deering spent months trying to arrange a photograph of the balloon. He had taken pictures of it during a hot air balloon festival in Albuquerque, New Mexico, but he wanted to shoot the picture from another balloon, so Lavorgna made arrangements with a friend who had a hot air balloon to fly Deering. All parties agreed, but that turned out to be the easy part.

Besides getting Deering's schedule to line up with Lavorgna's and the second ballooner's, the weather also had to be perfect. "I did this on my own time," Deering said, "and they had to work it in on their own time. A lot of times I could do it, but they couldn't, and vice versa. A lot had to do with the weather. We'd schedule one weekend that we could both do it, but the weather conditions wouldn't be right. It was too windy or too overcast or otherwise not conducive to hot air balloon flying. It took us well over six months to get that scheduled."

After months of trying, Deering received a call at his Houston home at 3:00 A.M. "I called him and said 'get up here,'" Lavorgna said. Deering did as he was told and met Lavorgna in Pflugerville.

Lavorgna remembers the day as being unique. "They came over the top of me two different times. I went up and flew over them, dropped back down and then they went over me," he said. "All the conditions were right. E. Joe caught an image of me running the burner. The sun was below the balloon and they were looking down on me from about 1 000 feet above me and the sun was just over the horizon. The picture is spectacular . . . but I am a little prejudiced."

Although the picture of the Texas flag hot air balloon looks pristine in the sunny skies, the hot air balloon in which Deering was flying got caught in a burst of wind and hit a fence post, crash landed, and dragged some fifty feet across a field. "We hit the fence and tumbled. I lost a roll of film," Deering said. "I went one way, the pilot went another way, the basket went a different way, and my camera gear went still another way. We found a couple of rolls okay. Fortunately, the one picture that was a good photo was on one of the rolls that we found. I totally lost one roll of film on that assignment. We just couldn't find it; it's out in that field somewhere."

During E. Joe's crash landing, the Texas flag hot air balloon and Lavorgna sailed serenely on.

Brazoria County was where Deering ran into Texas Land Commissioner Jerry Patterson. Patterson was attending a news conference in Lake Jackson where Deering was assigned to shoot photos for the *Chronicle*. Patterson, who loves to boast all things Texan, was wearing a crisp, white button-down shirt and a tie with waving Texas flags on it.

"I noticed his tie. I asked him if I could photograph it. I explained to him how I wanted to do it. I don't think he thought I was too sane but I did it. I explained that it was just the tie I was after," E. Joe said.

Patterson was a good sport and obliged. He was going to remove the two gold pens he had in his chest pocket. "No, no, no. We want to keep the pens," Deering insisted. The image E. Joe captured showed a little bit of Patterson's neck above the waving Texas flag with the white shirt as a backdrop.

Patterson wholeheartedly agrees that the Lone Star flag is recognized worldwide. During a week-long trip to Iraq, Patterson said he noticed numerous Texas-based National Guard units and reservists. "You can tell. Anybody from Texas has got their flag flying somewhere. That's just how Texans are. It's a flag recognized around the world. Show a California flag and a New York flag and you'd get people saying, 'What is that?' Show them the Texas flag, and they say, 'That's Texas.'"

It's true. Texans who move elsewhere in the United States or the world have a marked tendency to take the Texas flag with them. You'll find it decorating their living rooms, their kitchens—sometimes flying from their front porches.

In his travels, Patterson said he has found that most Americans, when traveling abroad and asked, "where are you from?" will say, "I'm from the U.S." Ask any traveling Texan and the answer will be, "I'm from Texas." "It's the same thing with the flag," Patterson said. "It's state pride."

One of Deering's favorite stories of his flag-hunting expedition began when he was in New Braunfels in Comal County for an assignment. A gentleman who overheard him talking about his pet project asked Deering if he knew musician Doug Moreland from Manchaca. "He has a Cadillac that's painted like a flag," the man told him.

"How do I get hold of him?" Deering asked. The man handed E. Joe Moreland's telephone number.

With Moreland's travel schedule, it took about a year for Deering to connect with him. The plan was for Deering to meet him at his home, on the outskirts of Austin. Moreland and his wife would drive the restored 1972 Cadillac, complete with a pair of longhorns on the hood, and Deering would follow behind as they headed downtown to the state Capitol.

"It was like a one-car parade," E. Joe chuckles. "People were honking and waving at them. At every stop people were taking pictures. It was all because of the car. Everybody was just getting a big kick out of it."

Deering envisioned Moreland driving down Congress Avenue while he snapped a picture with the Capitol in the background. Once they got to the state Capitol, they put the plan in action, with Deering shooting from the back of a pickup truck driven by one of Moreland's friends.

"But it wasn't working," E. Joe recalls. "There was too much traffic." So he pulled over and told Moreland he needed to get closer to the Capitol. Scoping it out, Deering found the perfect location: the sidewalk near the circular drive of the Capitol. He wanted Moreland to back up his car onto the sidewalk. Moreland didn't see a problem with that, but a trooper from the Texas Department of Public Safety soon did.

Deering and company had to explain the project to the female trooper, who fortunately proved understanding. "She walked up to me and said, 'I'll give you five minutes.'"

The trooper ended up redirecting traffic around Deering, giving him a clear shot of Moreland and his car with the Capitol in the background. The trooper's car also made it into the picture (p. 41).

Deering had a particularly strong personal interest in a series of photos he took at a Loyola University graduation ceremony—the only pictures for the exhibit taken outside the borders of the Lone Star State. If folks attending the event were not familiar with the Texas flag before then, they were after Hope Arnold of Houston, Deering's goddaughter, graduated.

Hope's late father had been E. Joe's best friend, and after his death, Hope and her sister, Joy, had maintained a close relationship with Deering. The girls knew of his flag project, so when Hope was about to graduate, she and her sister fashioned the top of her graduation cap to look like the Texas flag. "She invited me to attend her graduation," Deering said. "She said, 'Uncle E. Joe, if I put a Lone Star flag on my cap, will you take a picture of it?'"

How could he refuse? The exhibit at the George Bush Presidential Museum included a collage of six pictures of Hope.

A Single Star among Many?

Texans like to think of their flag as unique, and boosters often claim that it is. But other states use stars on their flags, and most have adopted some combination of the red, white, and blue colors. Not counting those which use stars in their great seals, seventeen other states have five-pointed stars on their banners. Four states (besides Texas) use single stars. On most flags, the stars represent either the original thirteen states or the number of states when they entered the union.

As the *Texas Almanac, 2006–2007* points out, Texas is one of only two states whose flags have flown as national flags; Hawaii is the other. Although Californians sometimes point to their Bear Republic flag (now the state flag) as another, the Bear Republic was in fact a failed revolt and never achieved recognized status.

The Flag We Love

The Lone Star flag was first adopted as the standard of the Republic of Texas in 1839, three years after the revolutionary birth of the nation. As Texas prepared to enter the United States, the Texian (a term often used to refer to Texans of the Republic period and before) legislature specified that the flag would serve the new state as it had the republic. As part of constitutional overhaul in 1879, the legislature scrapped all previous laws and substituted a new legal code. The solons failed to notice, though, that they had not reinstated the state flag. The state could therefore claim no official standard until 1933, when they passed a law re-establishing the Lone Star flag and further specifying aspects of its design.

Did the lone star always represent the individuality and independence Texans like to claim, or was it a clear signal that the infant republic planned to see its star added to the flag of the giant nation to the north and east? Robert Maberry says it was both. "Despite the Texians' intention to create a flag that would emphasize their independence they had self-consciously produced a design that was nothing more than a simplified version of the U.S. Stars and Stripes." Hurt pride at the refusal by the United States to admit Texas to statehood when it first won independence led the Texian flag committee to oppose "the transition of the single star into the American constellation." Hurt pride is, after all, still pride.

Once Texas entered the American union, the Republic's flag became the state flag. But during the mid-nineteenth century, state flags were not highly valued as symbols. The Stars and Stripes and the Confederate banner took center stage, depending on one's position north or south of the Mason-Dixon Line. It is perhaps not surprising, then, that the de-establishment of the state flag in 1879 slipped by without concern. Then how did Texas identity revive, to the point the state could credibly adopt slogans like "a whole other country" and "Don't mess with Texas"?

In 1906, the "Flag Song of Texas," composed by Aldridge B. Kidd with words by Lee C. Harby, was published with a picture of the Texian banner (a picture of this sheet music appears in *The Shape of Texas* by Richard V. Francaviglia). That song notwithstanding, state sentiment lay largely dormant in the late nineteenth and early twentieth century, in Texas as elsewhere. A nation was on the rise, and the imagery of nationalism held sway. After World War I, however, regionalism began to grow in popularity. In art, in literature, in popular culture, and even in urban planning, people started embracing the local. With the coming of the Depression, many looked to a romanticized past for comfort, identity, and hope. When the New Deal commissioned artists to create murals for post offices and other public buildings, the artists were expected to incorporate hope-inspiring local subject matter.

In Texas, there was an obvious focus for state identity: 1936 would be the 100th anniversary of the state's successful revolution against the Mexican government. In the 1920s the Advertising Clubs of Texas launched a movement to celebrate the centennial of Texas independence. Pride and patriotism were coupled with a large measure of economic self-interest in planning for the 1936 extravaganza, according to Kenneth B. Ragsdale's *Centennial '36: The Year America Discovered Texas*. When the Depression hit, many legislators and local business leaders worried that the cost of a centennial celebration was outlandish in a time of need, but others successfully argued that the movement would help advertise the state nationally and would stimulate both tourism and investment. In 1933 a series of legislative acts prepared for state observance of the anniversary. Among those acts was one that re-established the Lone Star as the state flag. Boosterism had found its symbol, and the forces of the State of Texas were enlisted in the cause of state pride, as well as state economic recovery. The flag flew again at the state Capitol, and its use soon spread with the swelling of Texas spirit.

Along with the flag, the state legislature in 1933 adopted a pledge to the flag that expressed and encouraged its celebratory spirit. The pledge was amended in 2007 to be recited as follows: "Honor the Texas flag; I pledge allegiance to thee, Texas, one state under God, one and indivisible." This pledge is recited in public school classrooms and assemblies around the state, but state law does not require this. Paragraph 3100.102 of the state code specifies "occasions at which the pledge may be recited" as "(1) public or private meeting at which the pledge of allegiance to the United States flag is recited; and (2) state historical events or celebrations."

The law also specifies how and when the flag is to be displayed. Longtime legend has it that the Texas flag is the only stage banner allowed to fly higher than the U.S. flag, but the legend is wrong. Both the U.S. flag etiquette code and Texas law treat the Lone Star like any other state flag. Among the many detailed provisions for displaying the Texas flag properly is the statement that it should not "be dipped to any person or thing, except as a mark of honor for the United States flag."

Nowhere does the state law say that the Lone Star pattern cannot be painted on walls, water tanks, or t-shirts. Our countryside would certainly be a lot less colorful if it did!

The law does suggest a "retirement" ceremony for flags that begin to look worn. The text of the ceremony, while a bit on the grandiose side, certainly reflects the uncritical enthusiasm with which many Texans view their state's banner:

I am your Texas flag!
I was born January 25, 1839.
I am one of only two flags of an American state that has also served
as the symbol of an independent nation—The Republic of Texas.
While you may honor me in retirement, the spirit I represent will never retire!
I represent the spirit of Texas—Yesterday, Today, and Tomorrow . . .
The blue field in me stands for the valor of our ancestors in the
battles for our country.
Let us retire the blue—Salute!
My white field stands for the purity in all our Texas hearts! It represents the honor
that each of us should pay to our State each day.
Let us retire the white—Salute!
The red is for all of the men and women who have died in service of our state—
whether as members of our armed services or as citizen Samaritans.
Let us retire the red—Salute!
My lone, independent star is recognized worldwide
because it represents ALL of Texas
and stands for our unity as one for God, State, and Country.
Let us retire the lone star—Salute!

Historian W. Fitzhugh Brundage has written (in *Lone Star Pasts: Memory and History in Texas)* that "mythic Texas is loud, brash, extravagant, and rustic." Nowhere is that more true than in this ceremony and the many other tributes to the Lone Star flag.

The Signs of Pride

Although the flag is known to almost any schoolchild in Texas, it is not the only symbol of state pride. The shape of the state itself has achieved the status of an icon. It is used in advertising, product design, and even landscaping. A whole book has been written about the symbolic use of the state map: *The Shape of Texas: Maps as Metaphors,* by Richard V. Francaviglia (Texas A&M University Press, 1995).

Besides the flag and the map, the state flower is probably the best-known symbol of the state. Who has not seen paintings and photographs of vibrantly beautiful bluebonnets in the Texas landscape? T-shirts, jewelry, wall plaques, and dishes are common carriers of the floral emblem of state pride. Jack Maguire has said that the bluebonnet is to Texas what the shamrock is to Ireland.

Among the lesser known emblems of the state are the state vegetable (the 1015 onion), the state fruit (red grapefruit), state pepper (jalapeno), state dish (chili), and state insect (monarch butterfly). Mammals are so abundant that it takes three to represent the state adequately: the state large mammal (longhorn), small mammal (armadillo), and flying mammal—yes, the official state *flying* mammal (Mexican free-tailed bat). And over them all flies the Lone Star flag.

So, how to account for Texas pride, as exemplified in Texans' eagerness to display their flag and its likeness at almost every opportunity? Historians demur at the explanations eagerly grasped by popular culture: the "Texas mythology" cobbled together from national independence, cowboys Comanches, pioneers, vaqueros, and Rangers. The true motivations for so many Texans' unmistakable pride in their state and its iconography may be both simpler and more complex than they know or would be able to verbalize. For whatever reason, Texans—both the native and transplanted varieties—have irreversibly wed themselves to their flag as an enduring symbol of the past, present, and future. It looms large in their consciousness. Wherever they go, it goes.

The Lone Star flag greets fans of Friday night high school football and flies outside the dance hall on Saturday night; it presides over town meetings and chili cookoffs. The flag of Texas drapes the walls of laundry-littered dorm rooms and provides a backdrop in austere courts of law. Not only that, but its irrepressible admirers have applied its image to pickups, caps, ties, water tanks, roofs, shirts, airplanes, stoves, bathtubs, and at least one hot air balloon.

I invite you to join me in appreciation of the proud Texans you'll meet in these pages. Enjoy the wide variety of their creative expressions of homage to the Lone Star State and its emblem. They are living evidence that for good or ill, amid sometimes annoying braggadocio, in good weather and bad, Texans certainly do love that Lone Star flag.

Flagatography

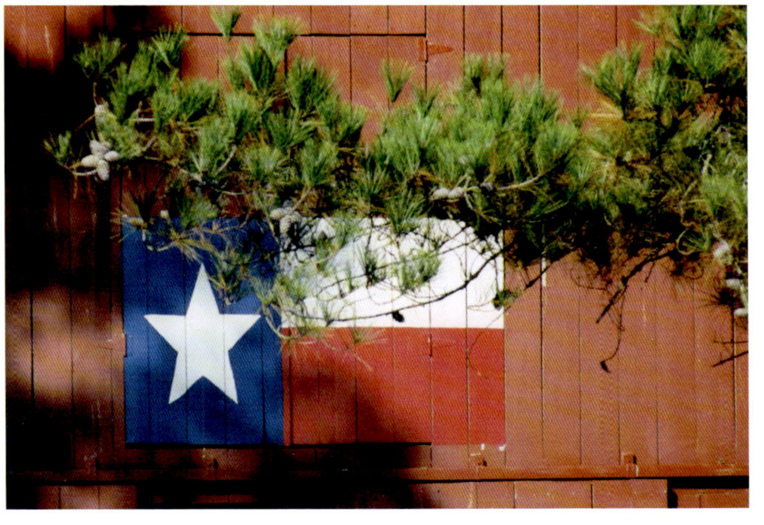

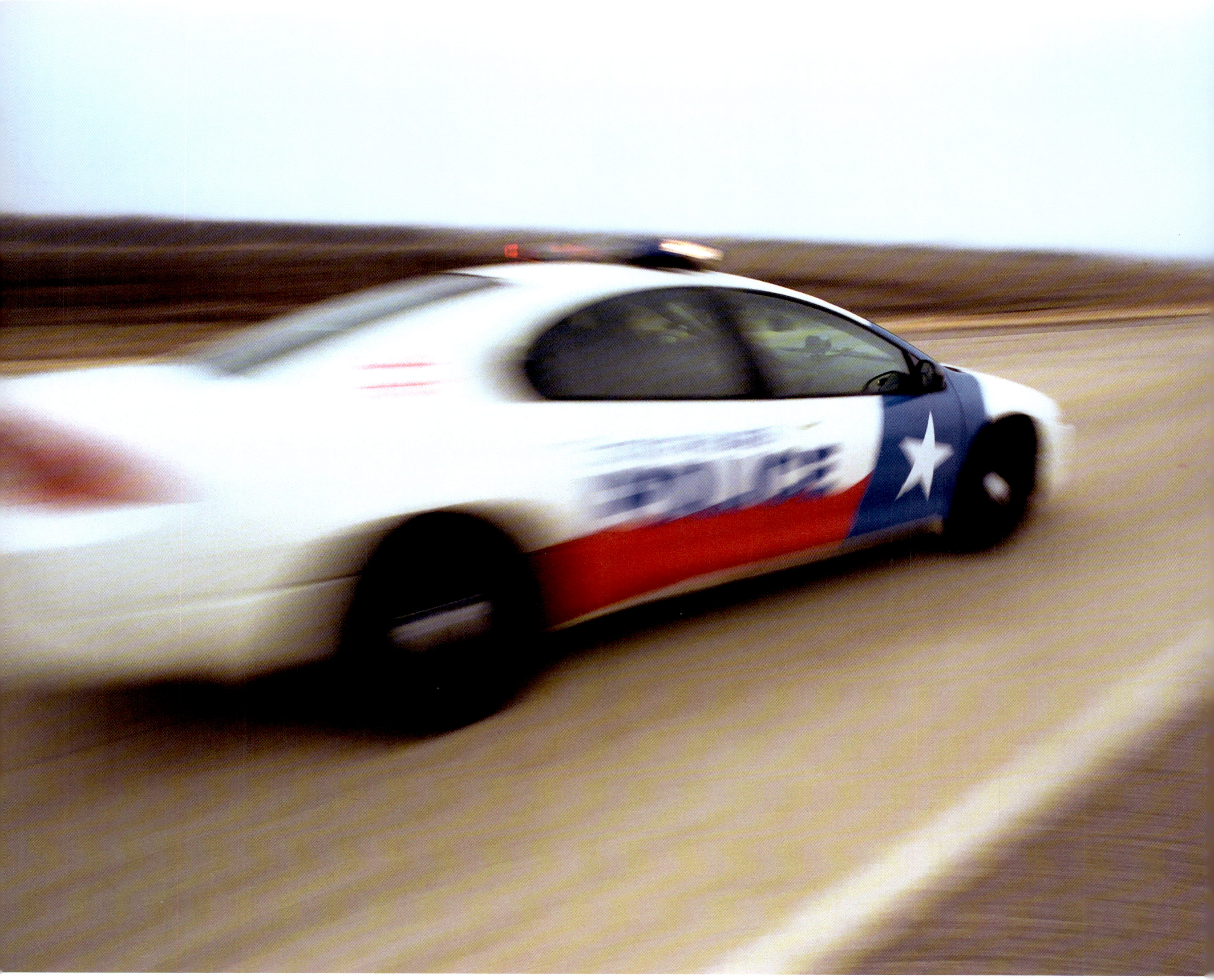

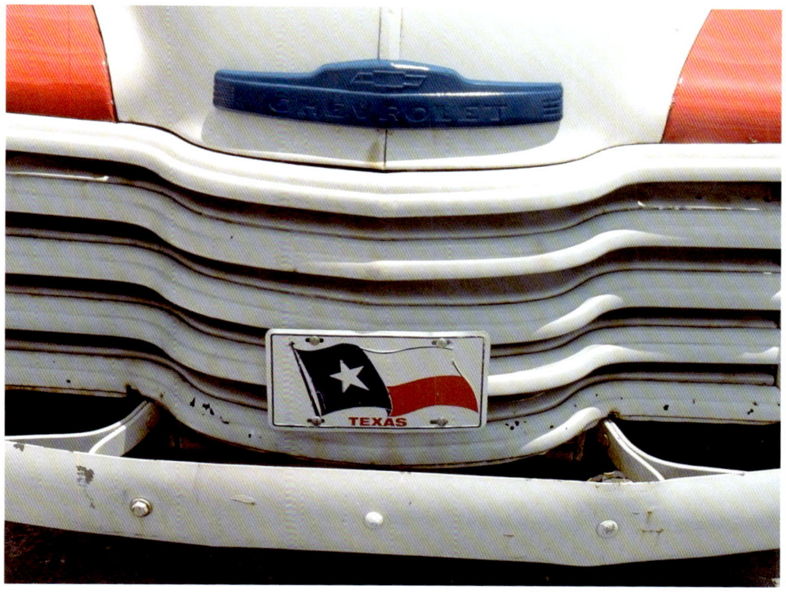

"Bumper"
(Rick Montana's 1949 Chevrolet truck, Houston), 2004

Rick Montana is a proud Texan who lives in Houston. His 1949 Chevy five-window pickup truck plate proudly displays the Lone Star flag.

"The Streak"
(Police car, Palmer), 2003

Stephen Sparks, chief of the Palmer Police Department, wanted his squad cars painted with the Lone Star flag to scream out their Texas pride. Palmer is a small north central country town located on Interstate 45 south of Dallas. Watch your speed.

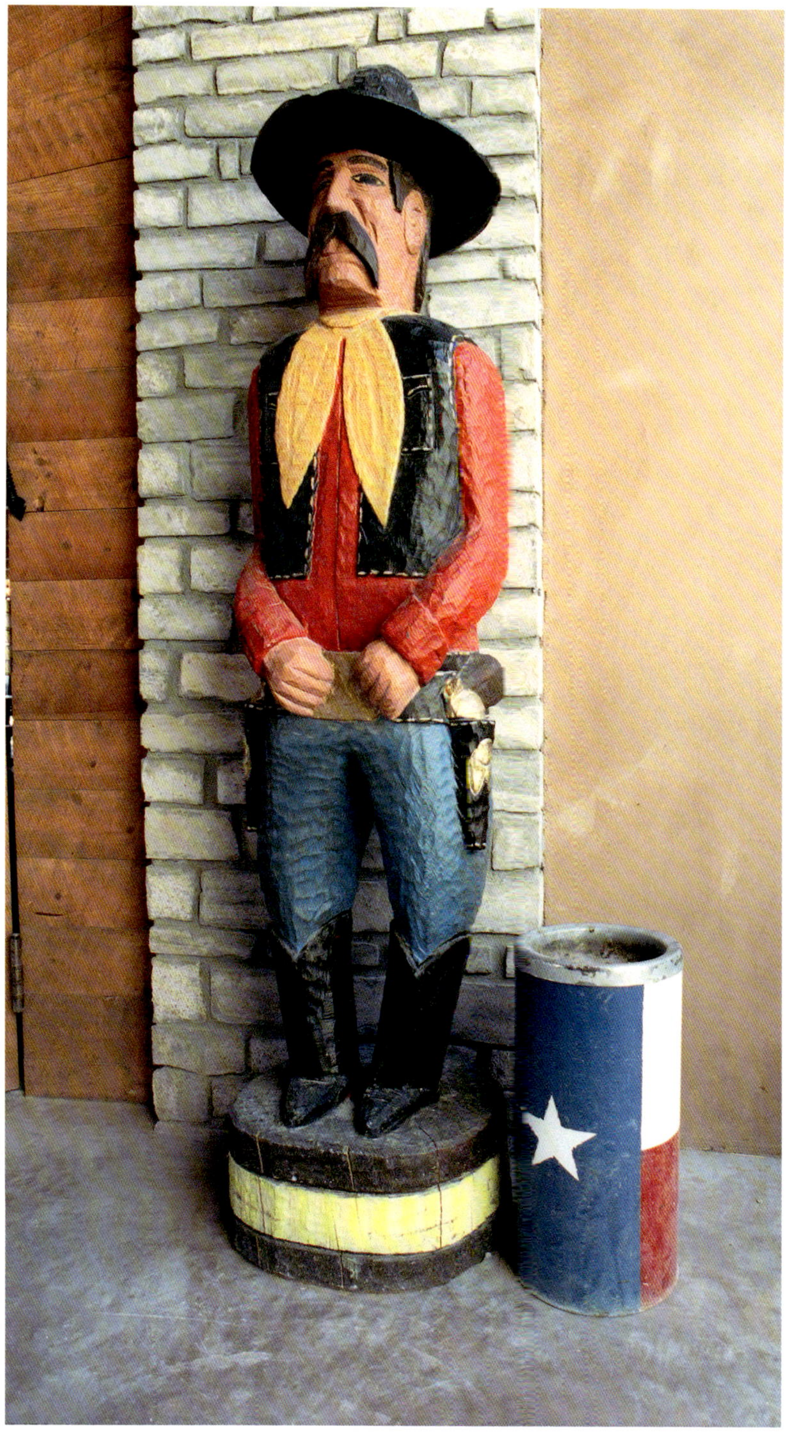

"Cigar Cowboy"
(Lajitas, Big Bend), 2002

This lone wooden drugstore cowboy with his Lone Star ashtray stands in one of the most secluded places in the state, Lajitas, in the Big Bend area of Texas. No smoking, please.

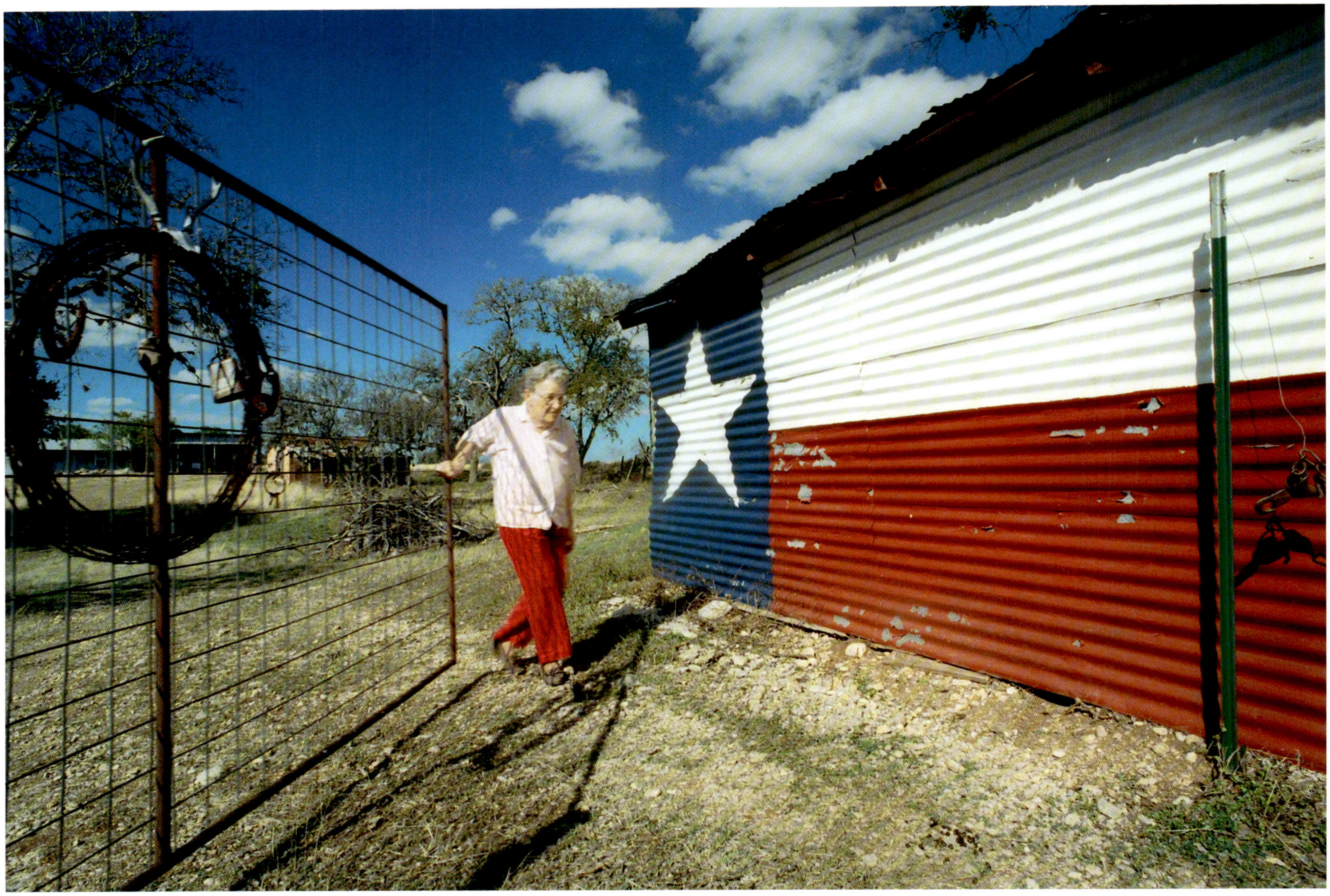

"Gate Closure"
(Christina Kalka, Bandera), 2004

Eighty-five-year-old Christina Kalka of Bandera, in the Texas Hill Country, raised eleven children on their farm located on State Highway 16. Son Samuel and daughter Helen painted the Lone Star flag on her garage. Drive by and honk.

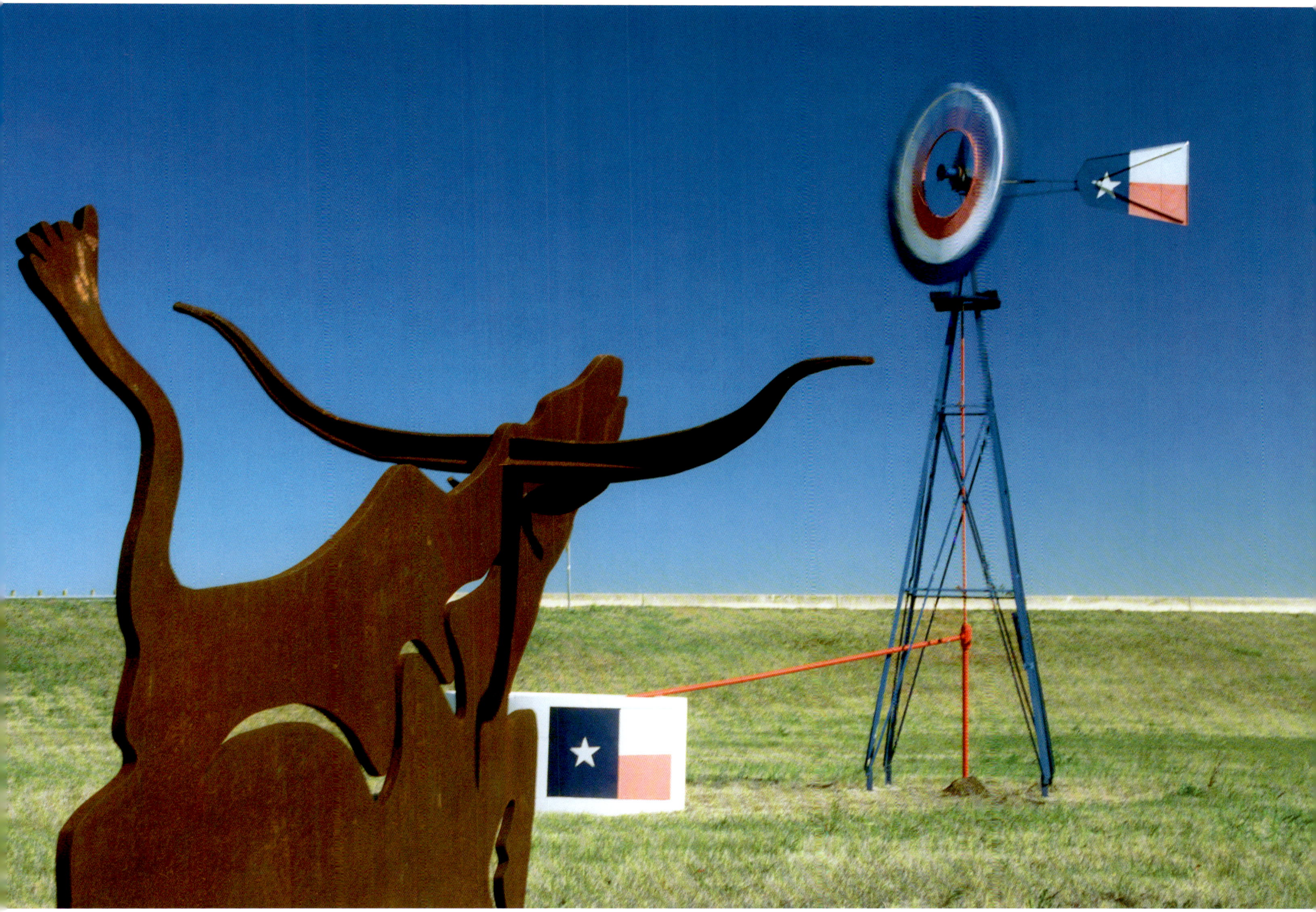

"Cow Mill" (Texas City, western area), 2004

Located on Emmett F. Lowry Expressway at Interstate 45, the city of Texas City wanted to greet visitors with a western theme and to show their Lone Star pride. Holy Cow.

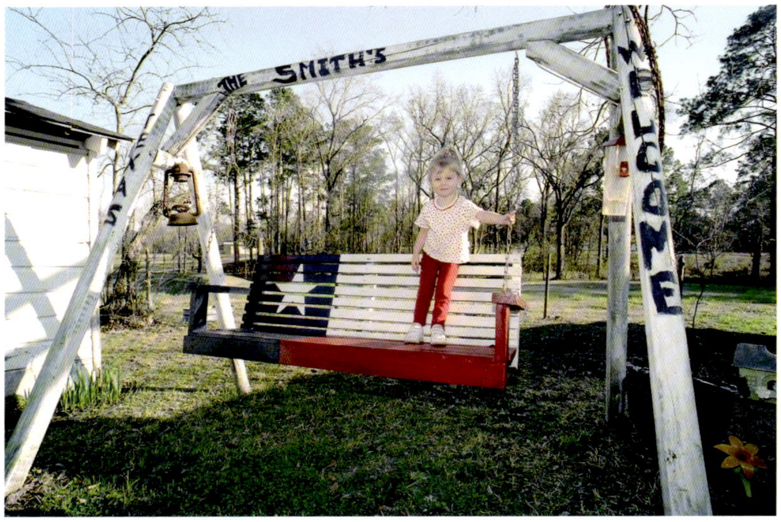

"Patriotic Swing" (Smith family swing, Corrigan), 2002

Makenna Hughes likes to visit her neighbors, the Smiths, in Corrigan, a small East Texas town. She enjoys their swing, which is painted Lone Star proud.

"Skeeter's Barn" (Diboll, Polk County), 2002

Cowboy Skeeter Scarborough of Diboll in Polk County sweeps a concrete flag he built in the hillside along U.S. Highway 59 in East Texas. His stepson Dewayne Dunn painted his barn, in the background.

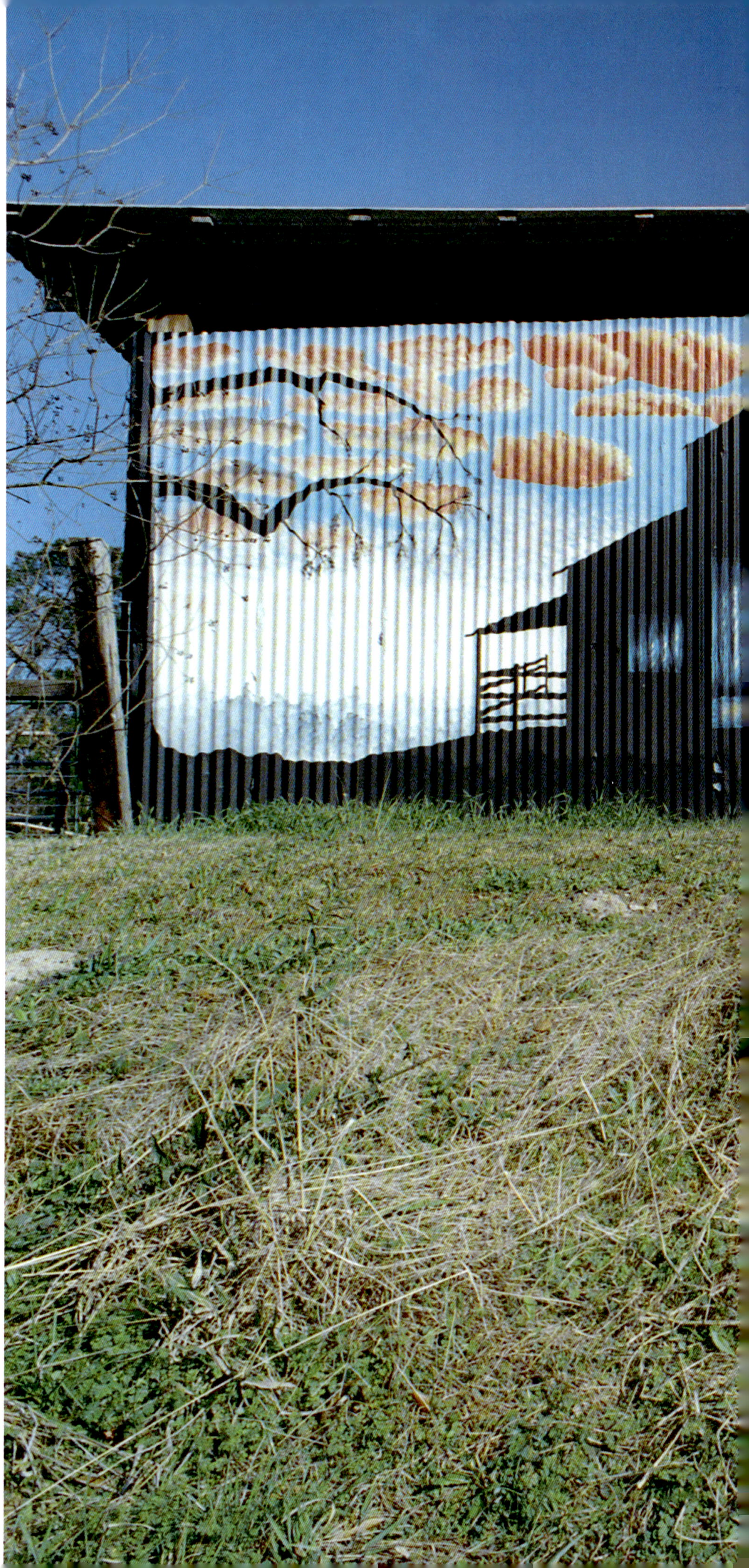

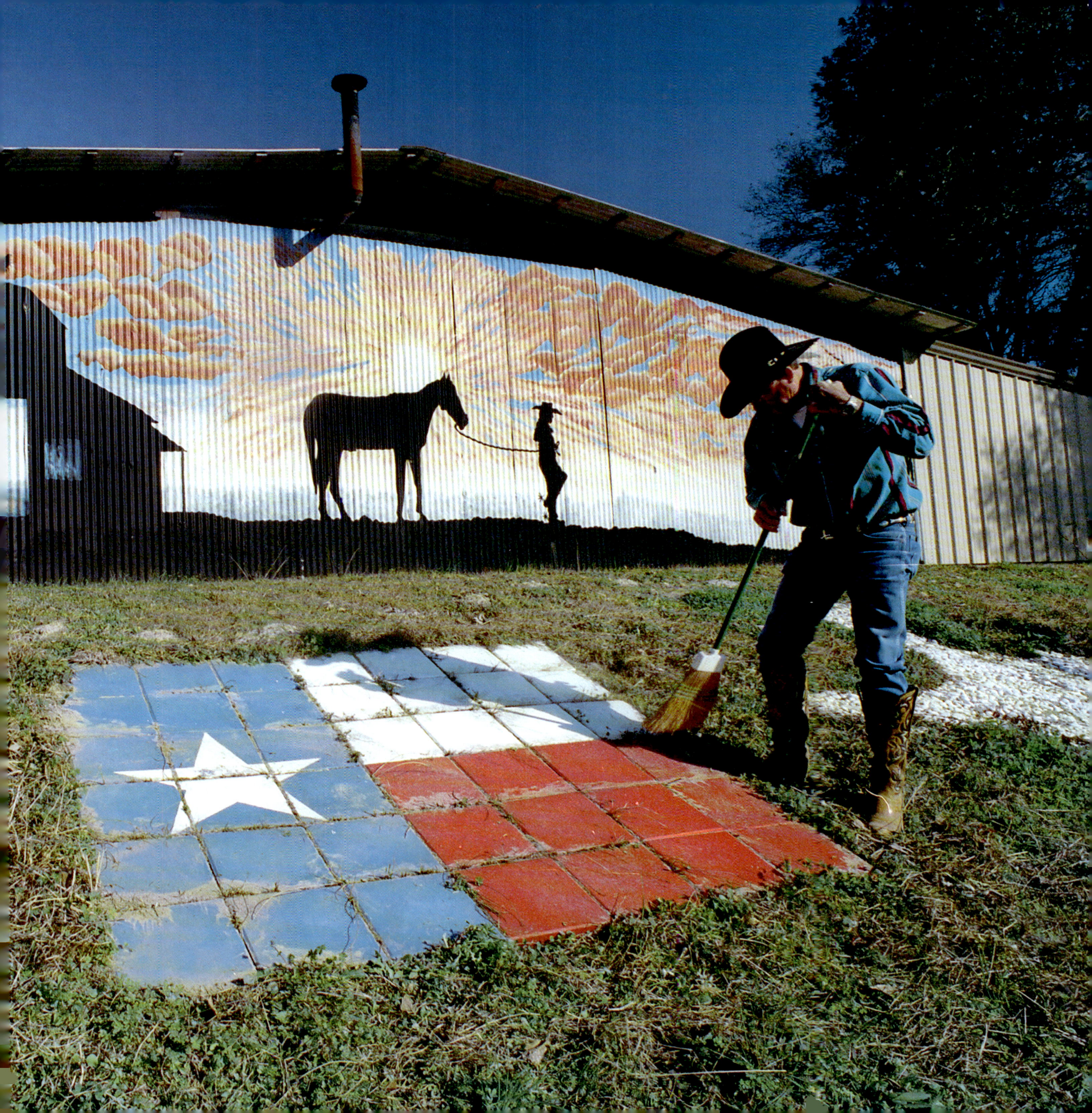

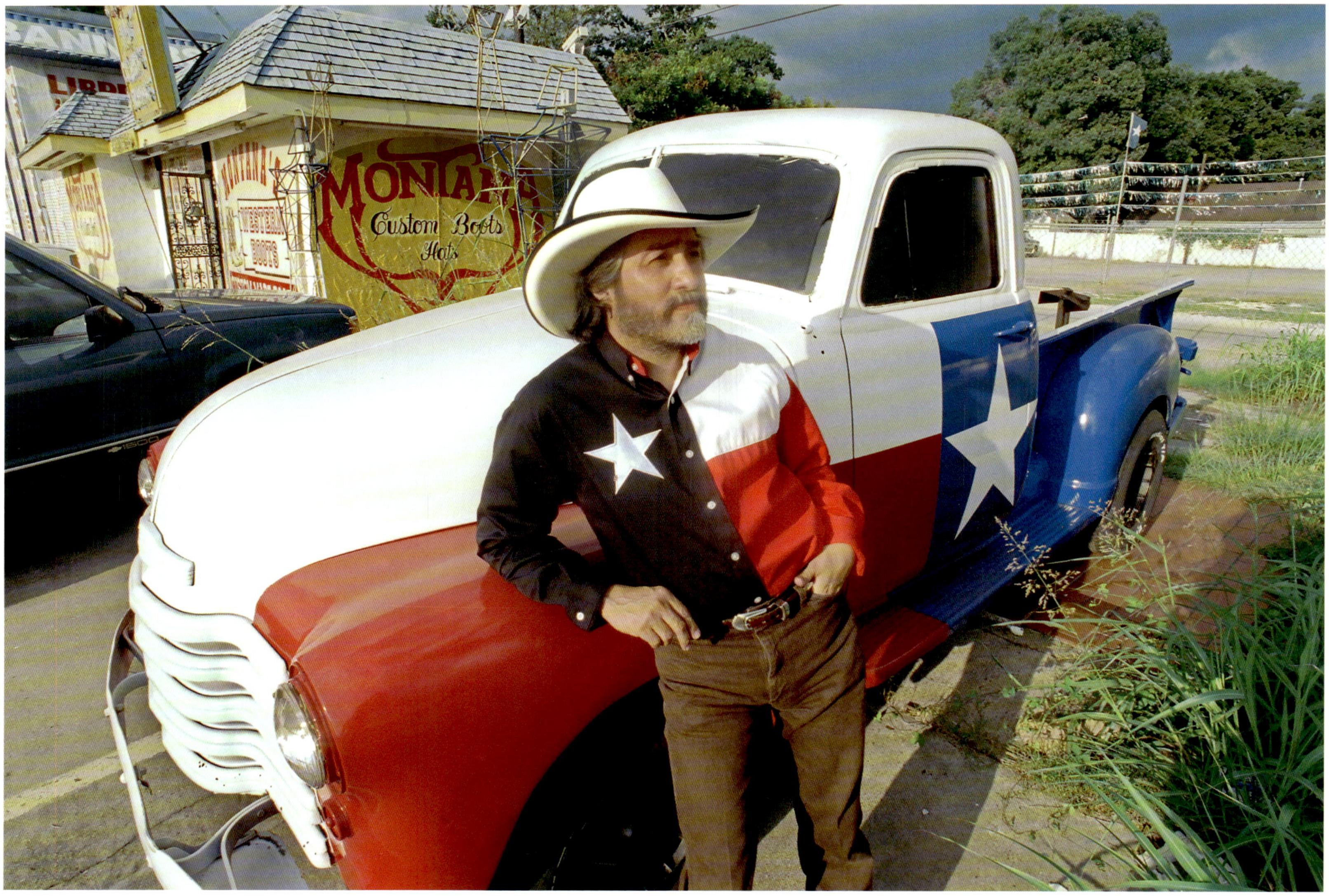

"1949 Chevy" (Rick Montana's truck, Houston), 2002

If his shirt doesn't convince people that Houston bootmaker Rick Montana is a proud Texan, a 1949 Chevy five-window pickup truck he restored does. Rick's boot shop is located in Houston's Fifth Ward. High Five.

"Hill Country Studio" (Pat Glenn, Blanco), 2003

Transplanted Houston artist Pat Glenn and his dog Spot enjoy the hills of Blanco. Pat's studio, where he goes to make "stuff," shows his artistic side and his Lone Star pride. A beautiful picture.

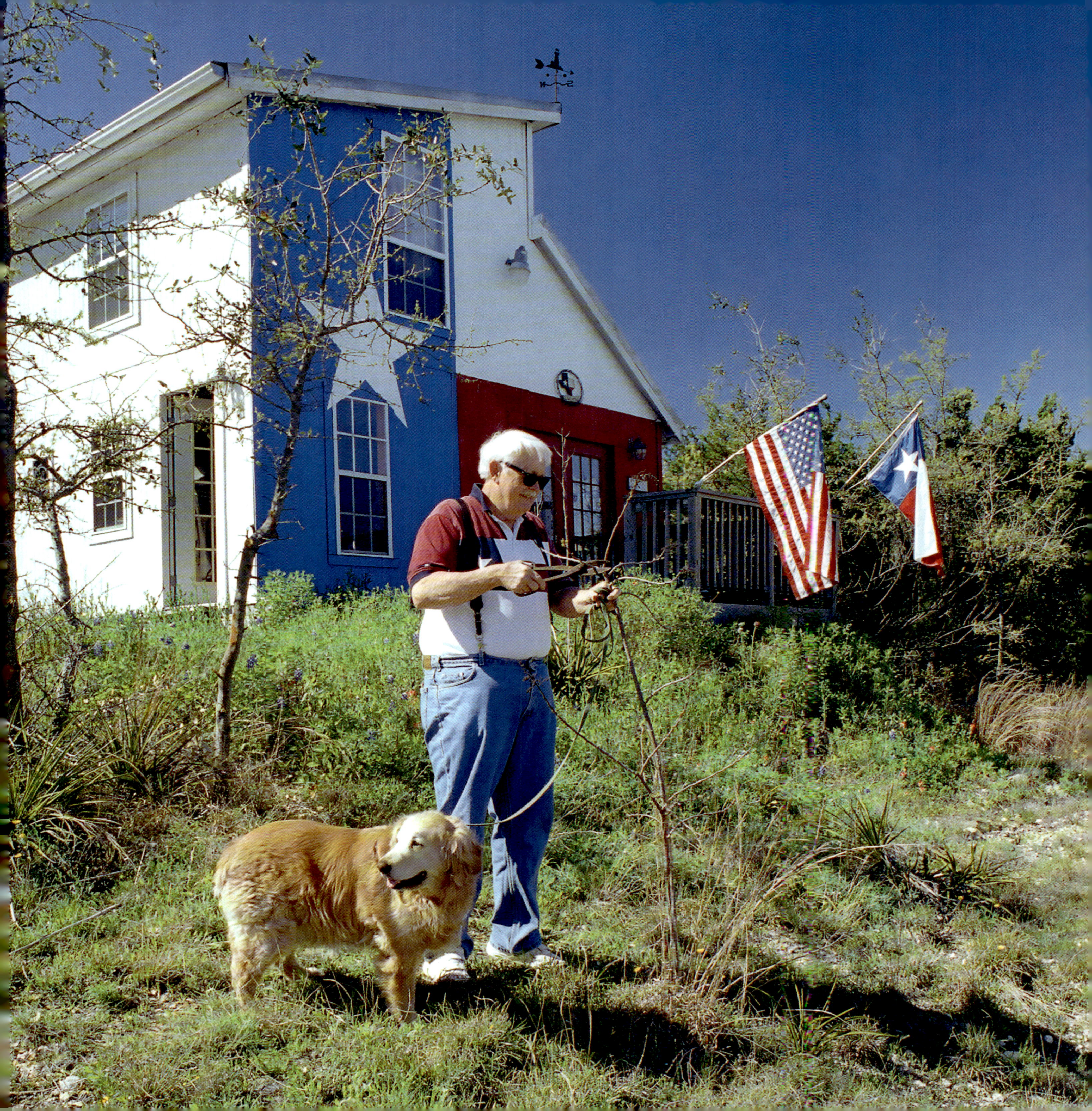

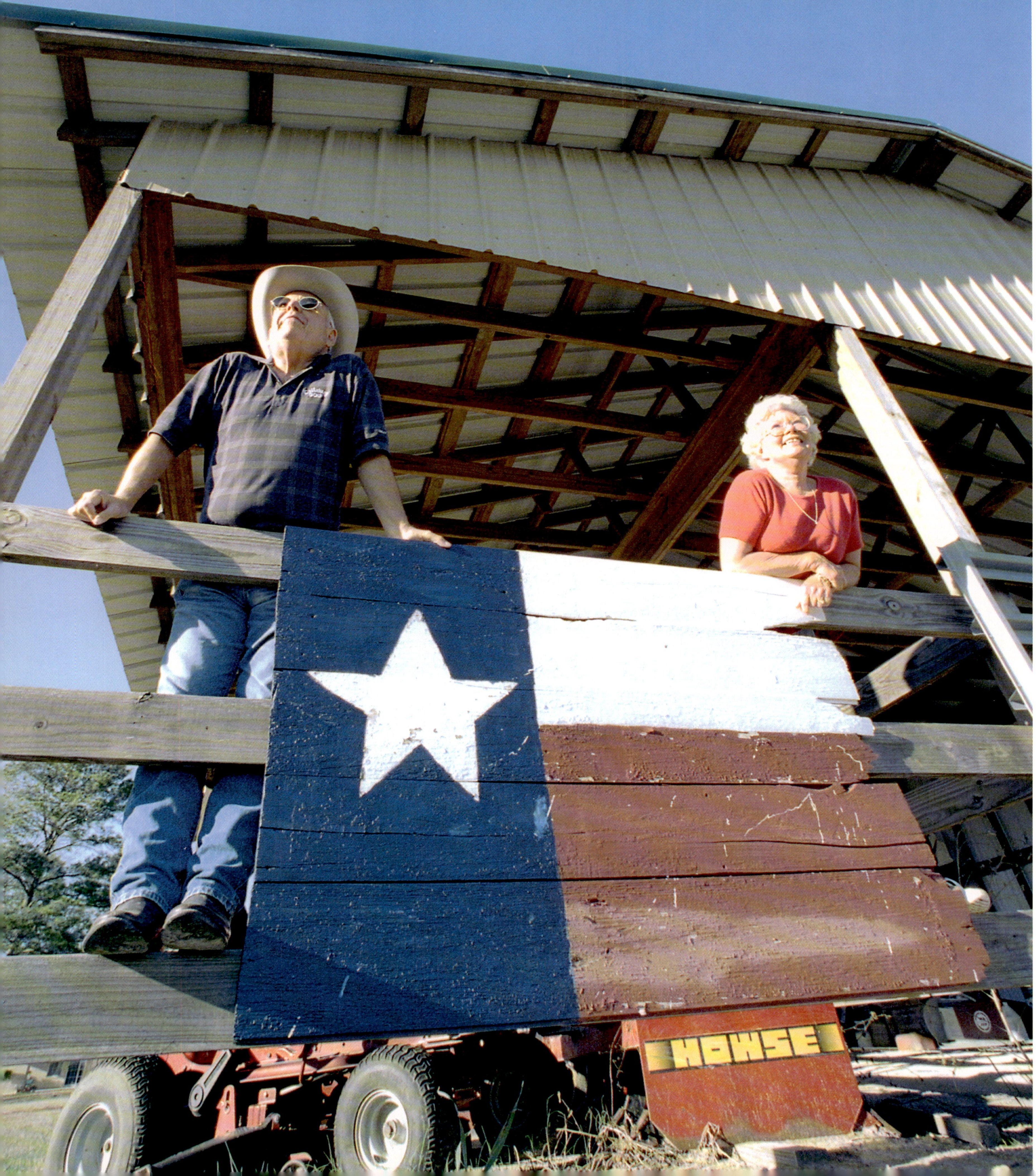
HOWSE

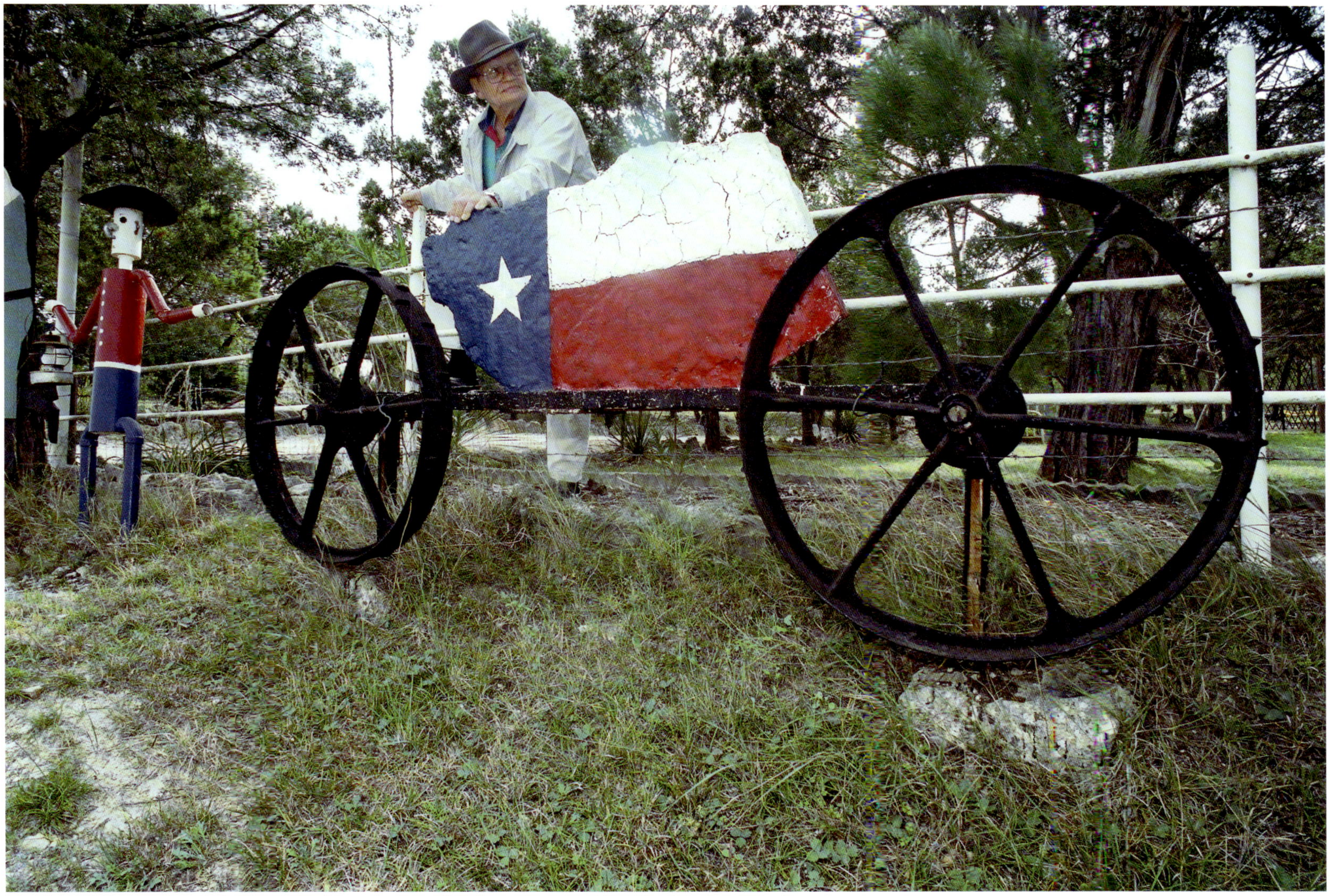

"Stone Wagon" (Arnold Heikkila, Canyon Lake), 2004

Arnold Heikkila of Canyon Lake dug up this large rock on his property. It looked like a covered wagon. Arnold added wheels, painted it with state pride, and placed the Lone Star Stone Wagon on his front fence. Westward ho.

"Old Woody" (T-Boy and Donna Tyner, Sour Lake), 2002

Warren (T-Boy) and Donna Tyner of Sour Lake frame a Lone Star flag painted on hundred-year-old wood by daughter Tracie. The Tyners proudly display their flag on an equipment barn located on State Highway 105. That-a-boy.

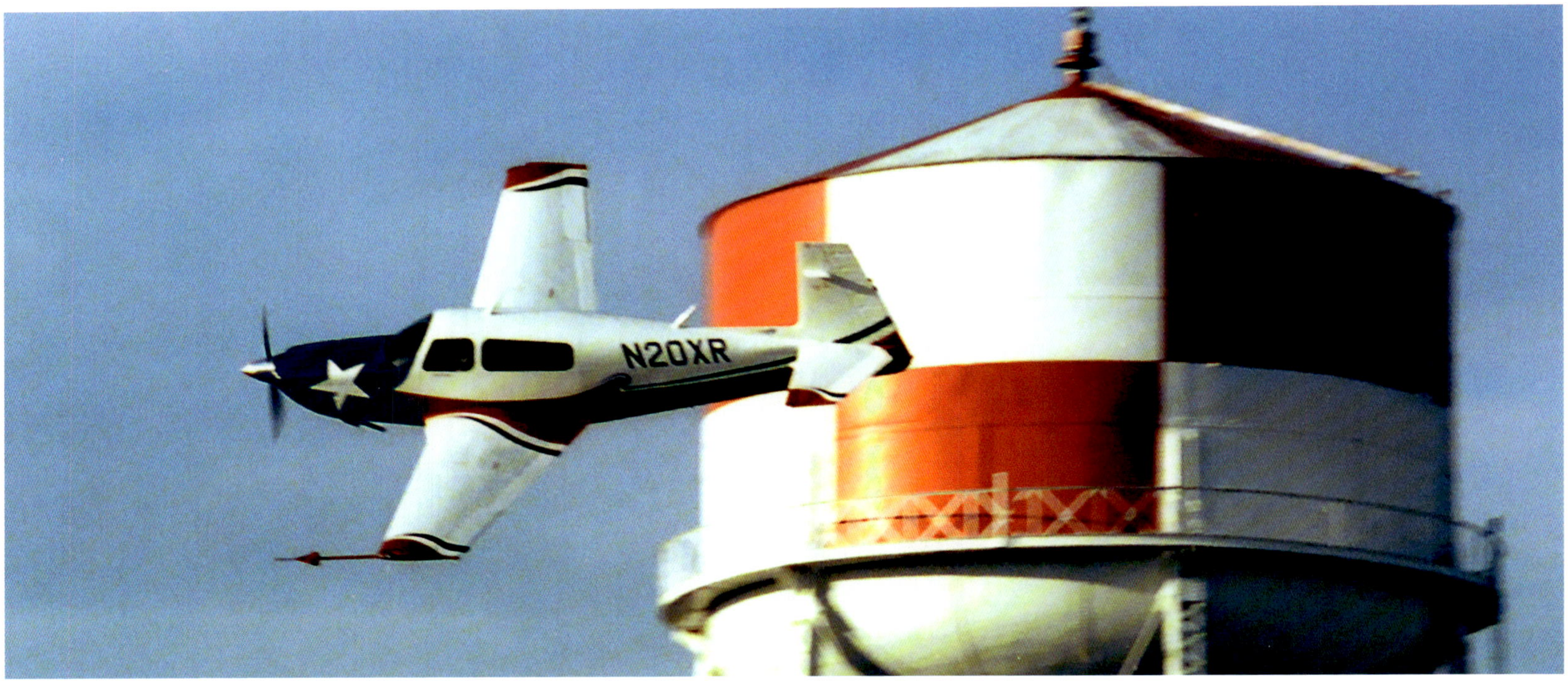

"Planeing Water" (Mooney Aircraft Company, Kerrville), 2003

Hand-built at the Mooney Aircraft factory in Kerrville, this aircraft with its distinctive Texas theme is the pride of the company. *Flying Magazine* declared it the "plane of the year" in 1995. The stuff pilots dream of.

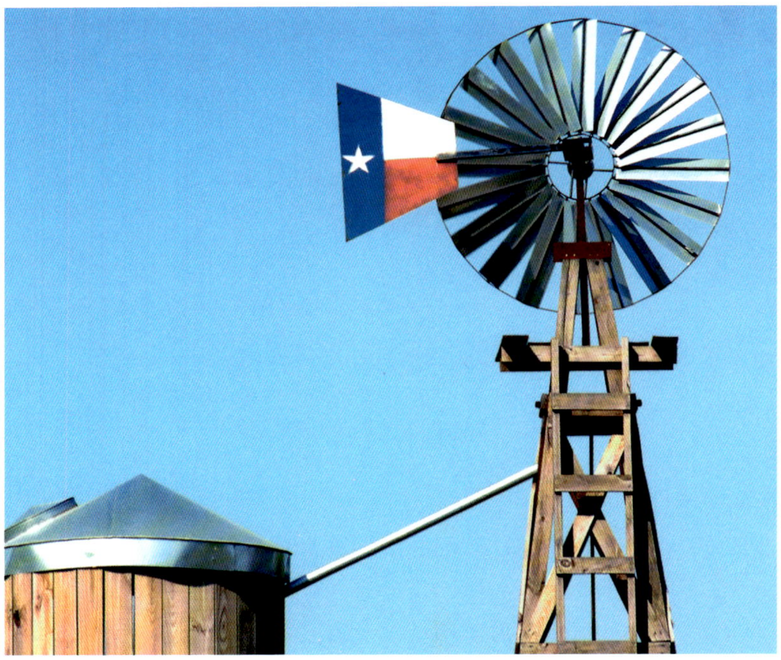

"Creek-Mill" (Don and Sharon Walker, Caldwell), 2002

The Shallow Creek Ranch owners Don and Sharon Walker have developed an old western theme out front, anchored by their Lone Star windmill, just northwest of Caldwell on Highway 36. Hear the wind blow.

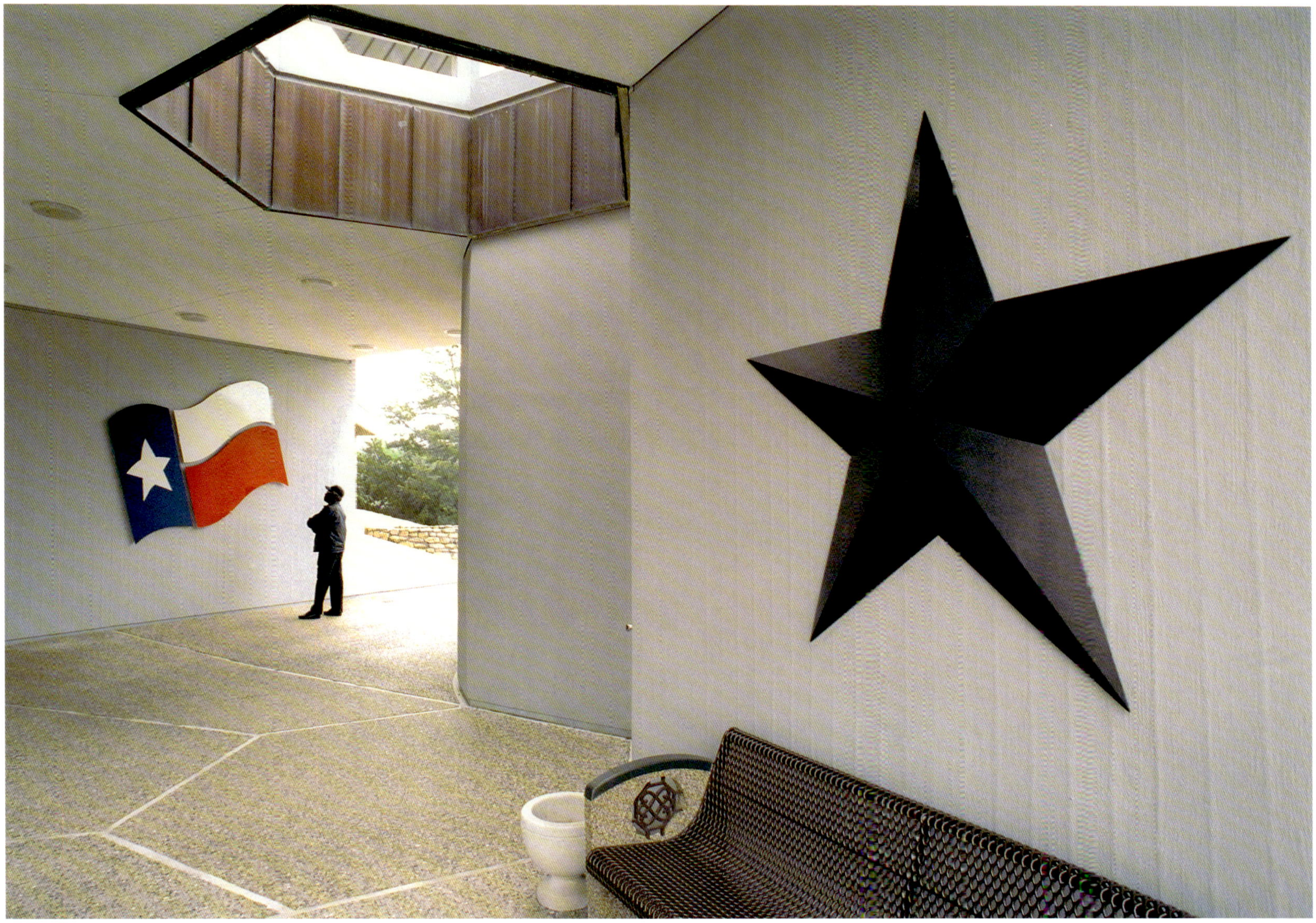

"Birthplace" (Washington-on-the-Brazos), 2002

Floyd Smith of Houston checks out the Lone Star artwork on display at the Star of the Republic Museum, Washington-on-the-Brazos. Washington-on-the-Brazos State Historical Park preserves the site of the last capital of the Republic of Texas so that all can experience the birthplace of the Lone Star State.

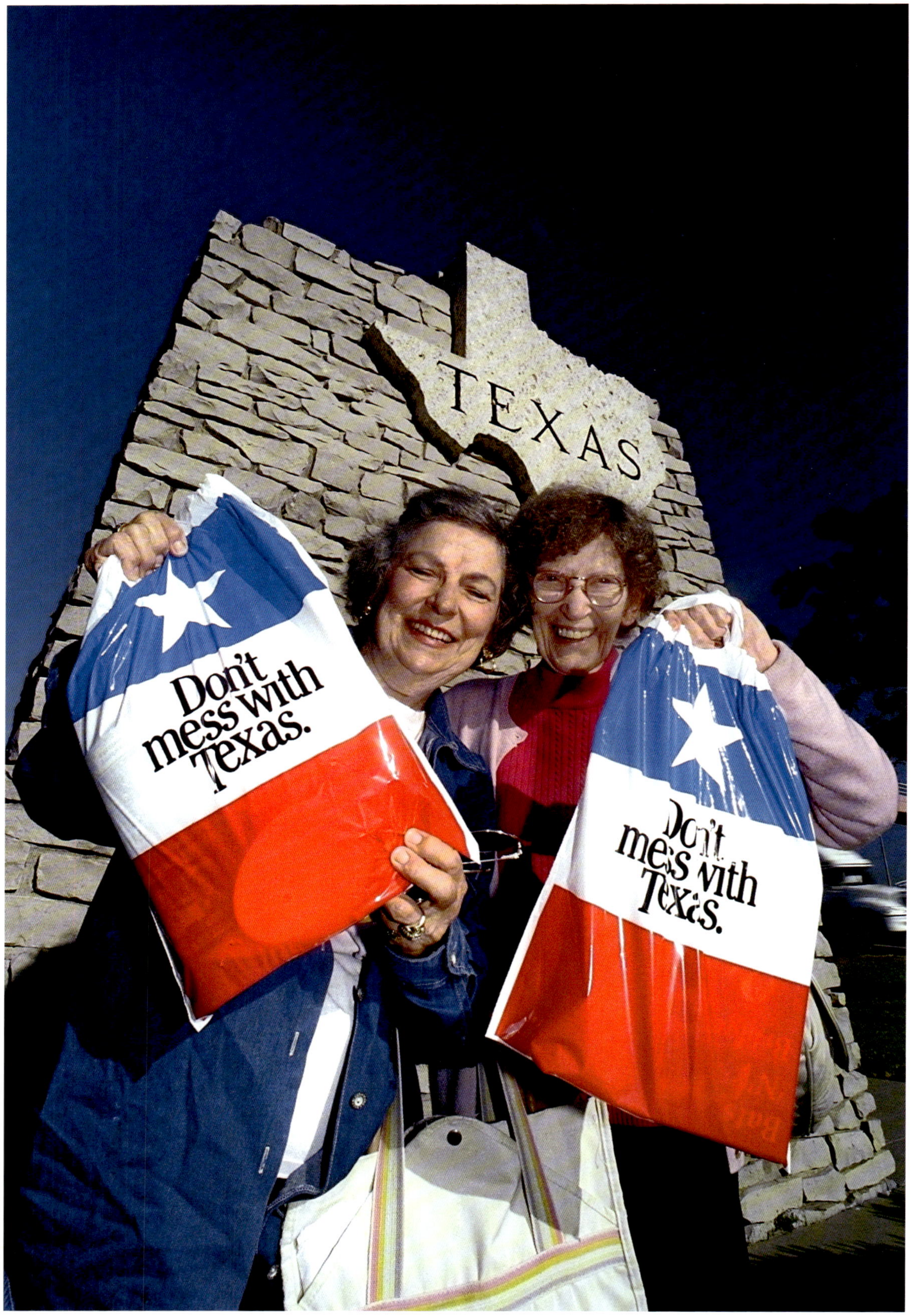

"Panhandle Visit" (Texas Visitor Center, Amarillo), 2003

Stopping at the visitor center located in Amarillo in the Texas Panhandle, Georgia residents Annie Frady Stevens, left, and her sister-in-law, June Stevens, get a feel for Texas hospitality. Don't Mess with Texas.

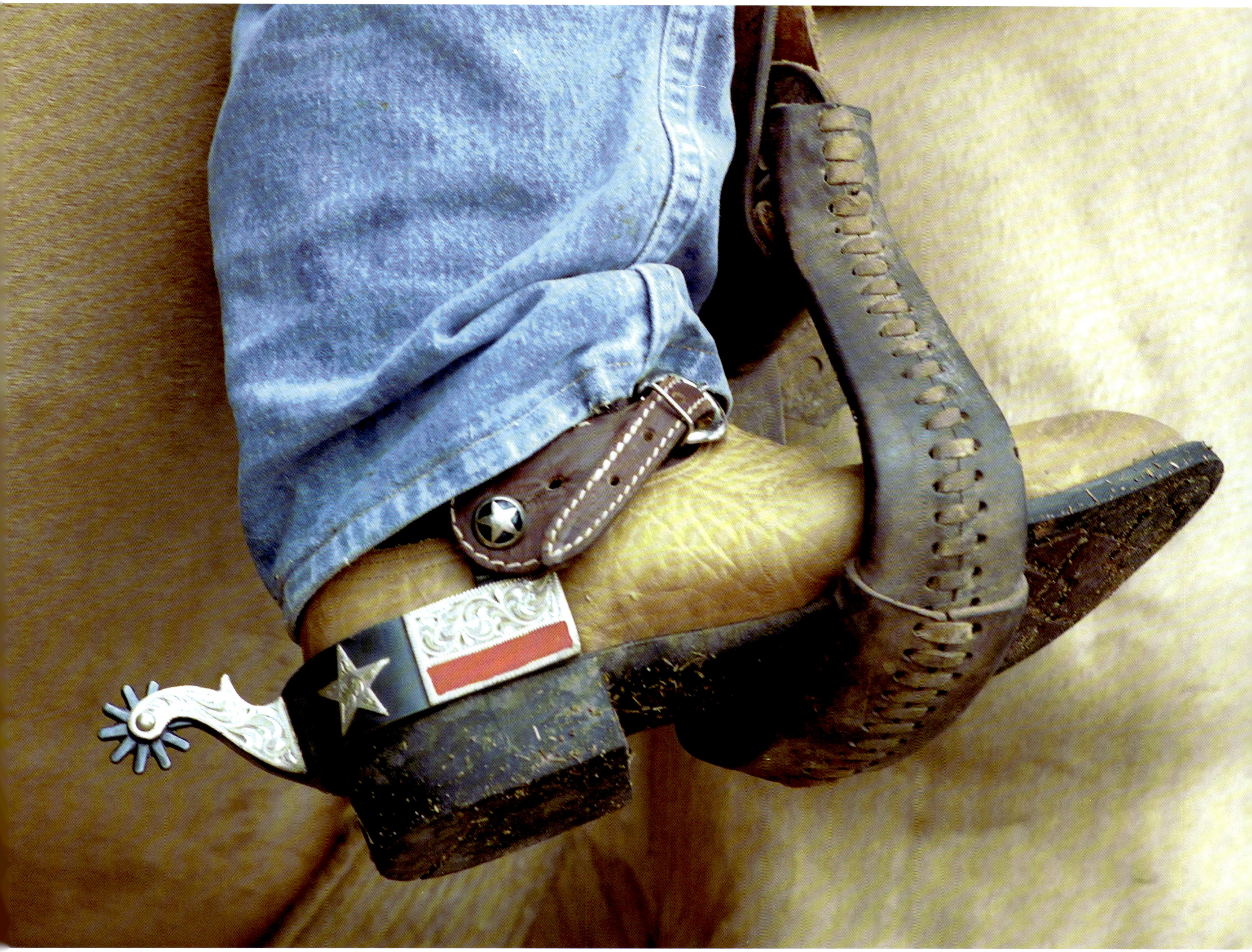

"Lone Spur" (Dana Nelson, Hempstead), 2004

Dana Nelson works his Cedar Hill Ranch in Hempstead with love and pride. Sitting on his ten-year-old quarter horse Sundae Cutta Pep, he sports his custom solid silver Lone Star spurs. Saddle up.

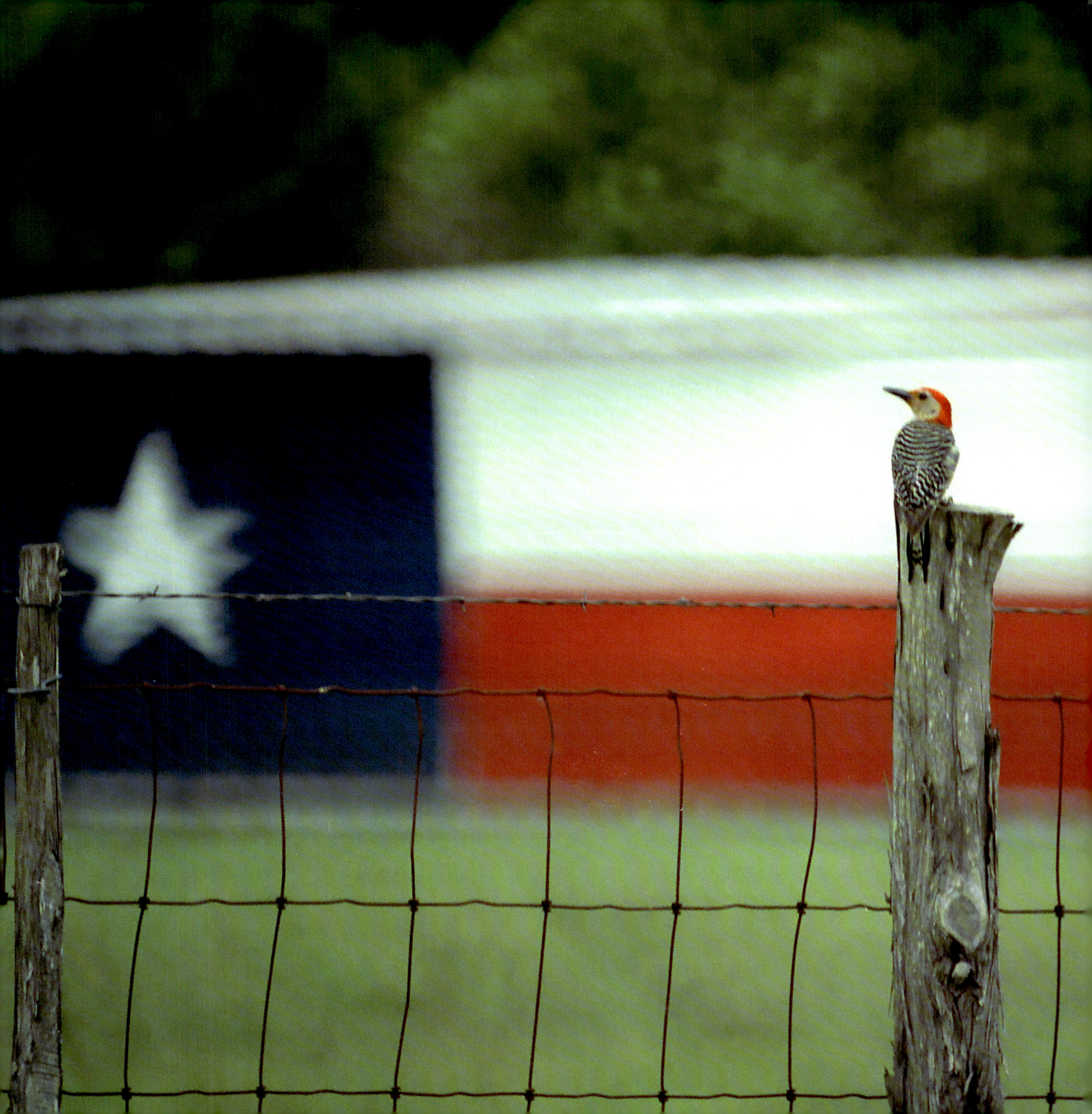

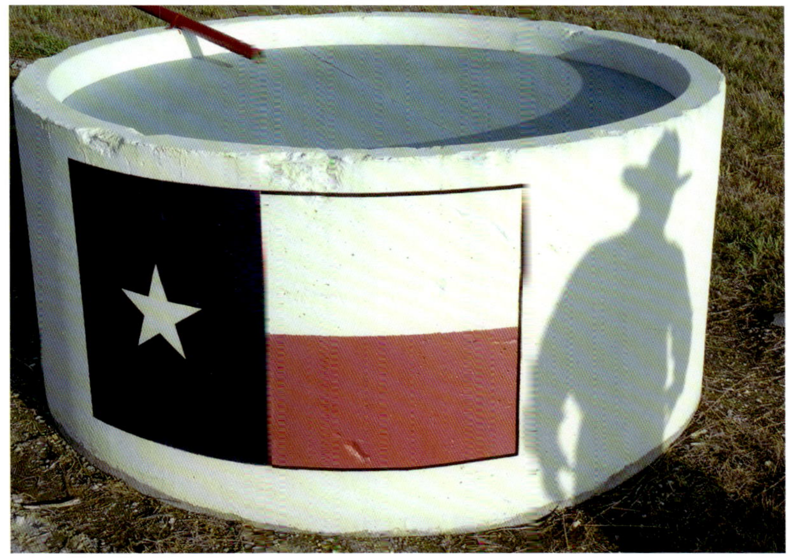

"Watering Hole" (Welcome water trough, Texas City), 2004

Located between Galveston and Houston, the city of Texas City greets its visitors along Interstate 45 and shows off its state pride. Mark Burns's shadow casts no shadow of doubt on the Lone Star water trough. Thirsty?

"Woody Peck" (Hughes family shed row barn, Washington), 2004

A woodpecker checks out the carefully painted shed row barn on the Hughes Ranch in Washington, Texas, located on State Highway 1155 north of Chappell Hill. The owners, Bubba and Kerry Hughes, painted the barn themselves.

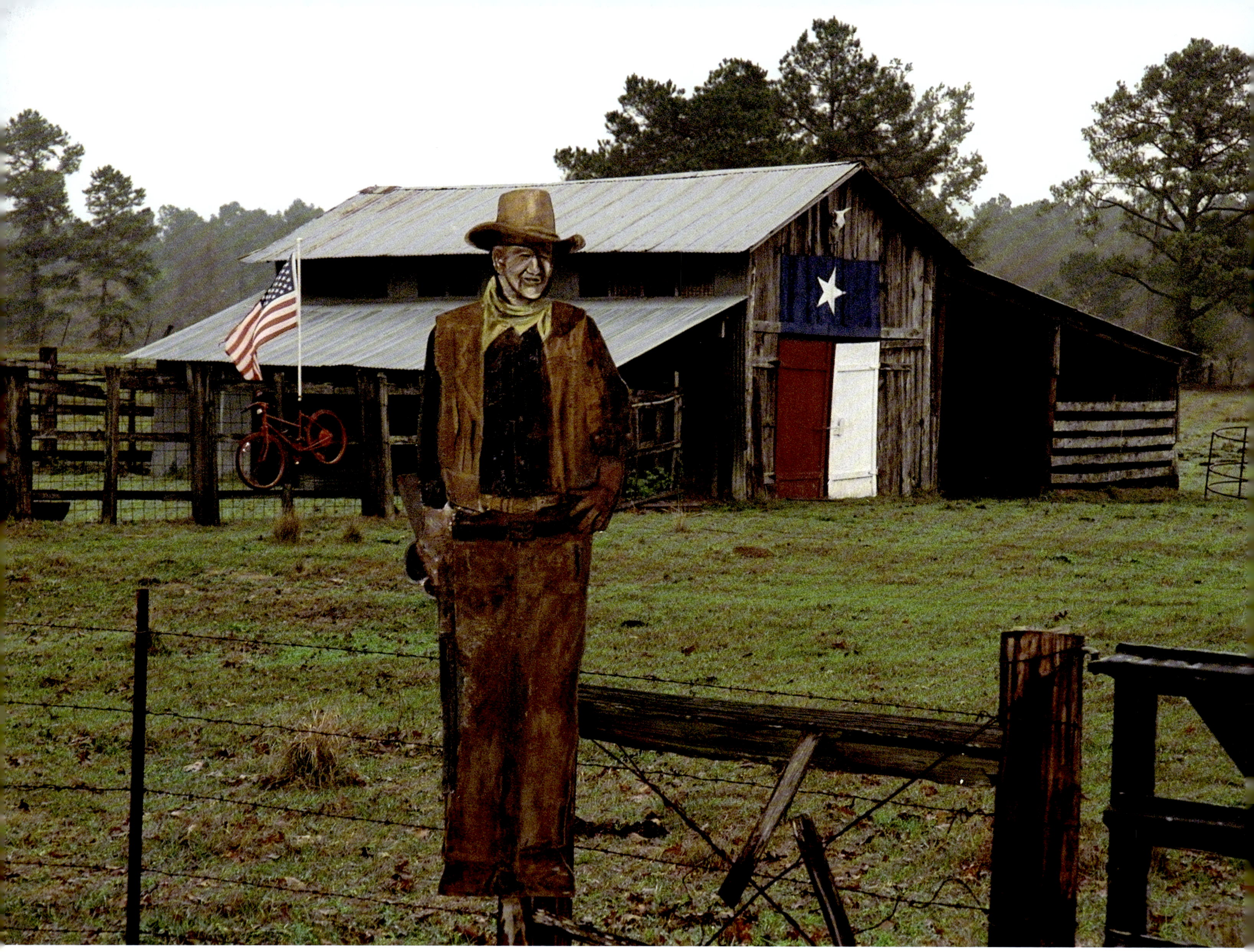

"The Duke" (Canterbury Tails Ranch, Karnack), 2003

Nigel and Shirley Shivers, owners of the family's Canterbury Tails Ranch in Karnack, have their utility barn protected by John Wayne. Nigel's father built the barn in the '40s with a door that always opens with state pride.

"Pointing West" (The Reynolds' old gift shop, Alvord), 2003

Karen and Ronnie Reynolds' Old Treasured Gift Shop on Highway 287 in Alvord, Texas specializes in Texas and western items. Point the way.

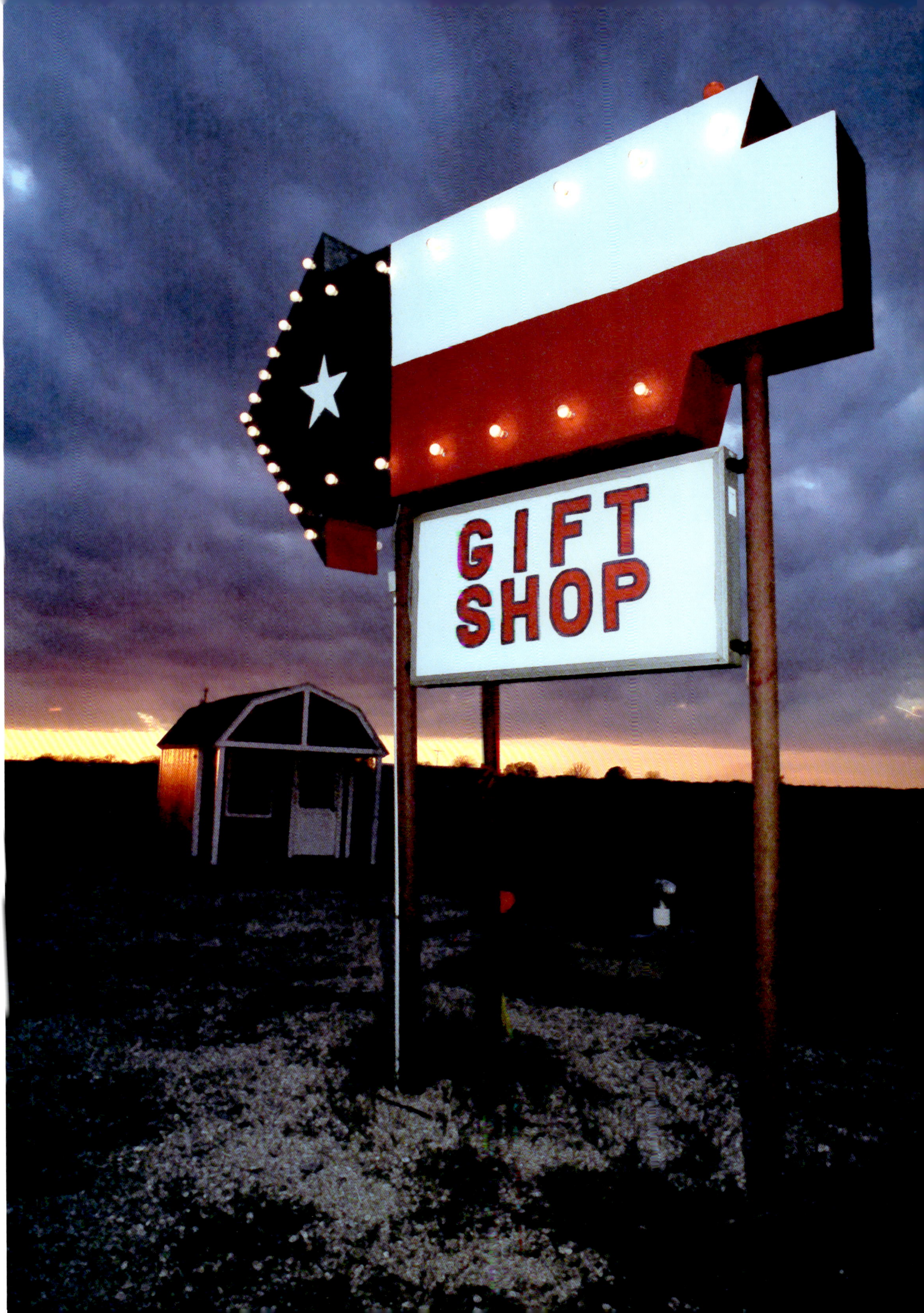

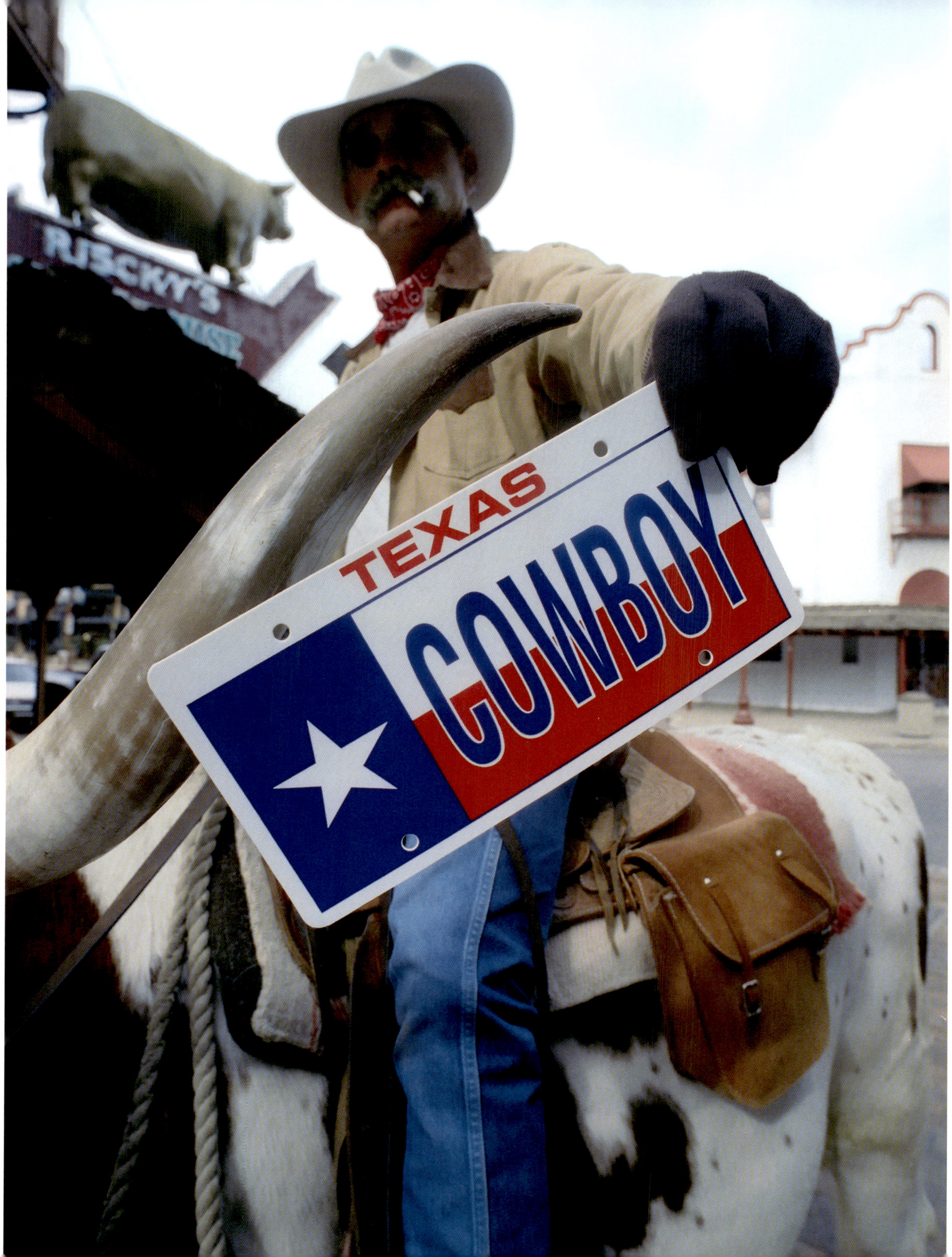
RISCKY'S
TEXAS
COWBOY

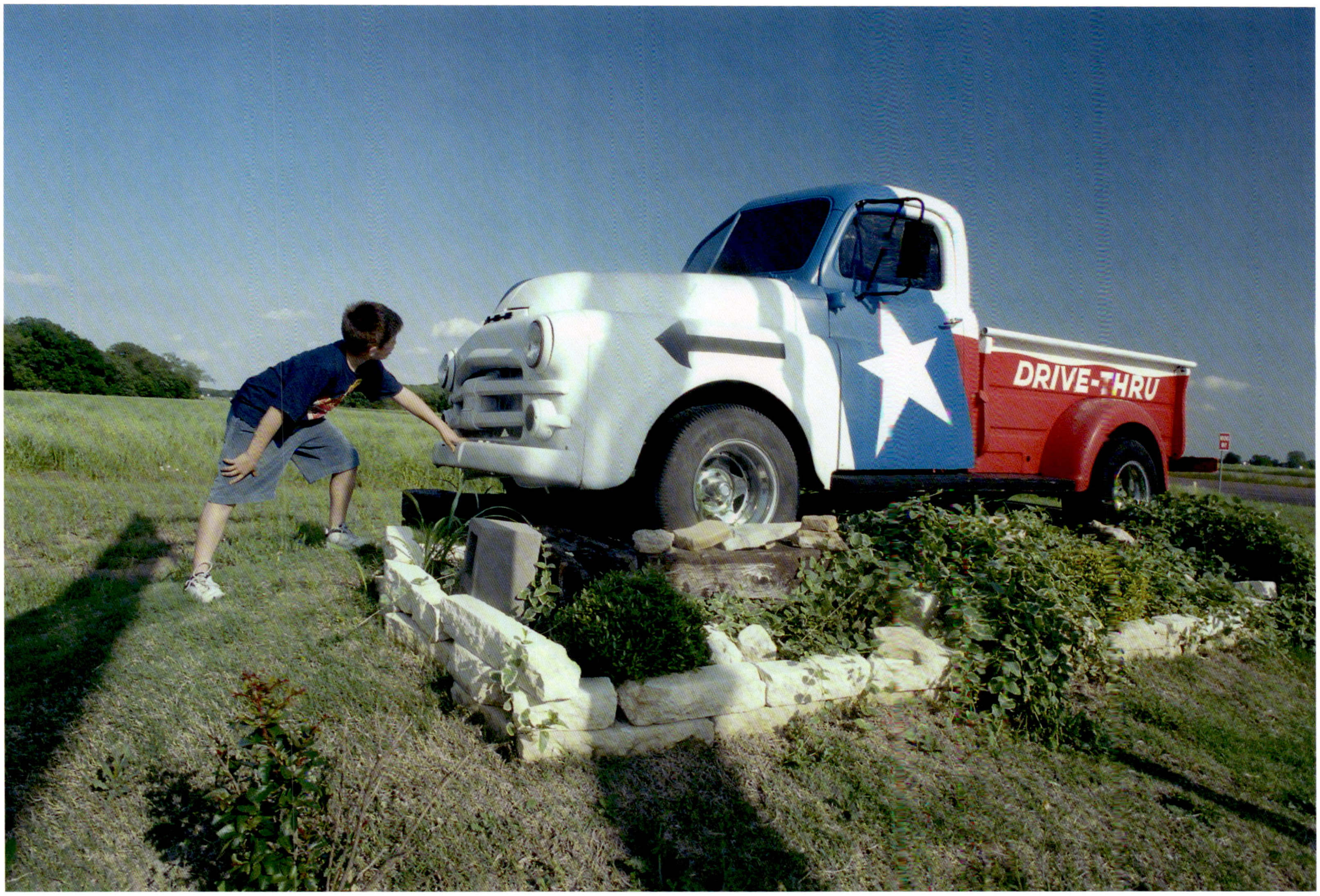

"1953 Dodge" (Reagor Springs Drive-Thru, Waxahachie), 2003

Ten-year-old J. T. Sakata of Waxahachie, Texas, checks out a 1953 Dodge pickup truck parked out front of the Reagor Springs Lone Star Drive-Thru. Gear down and pull in.

"Cowpuncher" (Ron Sitton, Fort Worth Stockyard), 2002

Cowboy Ron Sitton can be seen riding his longhorn steers in the Fort Worth Stockyards. Ron trains longhorns and is proud to be a real Texas cowboy. Steering you right.

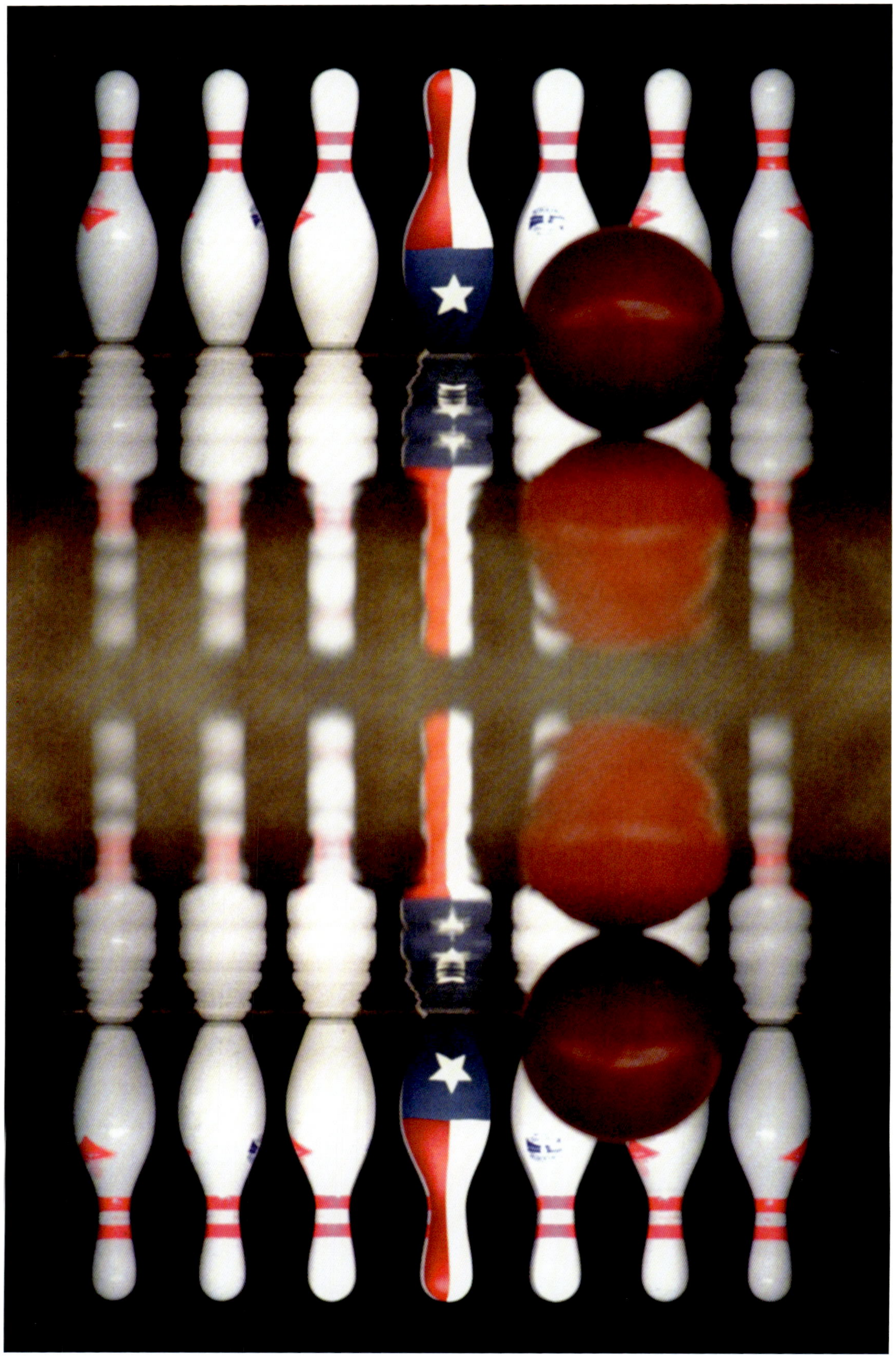

"Lone Strike" (The Texas Bowl, Lake Jackson), 2004

The Texas Bowl on FM 2004 in Lake Jackson is a family fun center—note the Lone Star king pin.

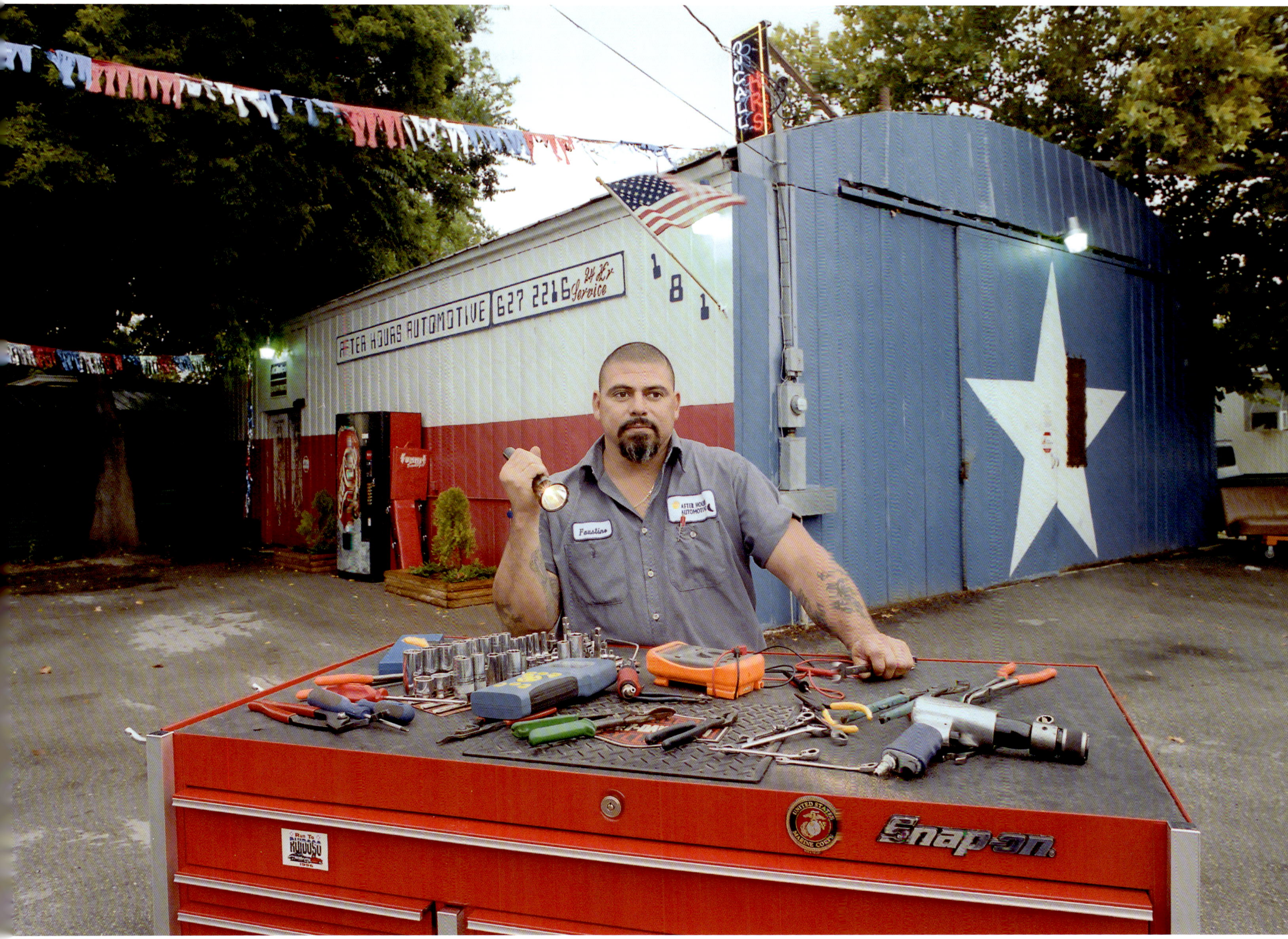

"After Hours" (After Hours Automotive, New Braunfels), 2004

Mechanic and owner Faustino Collazo runs the After Hours Automotive shop in New Braunfels. A community-minded man, Faustino says customers love the Texas pride he shows with his building. *Se Habla Español.*

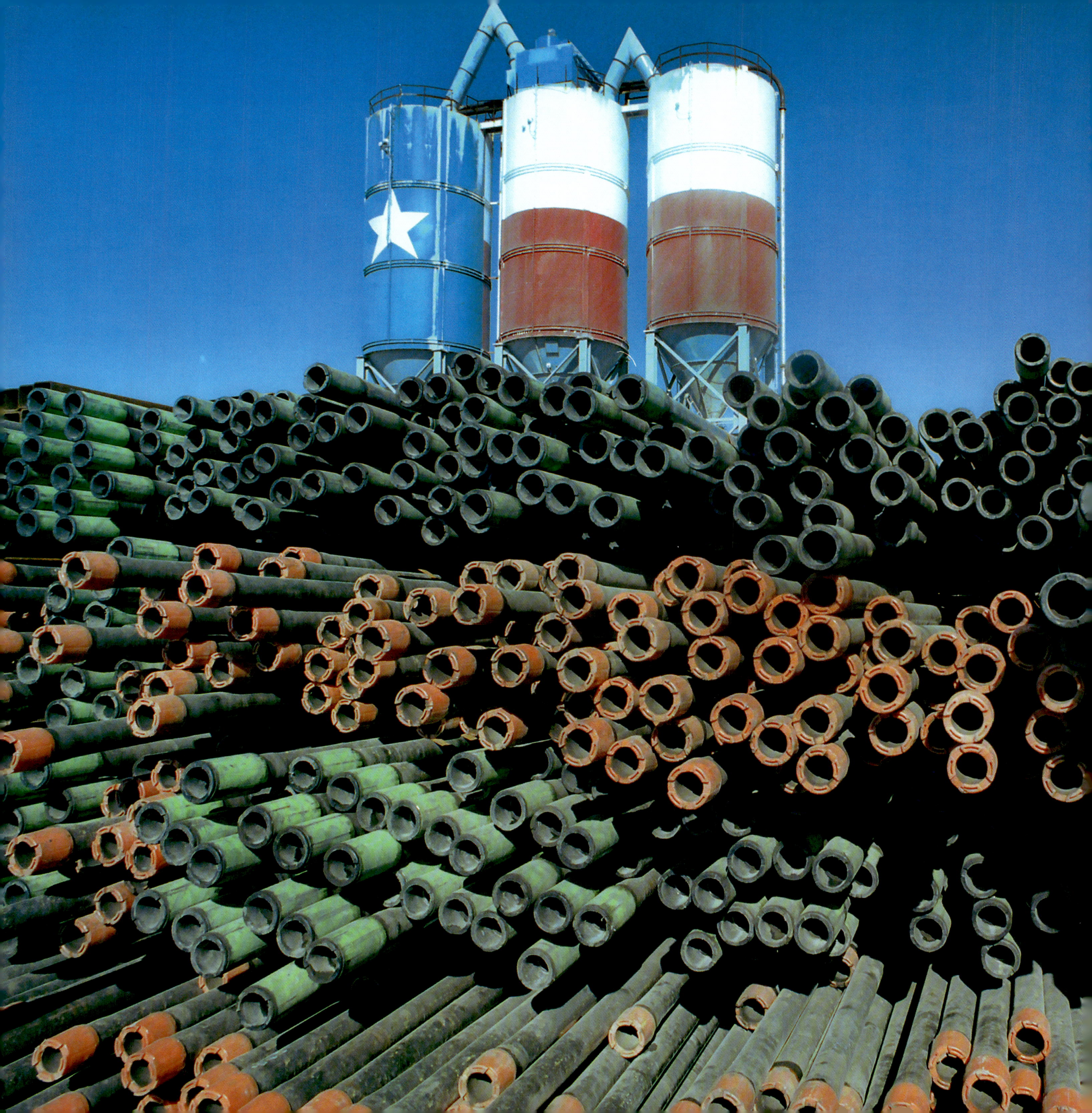

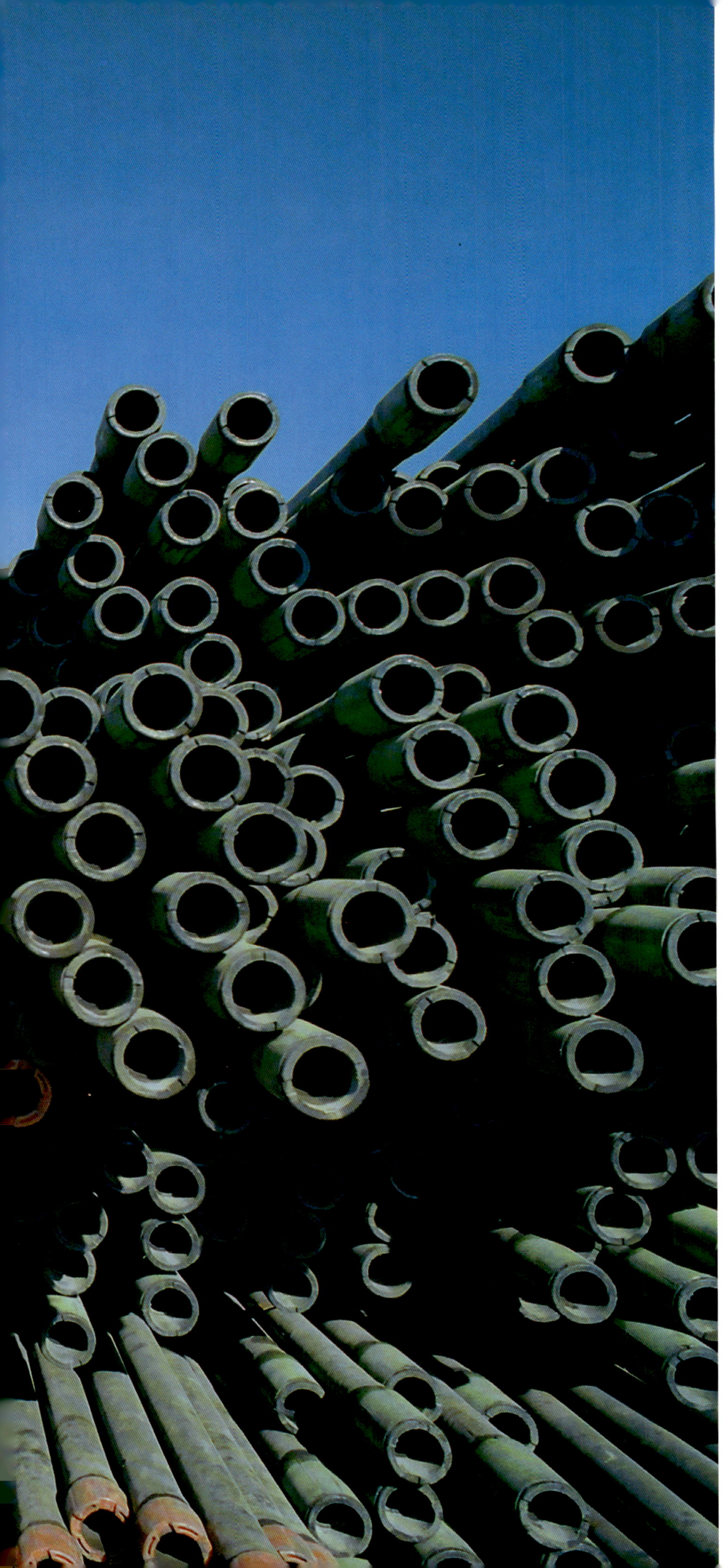

"Silos" (Houston Ship Channel), 2002

This stack of oil field pipes on the banks of the Houston ship channel at the New Terminal Stevedores Company Warehouse shows a carefully painted Lone Star concrete silo sailing high in the background.

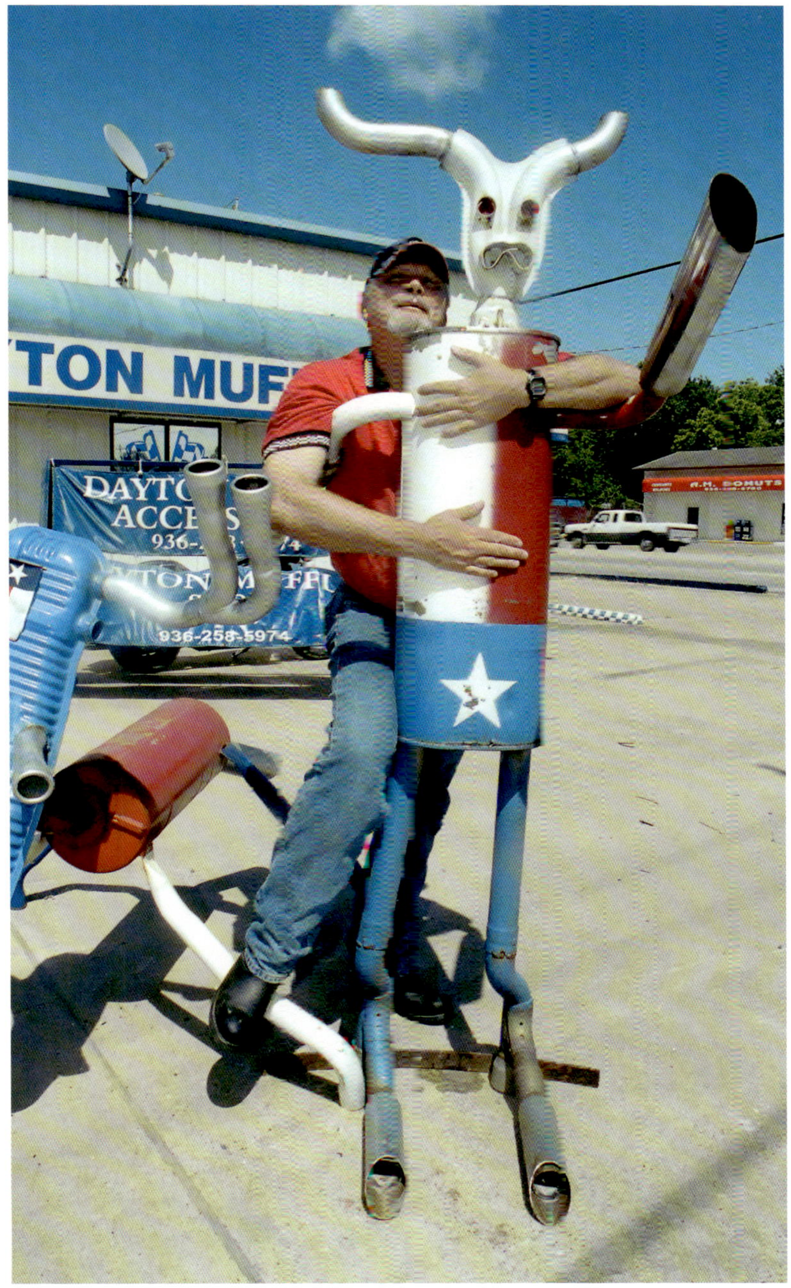

"Muffler Love" (Denny A. D. Talley, Dayton), 2004

Denny Talley, owner of the Dayton Muffler Shop, shows his love for his art and his state. Start your engine.

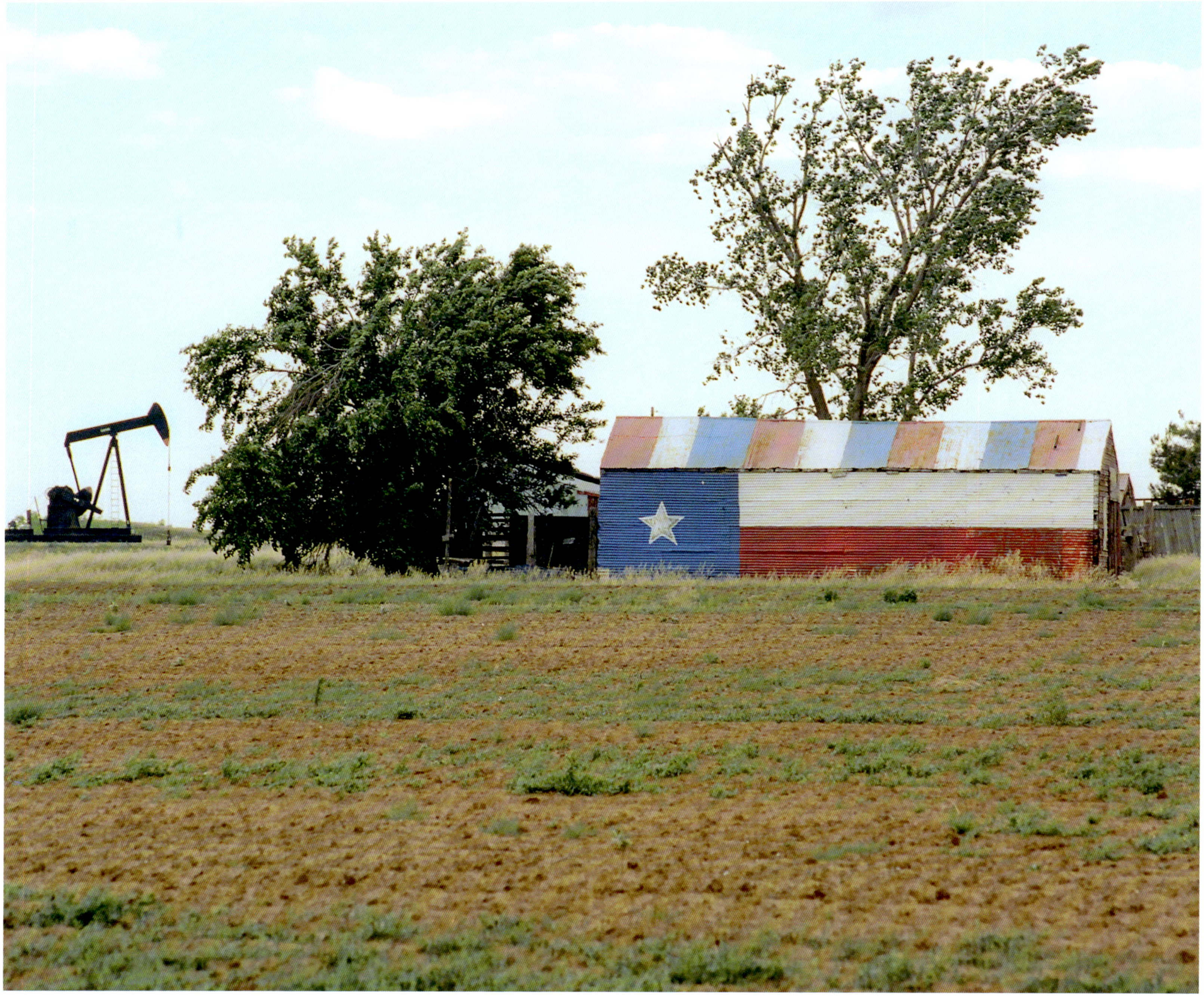

"Oil Barn" (painted barn, Post), 2002

A true Texas landscape in Post, along State Highway 84, pictures a lone pumpjack working next to the Lone Star–painted barn.

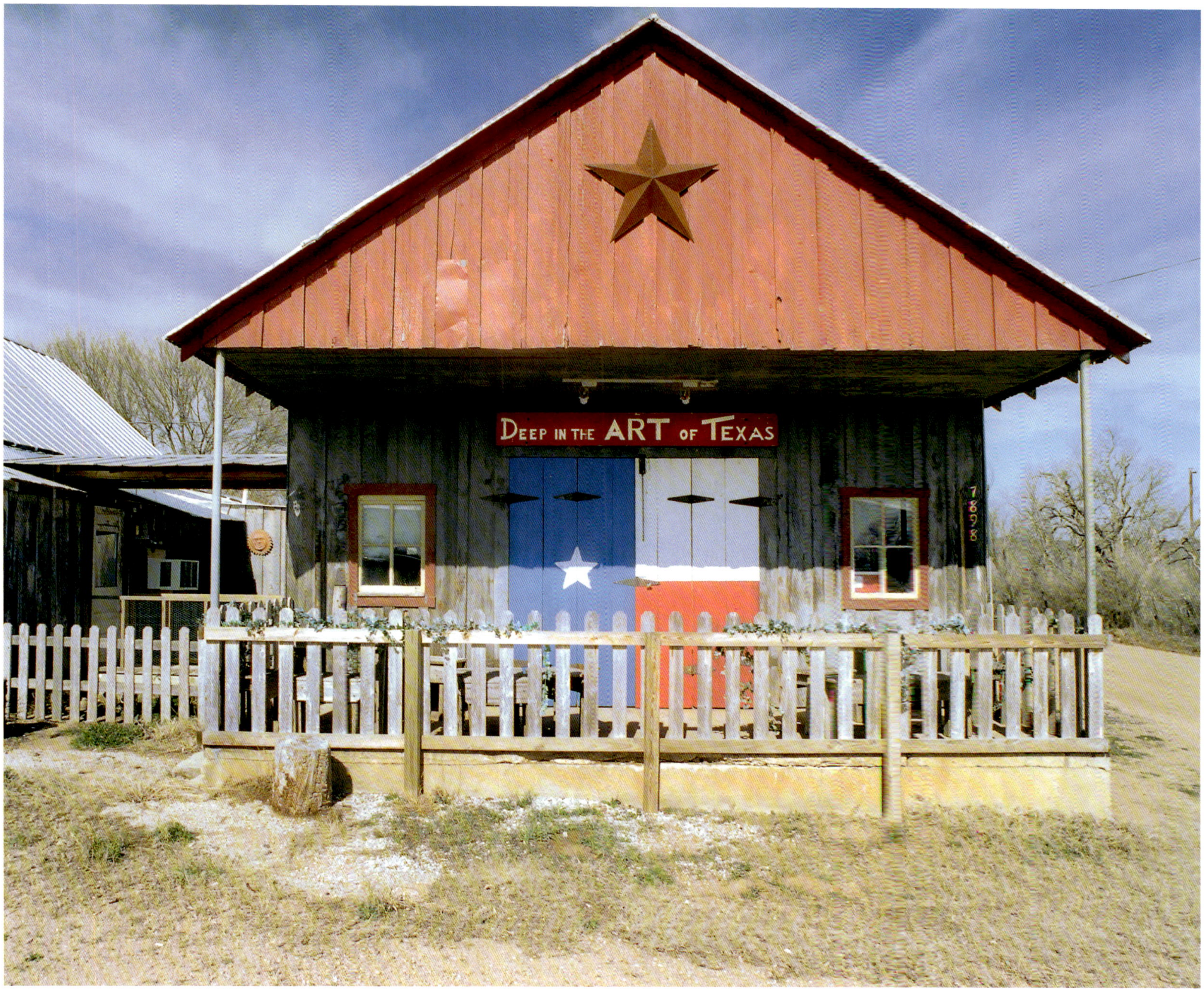

"Door Art" (Community Center and Museum, Art, Texas), 2002

The Community Center and Museum in the town of Art, Texas, do their artistic best to show state pride by painting a Lone Star flag on the front door. Knock three times.

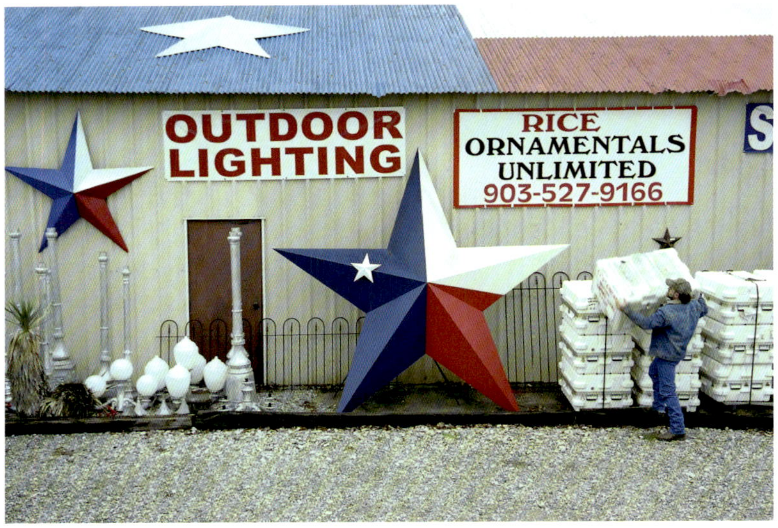

"Ornamental" (Philip Rice, Caddo Mills), 2003

Philip Rice, owner of Rice's Ornamentals in Caddo Mills, makes indoor and outdoor metal and iron works, furniture, windmills, and much more. Philip loves the Lone Star State and its flag.

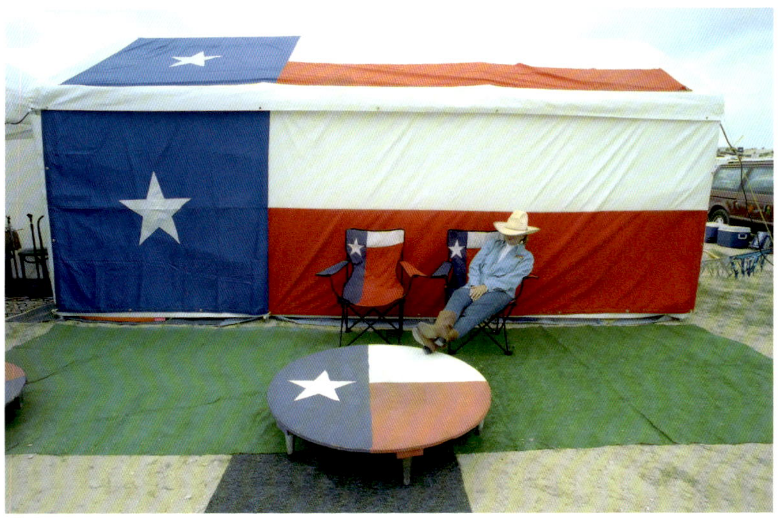

"Tent City" (Entertainment Now, Austin), 2003

Phyllis Greiner of Entertainment Now in Austin takes a breather between shows. The group was performing in Terlingua, located in the Big Bend area of Texas.

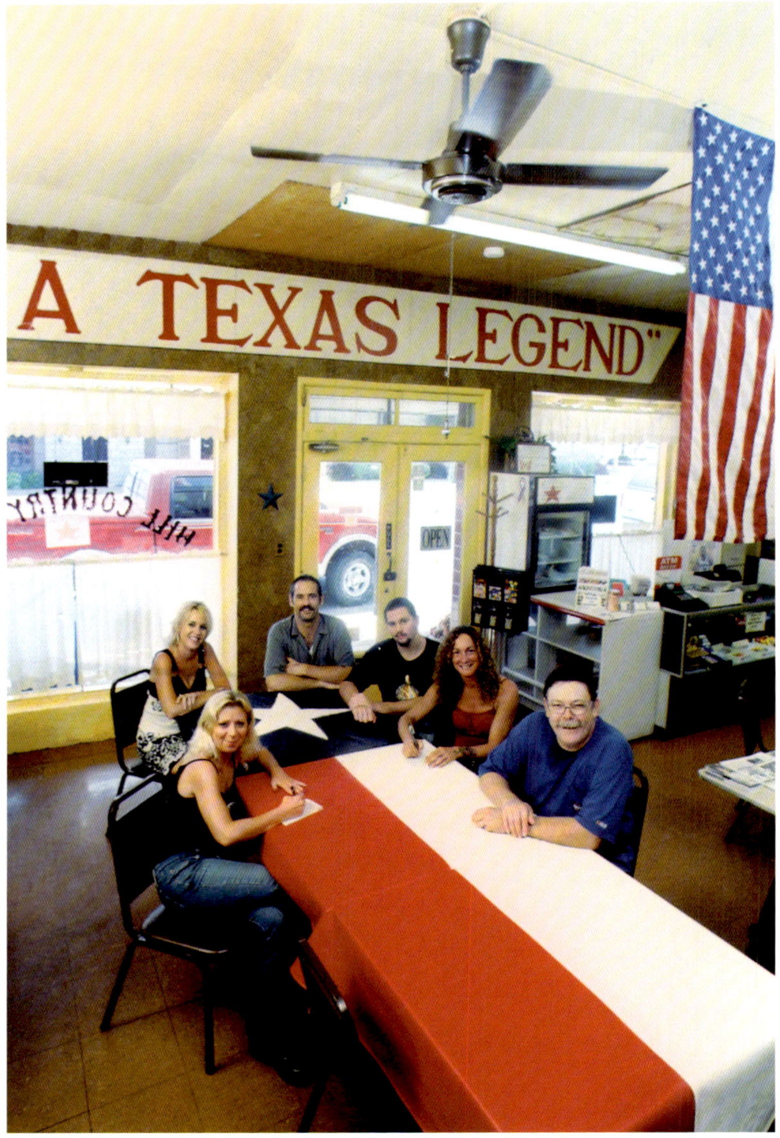

"Tables for Texans" (Hill Country Café, Kerrville), 2007

The 65-year-old Hill Country Café, owned by Cindy and Mike Piper, is famous for its Texas-sized breakfasts. Sitting clockwise around the Lone Star flag table are Rhonda Brown, Cindy, Mike, Harley Piper, Jeni DeBernardi, and Marty Morin. Coffee, please.

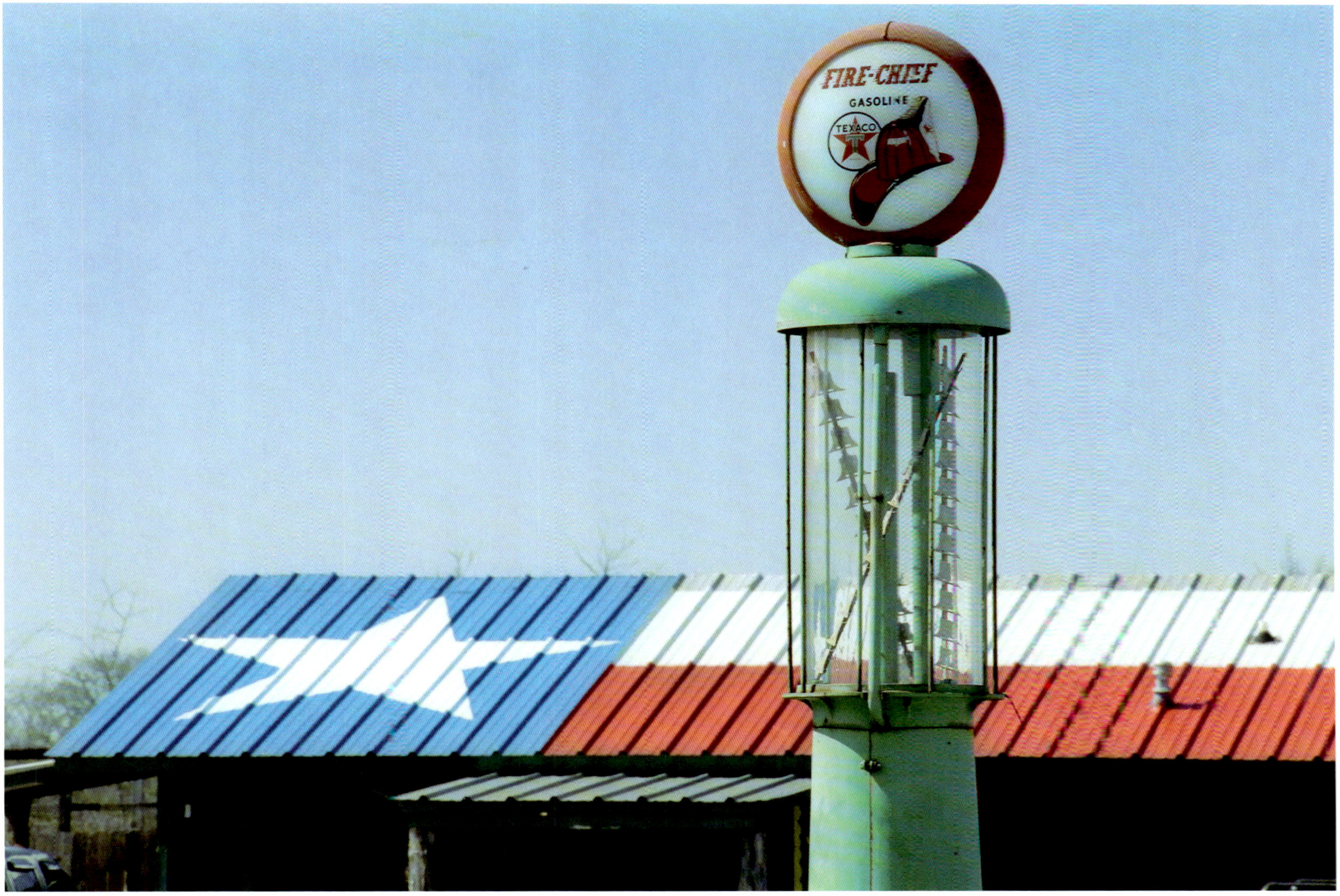

"Pumped Up" (Yellow Rose Store, Normangee), 2003

The Yellow Rose country store on OSR in Normangee is all about being nostalgic—and showing love for the Lone Star flag. High octane.

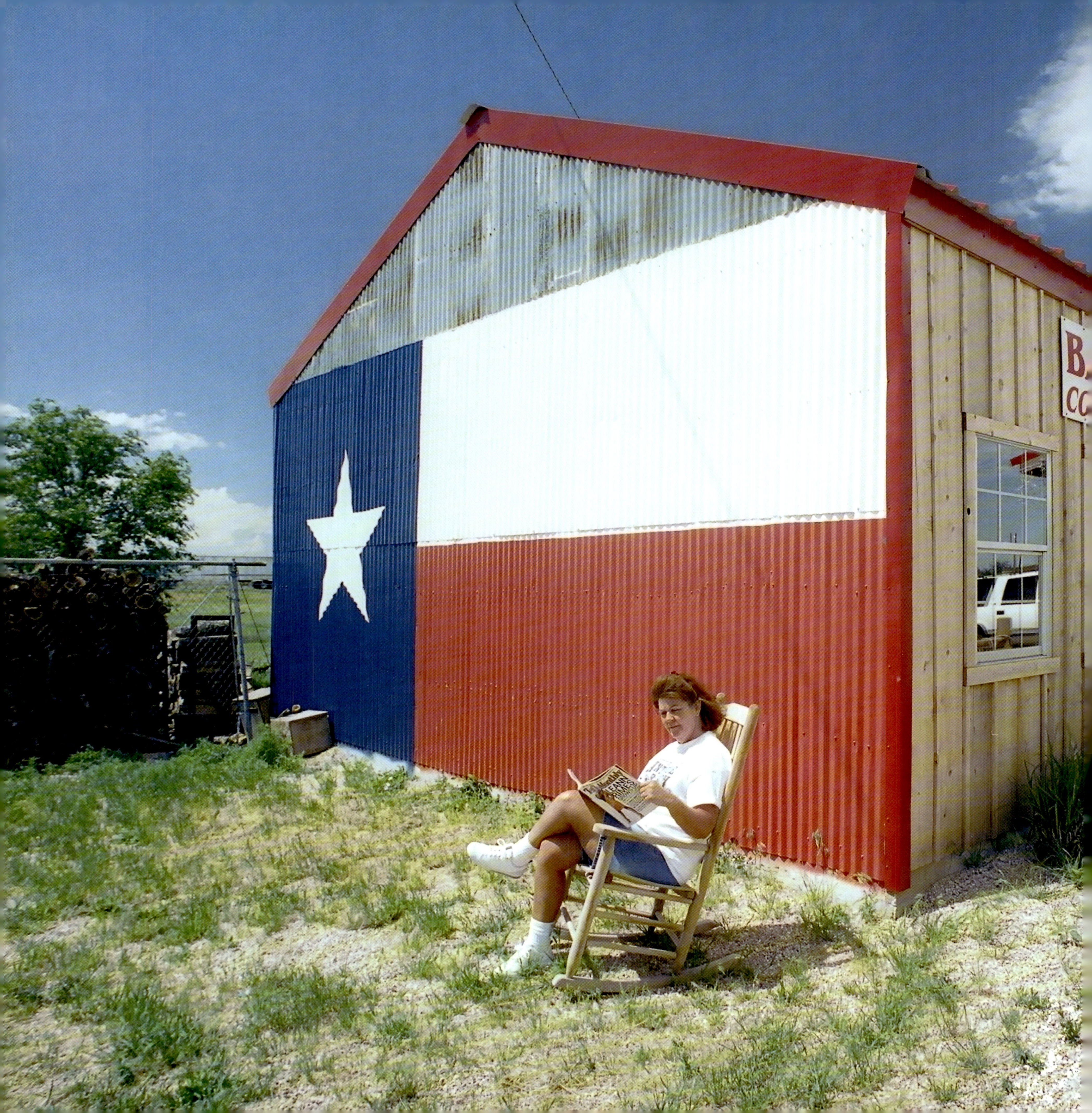

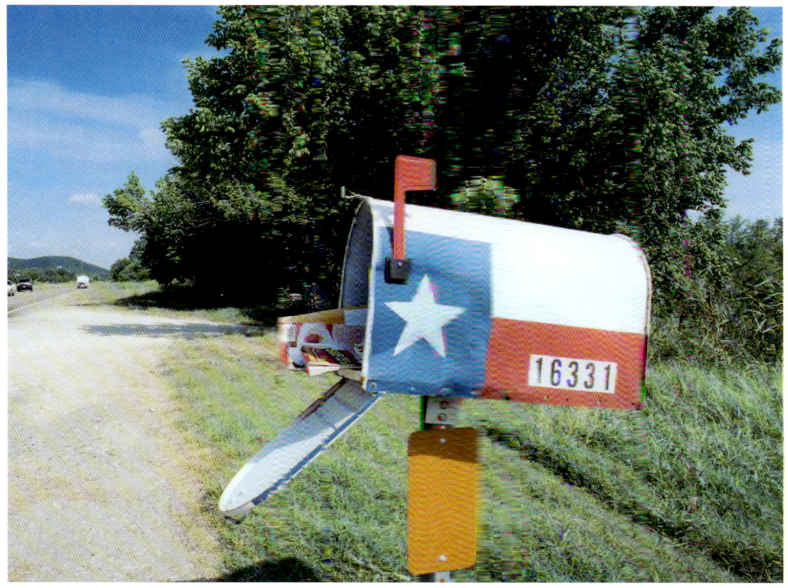

"Box 16" (Hubble Family mail box, Medina), 2003

The Hubble family of Medina lets passers-by know that their special delivery is love for the Lone Star flag. The Hubbles live along State Highway 16 in Bandera County.

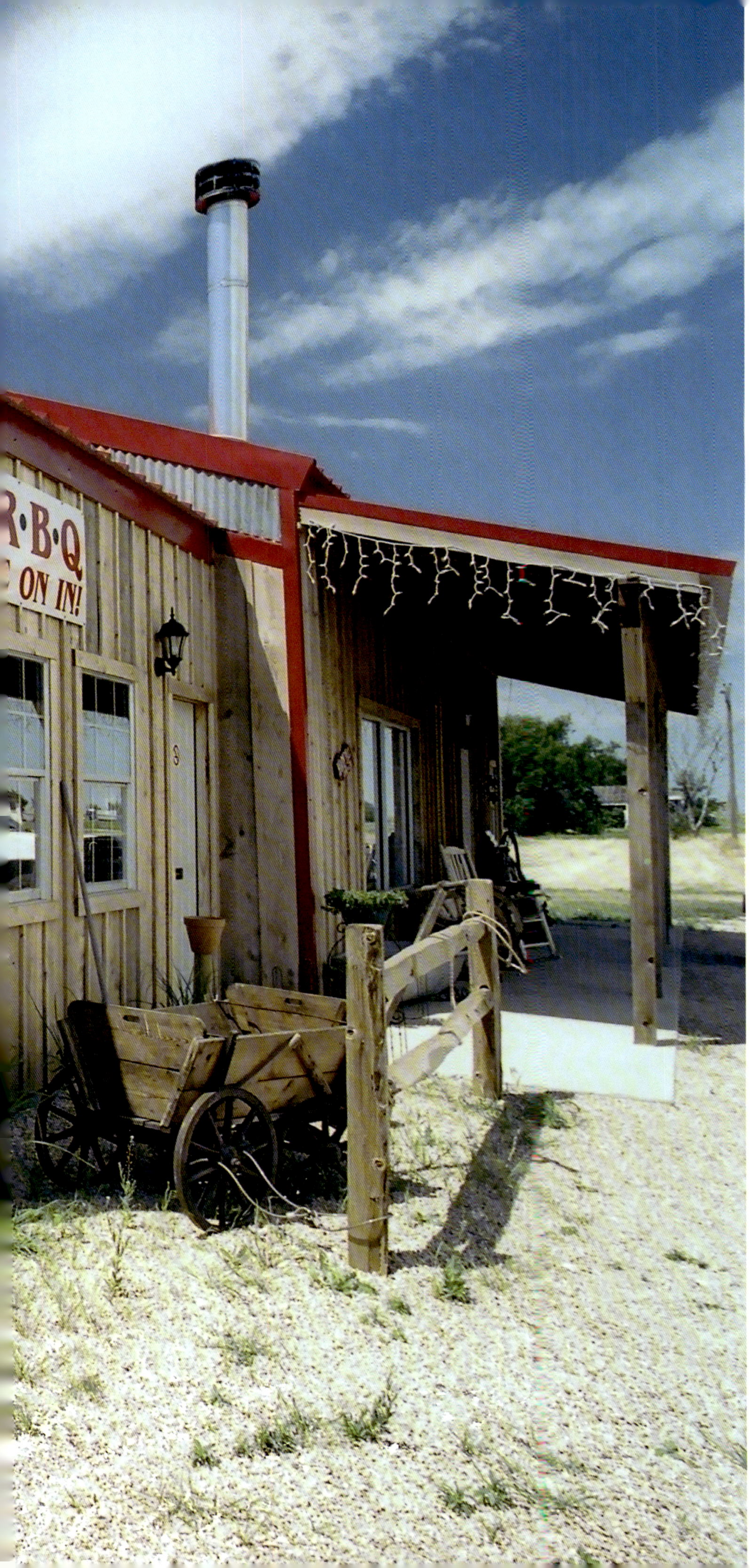

"BBQ Rock" (Antique Ranch BBQ, Adrian), 2002

Tracy Carnes, who works at the Antique Ranch BBQ in the Texas Panhandle town of Adrian, takes a little R&R after cooking up some ribs and brisket.

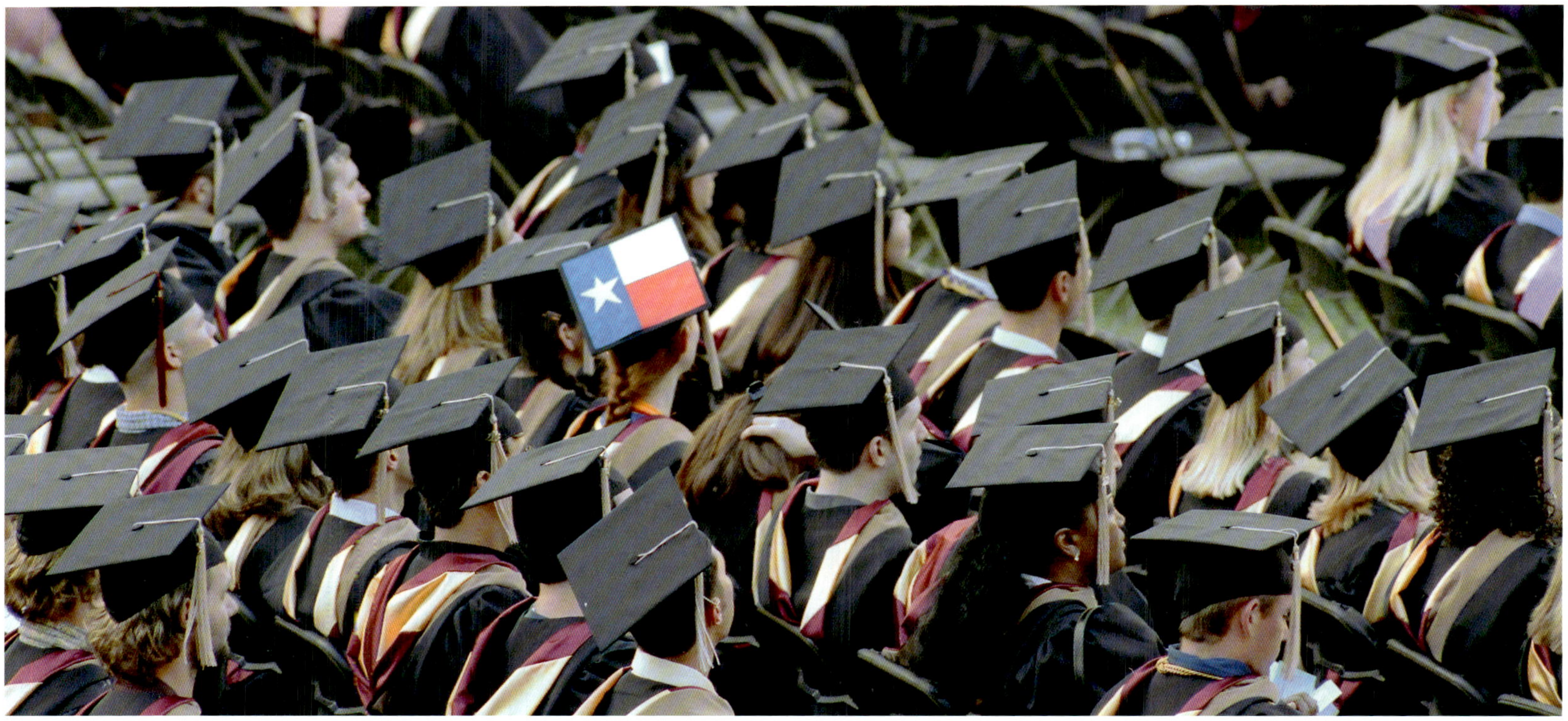

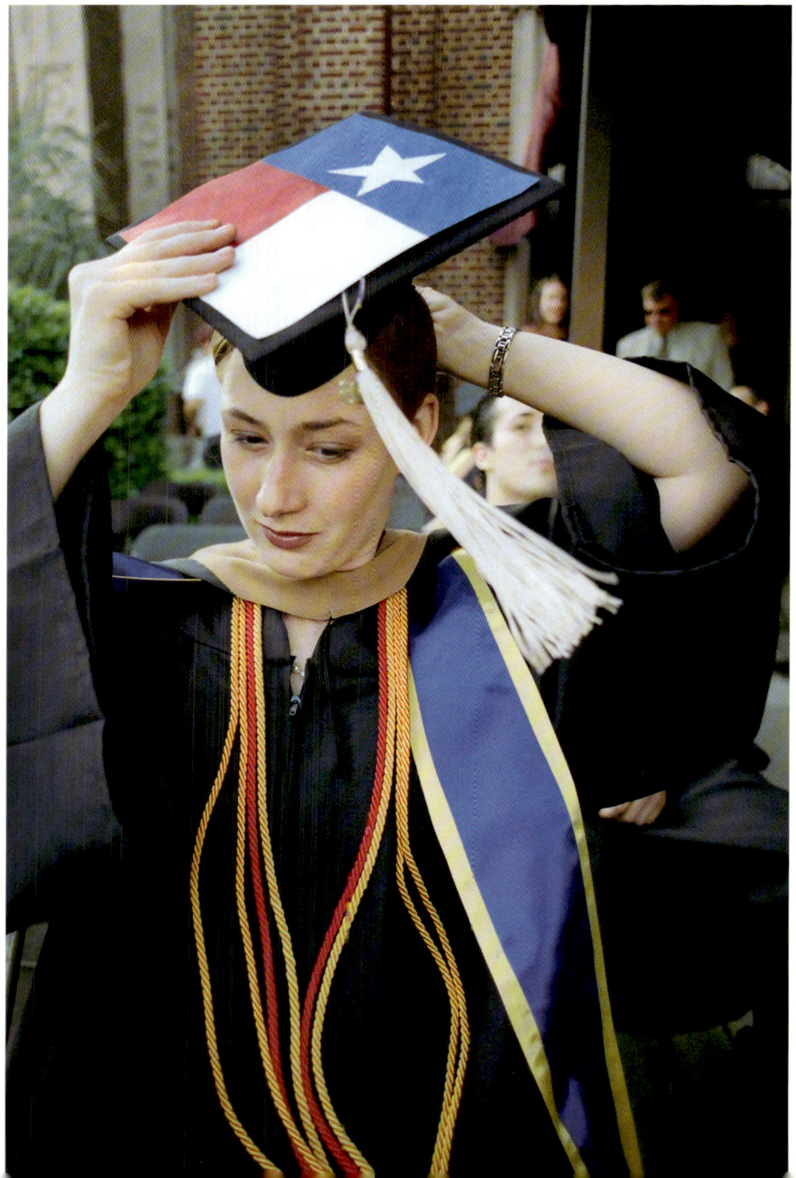

"Grad 3" (Hope Arnold, Loyola University, New Orleans), 2003

Hope Arnold is a stand-out at her graduation with her Lone Star mortar board. A star in the mix.

"Grad 1" (Hope Arnold, Loyola University, New Orleans), 2003

Hope Arnold, a native Texan from Houston, graduated from Loyola University in New Orleans, Louisiana, with honors––while also honoring her Lone Star State.

"State Caddie" (Doug and Suzan Moreland, Manchaca), 2005

Doug Moreland from Manchaca restored this 1972 Cadillac from scratch for the love of the Lone Star State. Doug, an artist, singer, and performer, can be seen throughout the state with his Caddie and wife Suzan by his side. ➡

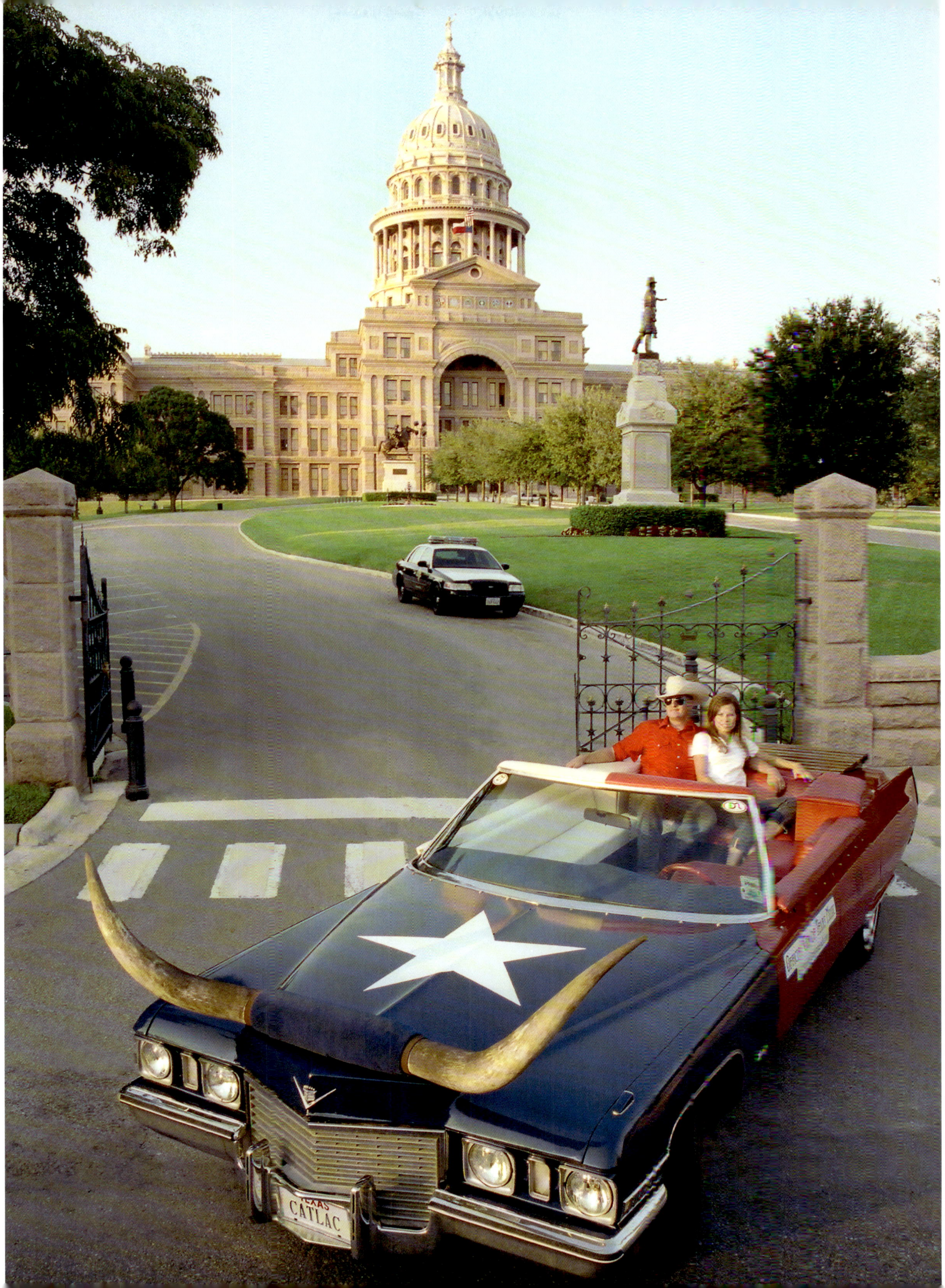
TEXAS
CATLAC

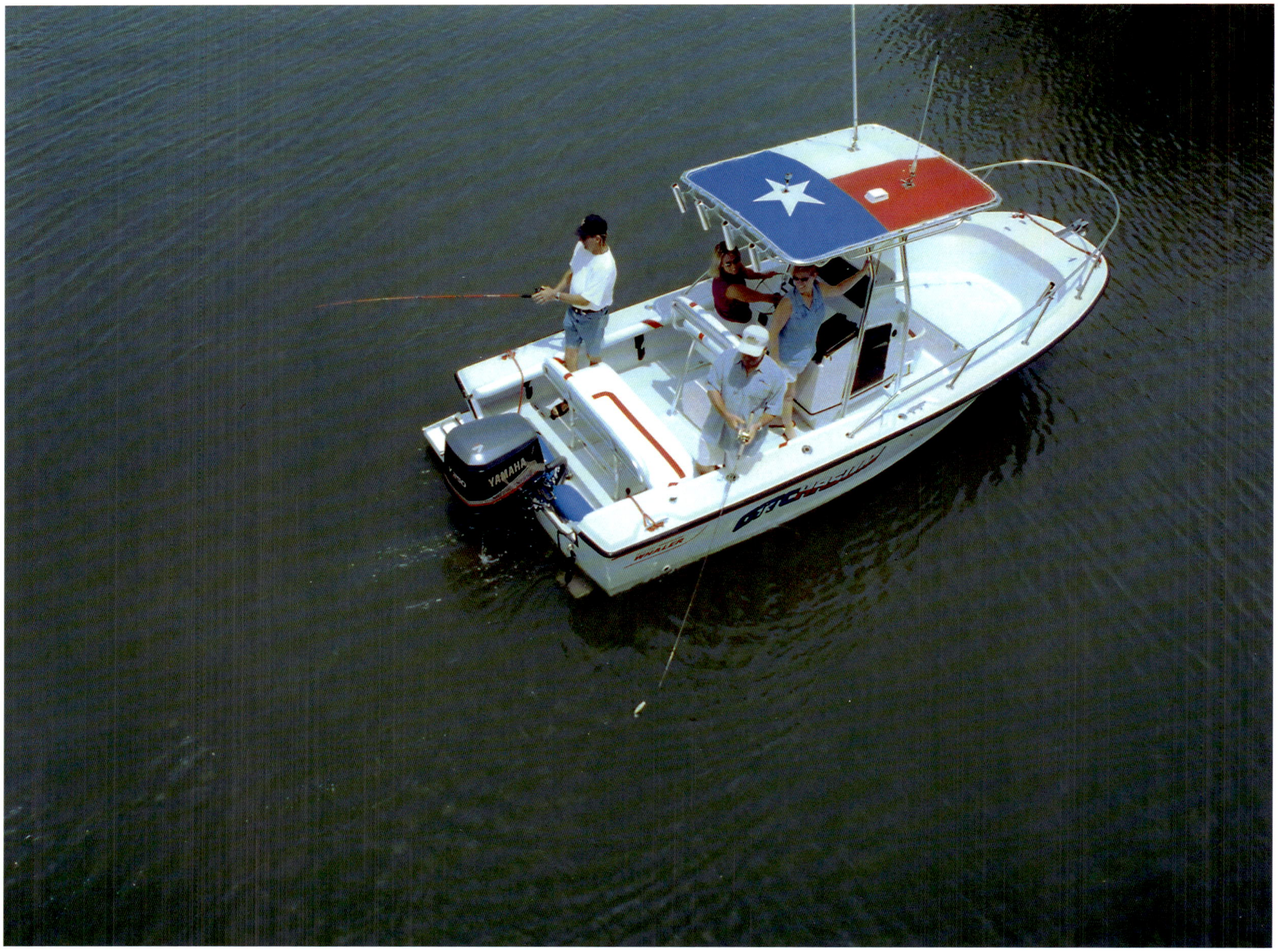

"Lone Boat" (West Bay, Galveston), 2004

Boat owners Howard and Lore Cordell of Terramar Beach fish the west bay of Galveston with friends Kenny and Debbie Klyng. Their twenty-one-foot Boston Whaler is all decked out with the Lone Star flag.

"Belt Buckle" (Jesse Campos, Houston), 2004

Jesse Campos of San Antonio bought the belt buckle after his discharge from World War II, just proud to be back in the Lone Star State. Jesse, who now lives in Houston, was attending a memorial for the war he served in.

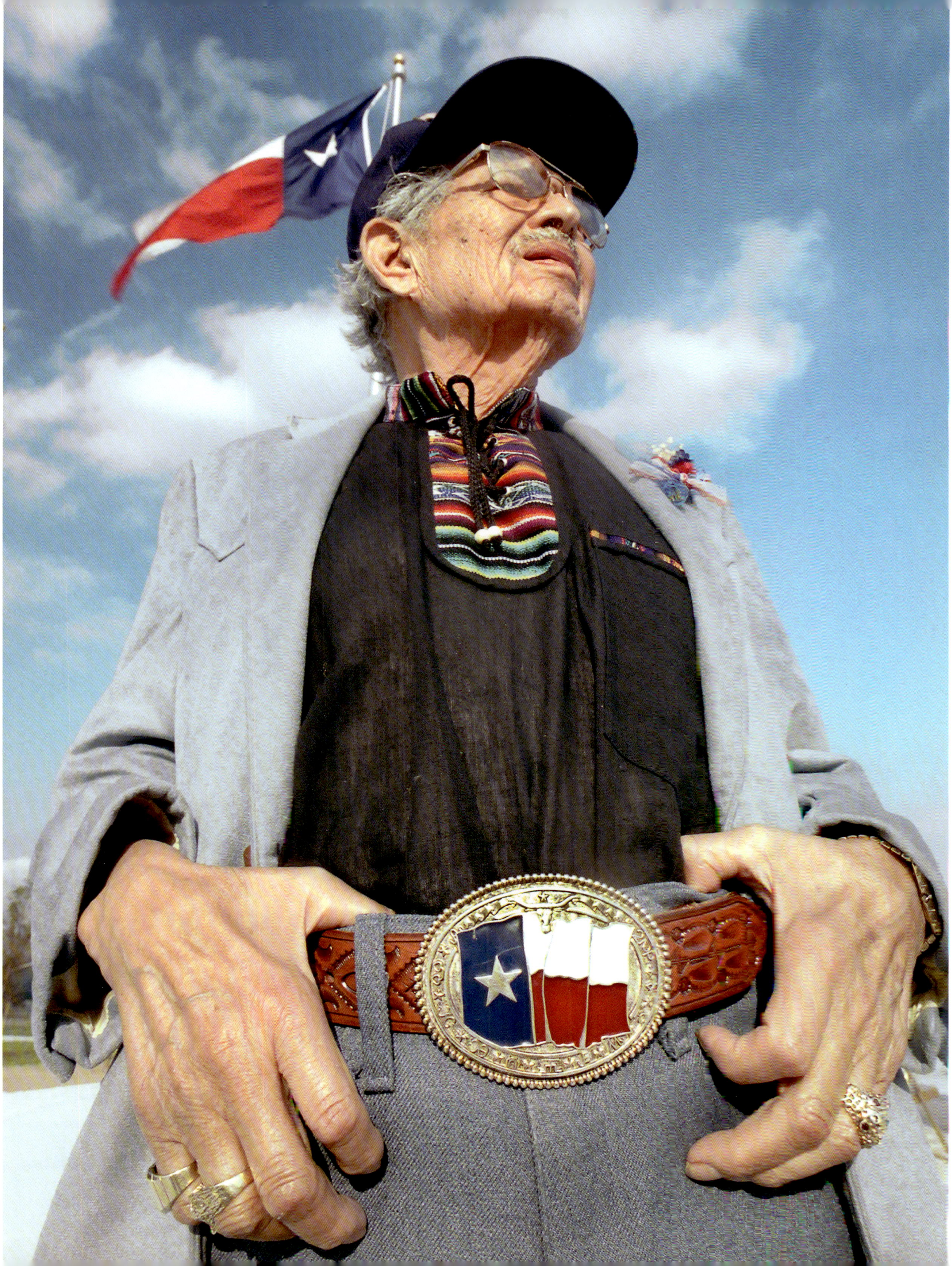

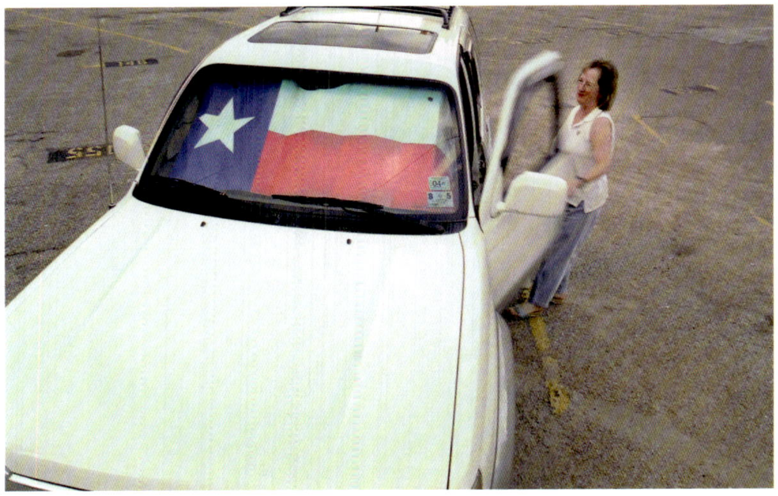

"Auto Shade" (Linda Daigle, downtown Houston), 2004

Linda Daigle crossed that Red River from her hometown of Shreveport, Louisiana, married a Texas boy, and is now all Lone Star proud.

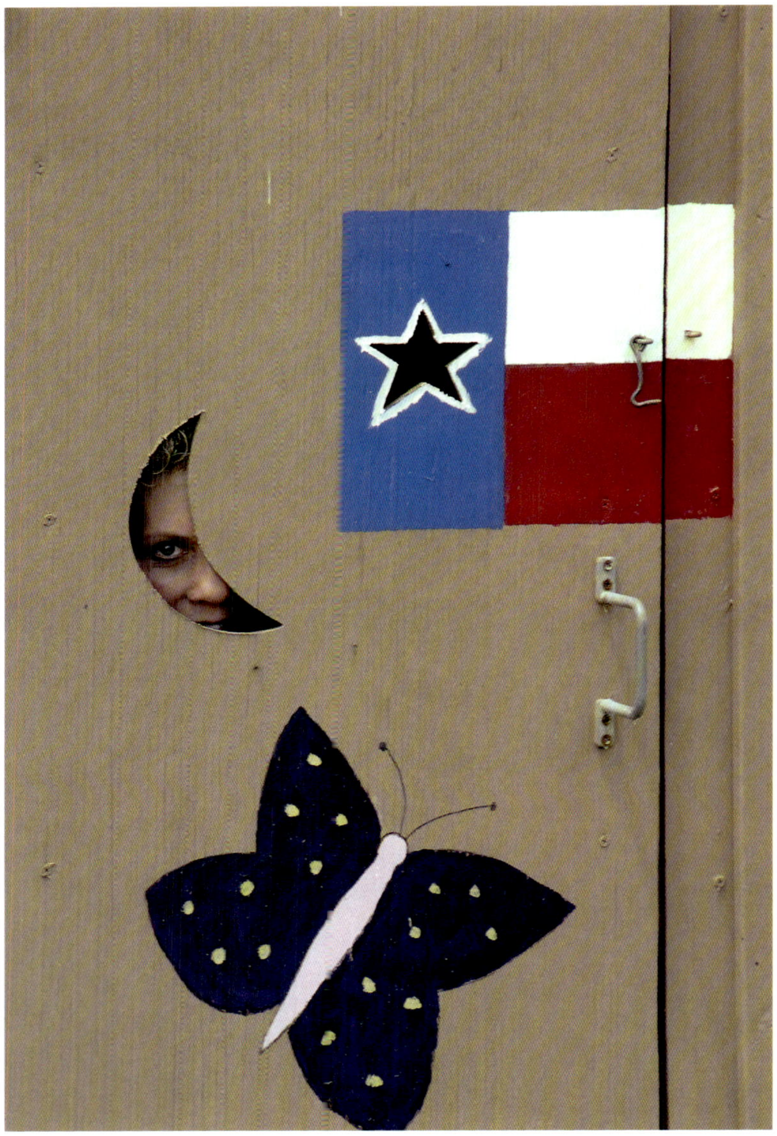

"Outhouse" (Ann Kainer, Schulenburg), 2004

Ann Kainer of Houston peeks from the outhouse on her family's country property in Schulenburg. Ann painted her outhouse to show her love of the Lone Star flag, then added the crescent moon to soften the appearance. Occupied.

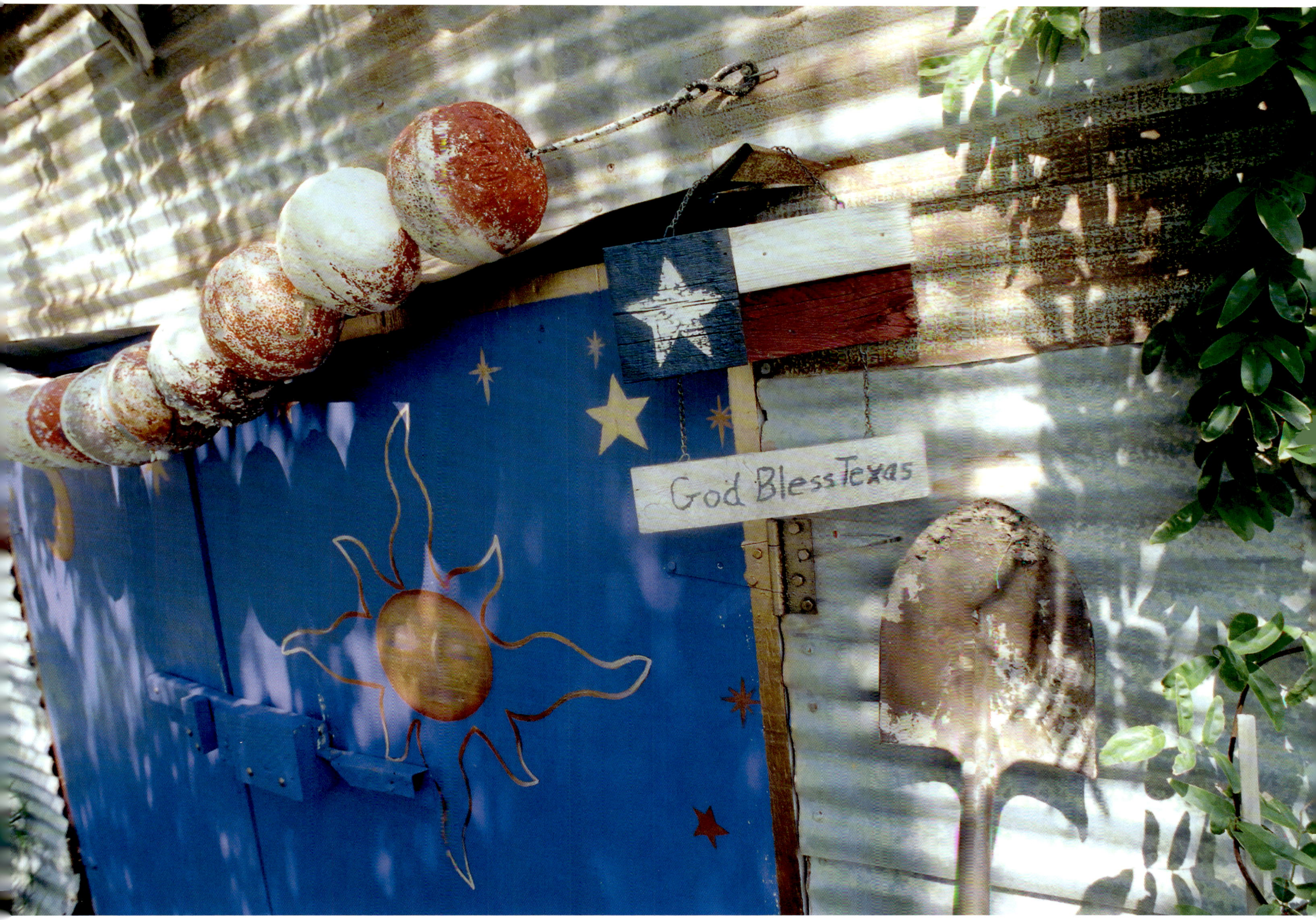

"Blue Pride" (Diane Wilson, Seadrift), 2002

Seadrift shrimper Diane Wilson catches state pride and casts for God's blessing with the homemade wood Lone Star flag that anchors her garage door.

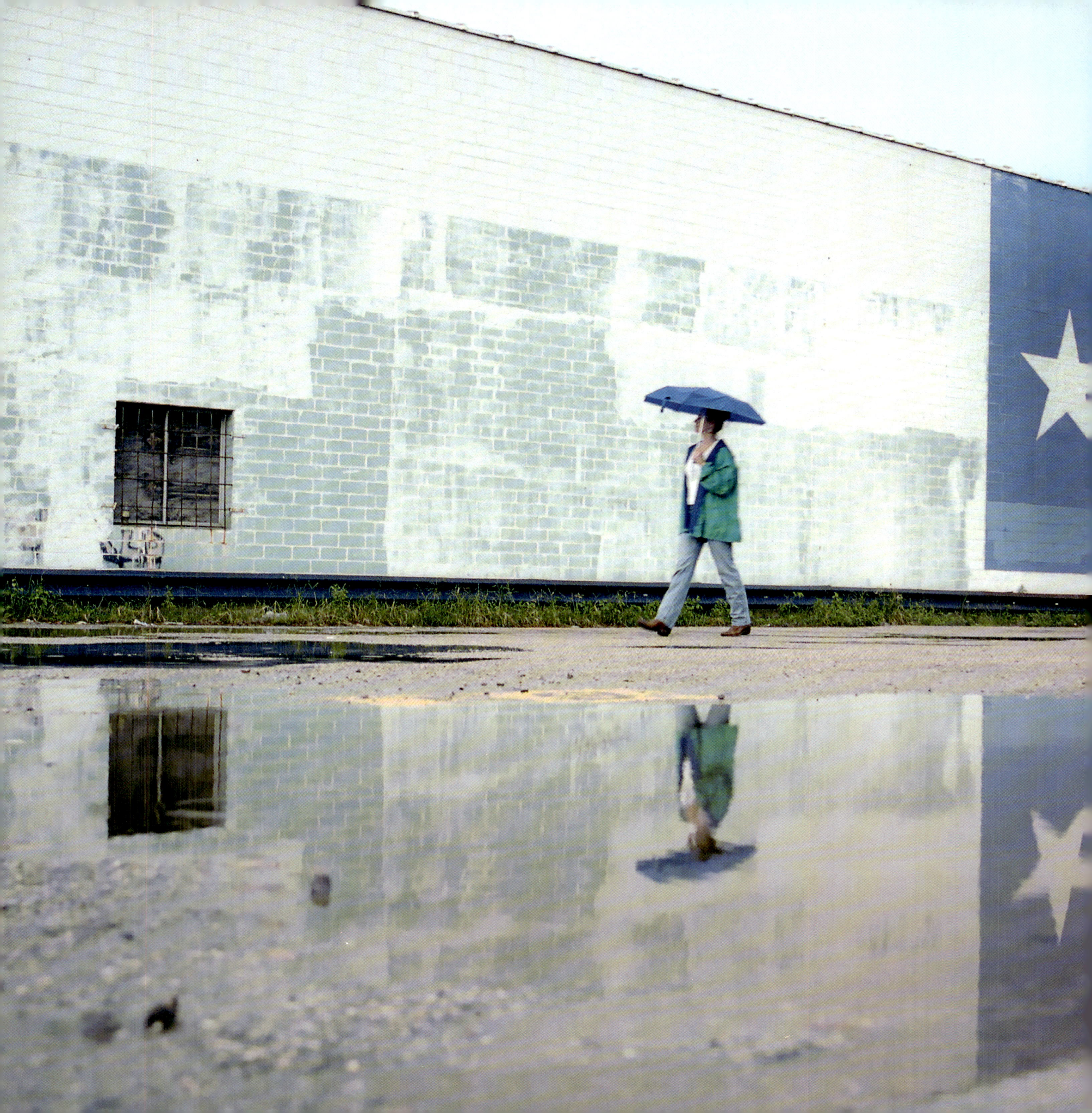

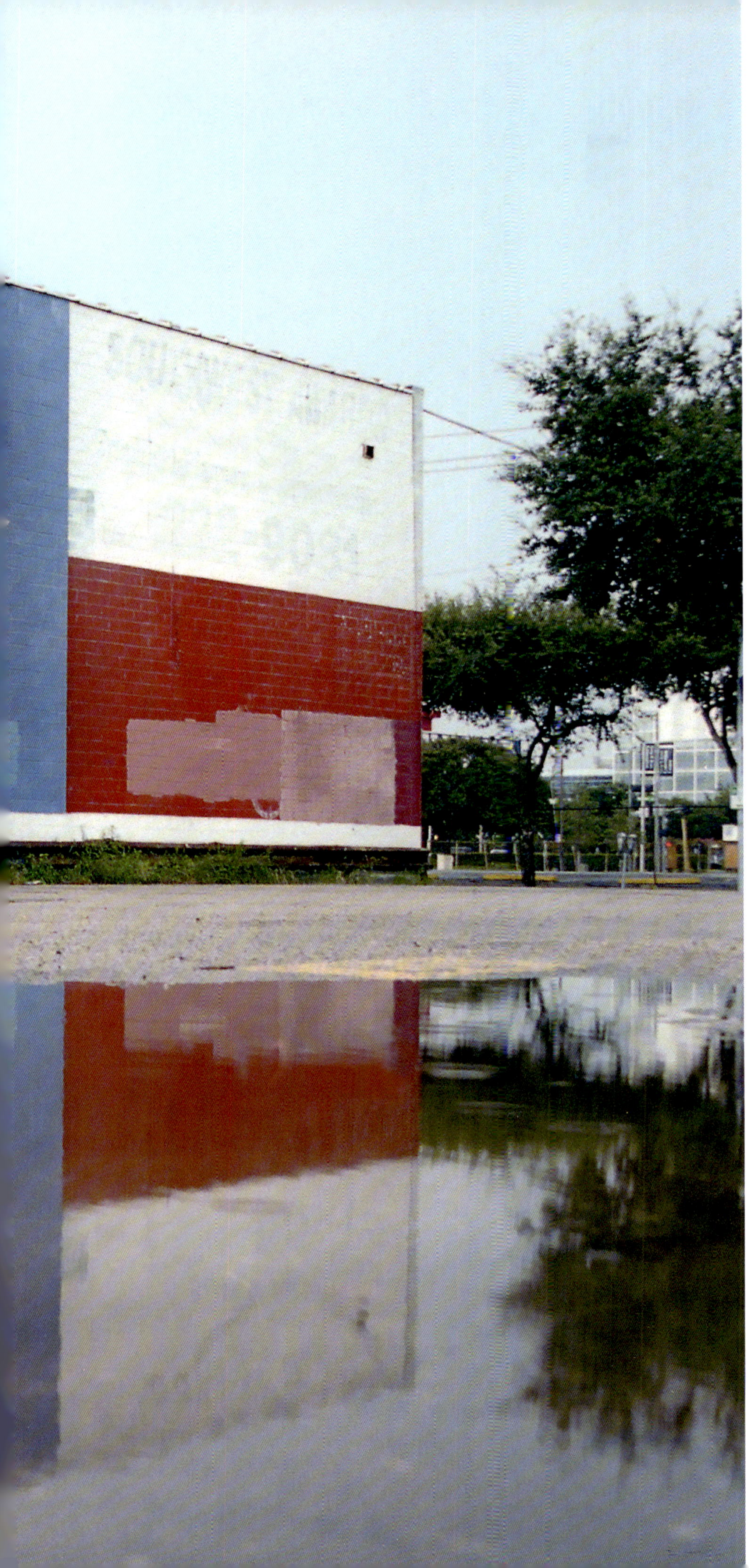

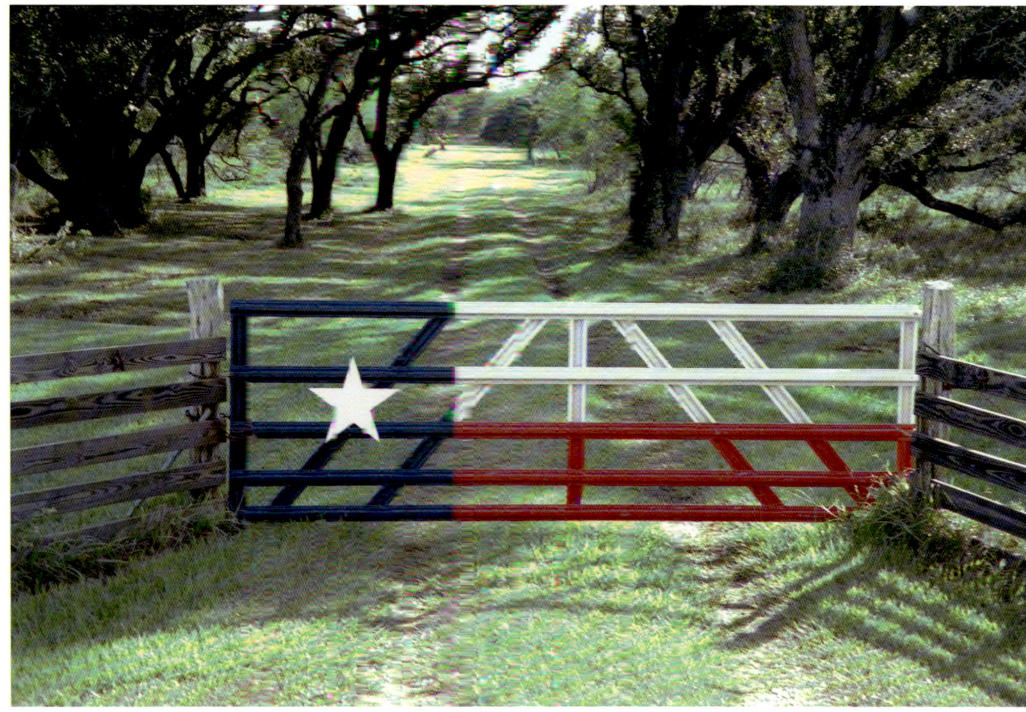

"Raisin Gate" (Royce Krueger's fence, Raisin), 2004

Live oak trees line the country road at the Krueger's family farm in Raisin. Their gate greets visitors with Lone Star pride. Swing on in.

"Lone Puddle" (Joy Arnold, Houston), 2005

After a rainstorm, Houstonian Joy Arnold walks back from a convention at the George R. Brown Convention Center. A puddle reflects one of Houston's old buildings decked out with the Lone Star flag.

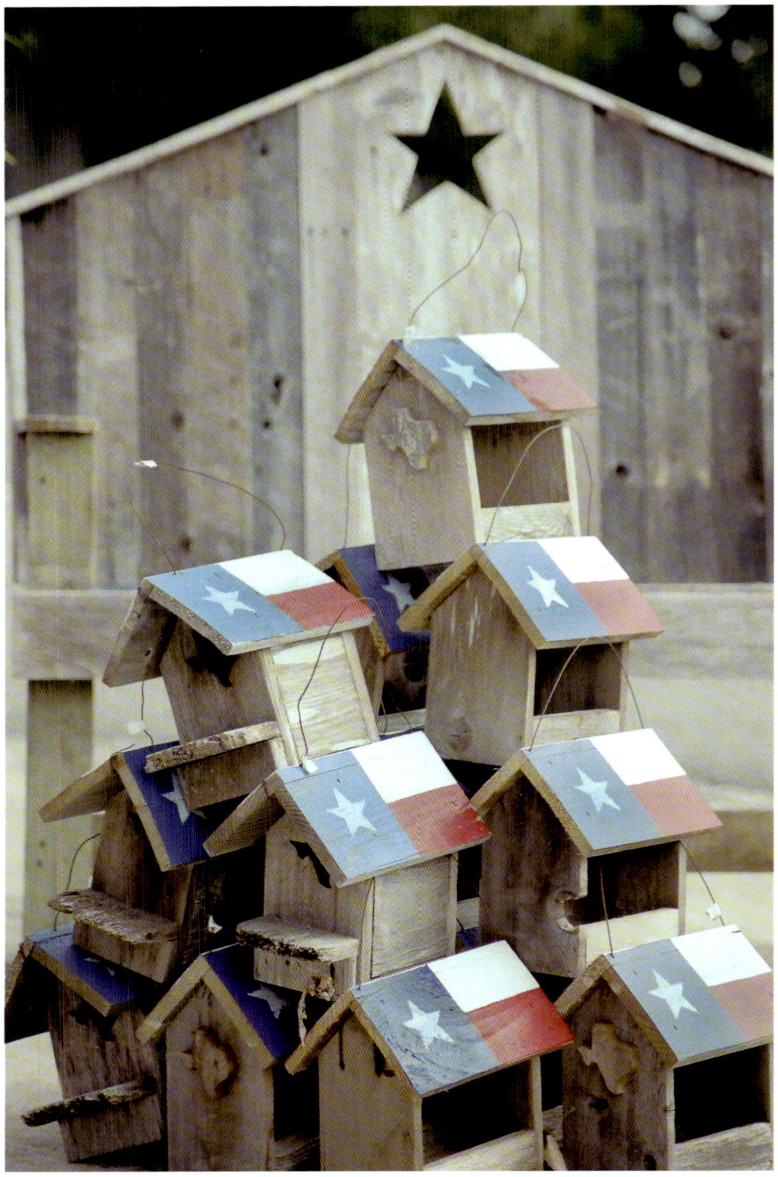

"High Rise" (Birdhouses, Johnson City), 2004

Carol Sorensen, owner of The Gazebo gift shop in Johnson City, specializes in western accents featuring the Lone Star State, like these birdhouses.

"Paint Bucket" (Painted Horse B&B, Kerrville), 2004

Bud and Sandy Bonner run the Painted Horse Ranch and Bed and Breakfast on fifty-five acres of beautiful Hill Country land. Their love of Texas paints the landscape. Sit a spell.

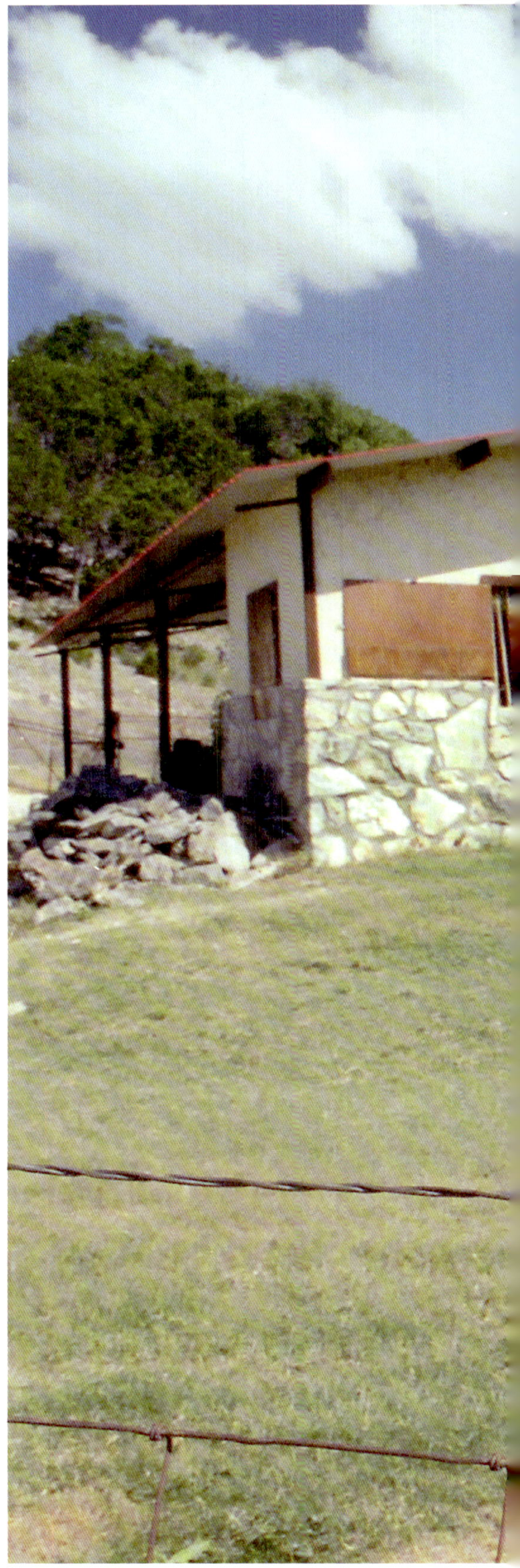

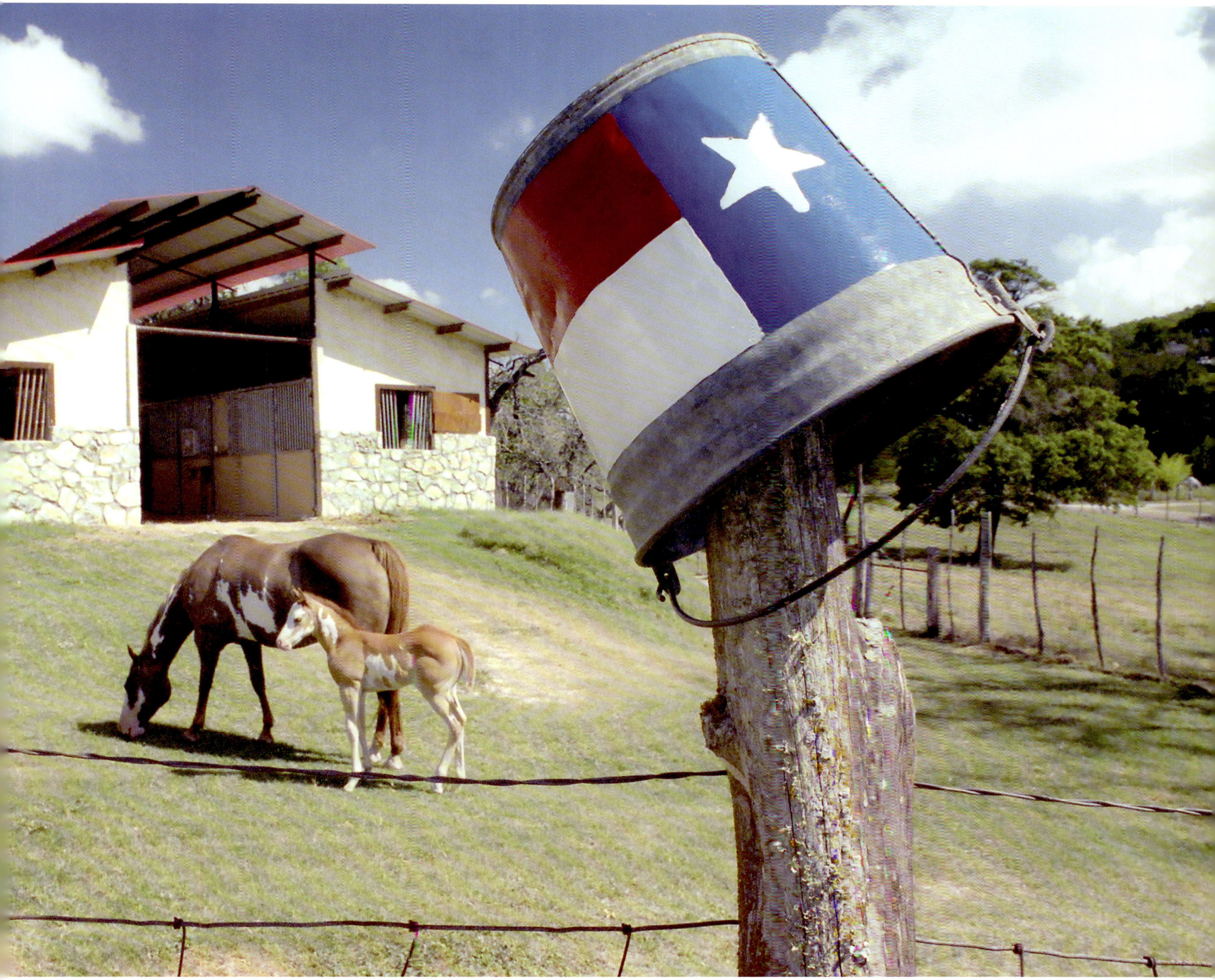

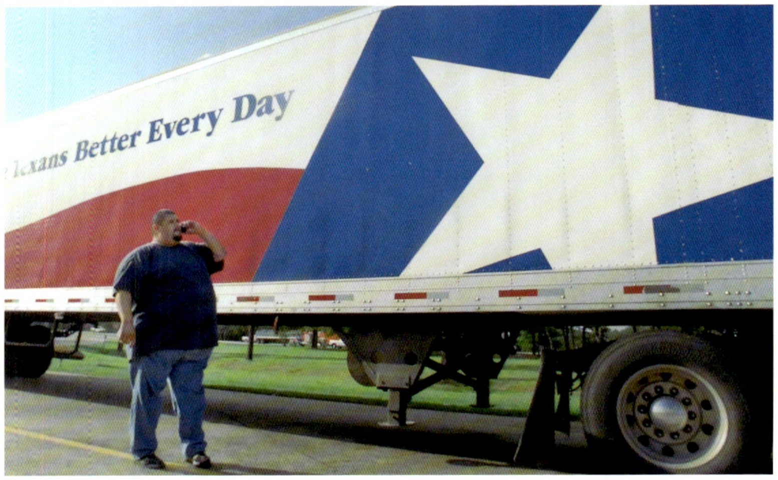

"Big as Texas" (Alfred Alvizo, San Antonio), 2004

Alfred Alvizo of San Antonio, driver for the HEB supermarket chain, takes a breather in Columbus on his way to Houston. Founded in Kerrville in 1905, HEB displays the Lone Star flag on most of the company vehicles.

"Mail Faith" (Steven Longino, Pasadena), 2003

Steven Longino of Pasadena retrieves his mail from a heavenly mailbox that proclaims the Lone Star State is God's country. Prayers answered.

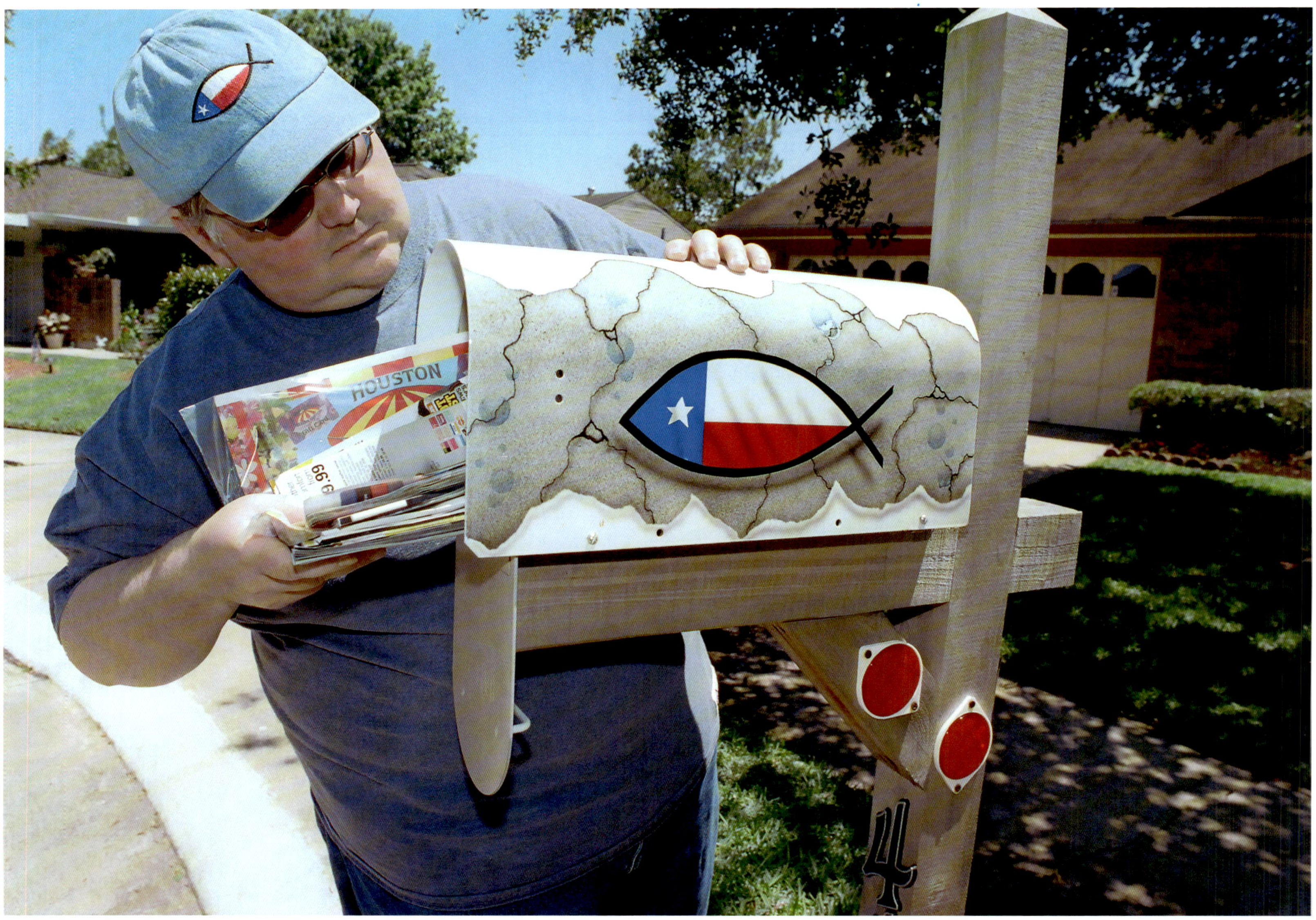

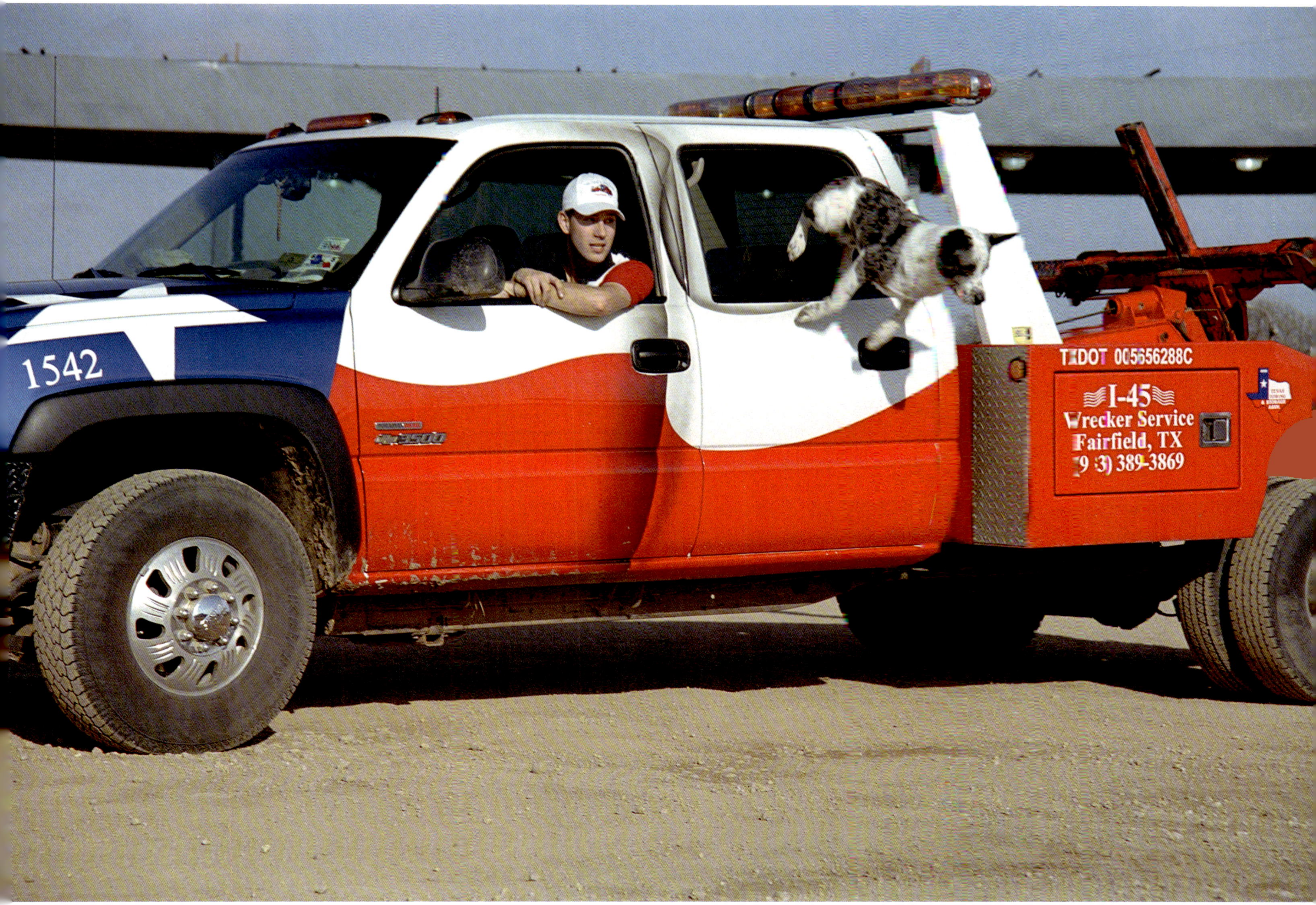

"Jump Start" (David James with his dog, Crash, Fairfield), 2004

David James pulls up in his Lone Star Chevy ton-and-half tow truck, as Crash gets a jumpstart for the house. Road service anyone?

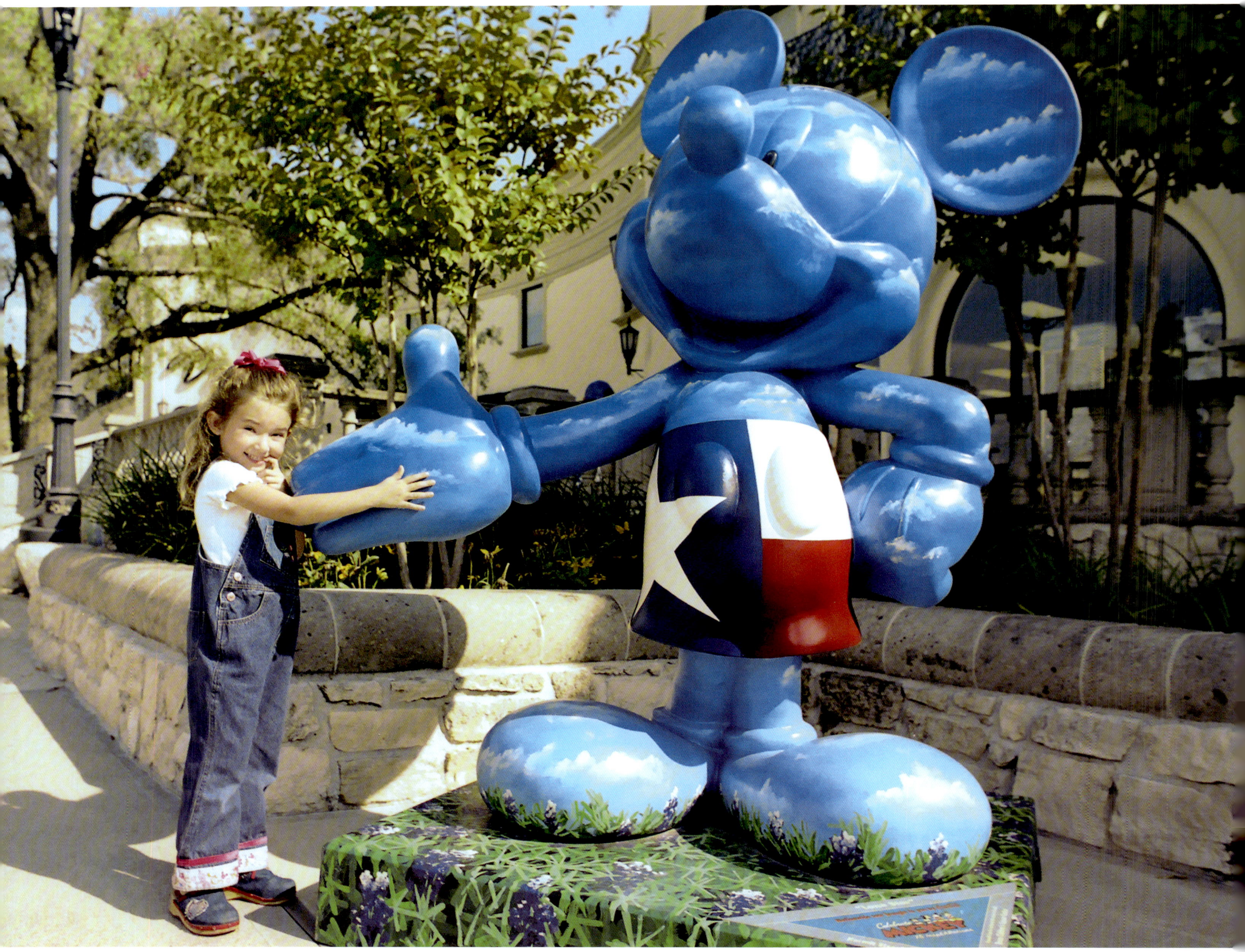

"Mickey" (Anna McGrath, Houston), 2005

Anna McGrath of Houston gives Mickey Mouse a bashful high five. The most famous mouse in the galaxy celebrates his seventy-fifth birthday. Lone Star Mickey is the work of Houston artist Kermit Eisenhut. Say "cheese."

"Miss Boots" (Rocky Carroll, Houston), 2004

Houston boot maker Rocky Carroll has gotten a lot of miles out of the boots he has fashioned for the rich and famous including U.S. presidents 41 and 43, and for just plain folks. He made these boots ("Miss Texas"), for his wife, Judge Denise Collins.

"Chron Cap" (Amanda Mason, Houston), 2005

Amanda Mason of Houston, whose parents Don Mason and Claudia Feldman work at the *Houston Chronicle*, shows her pride in the Lone Star flag and the newspaper.

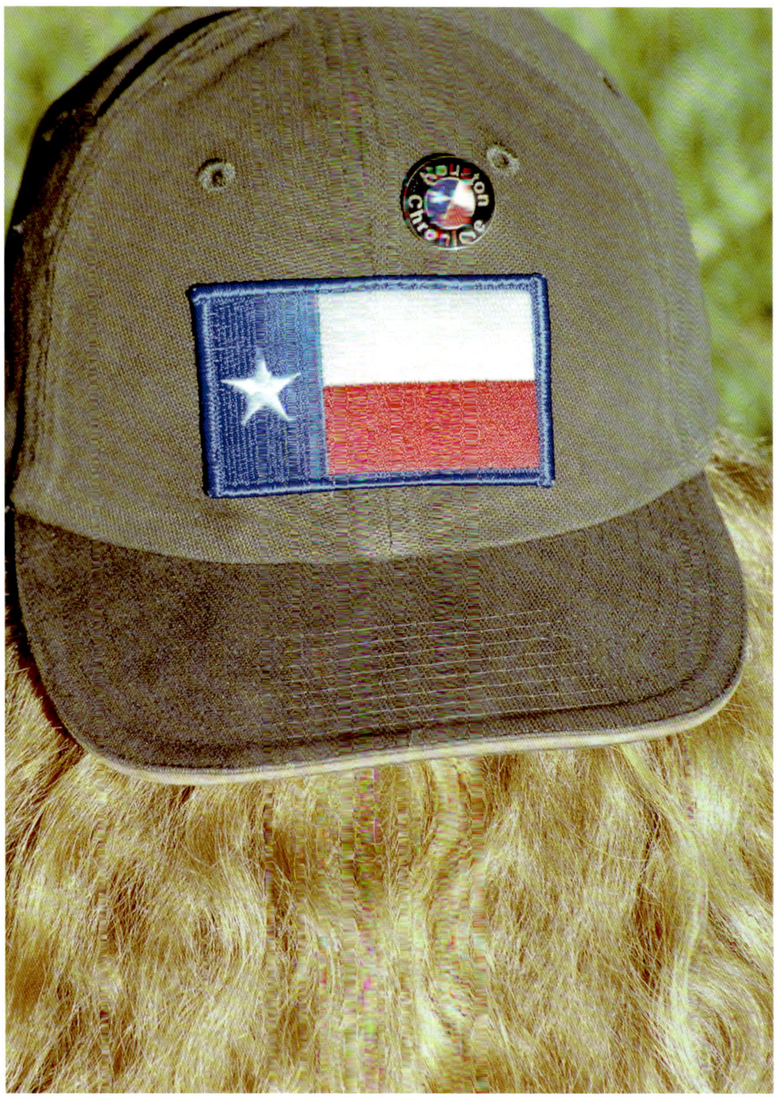

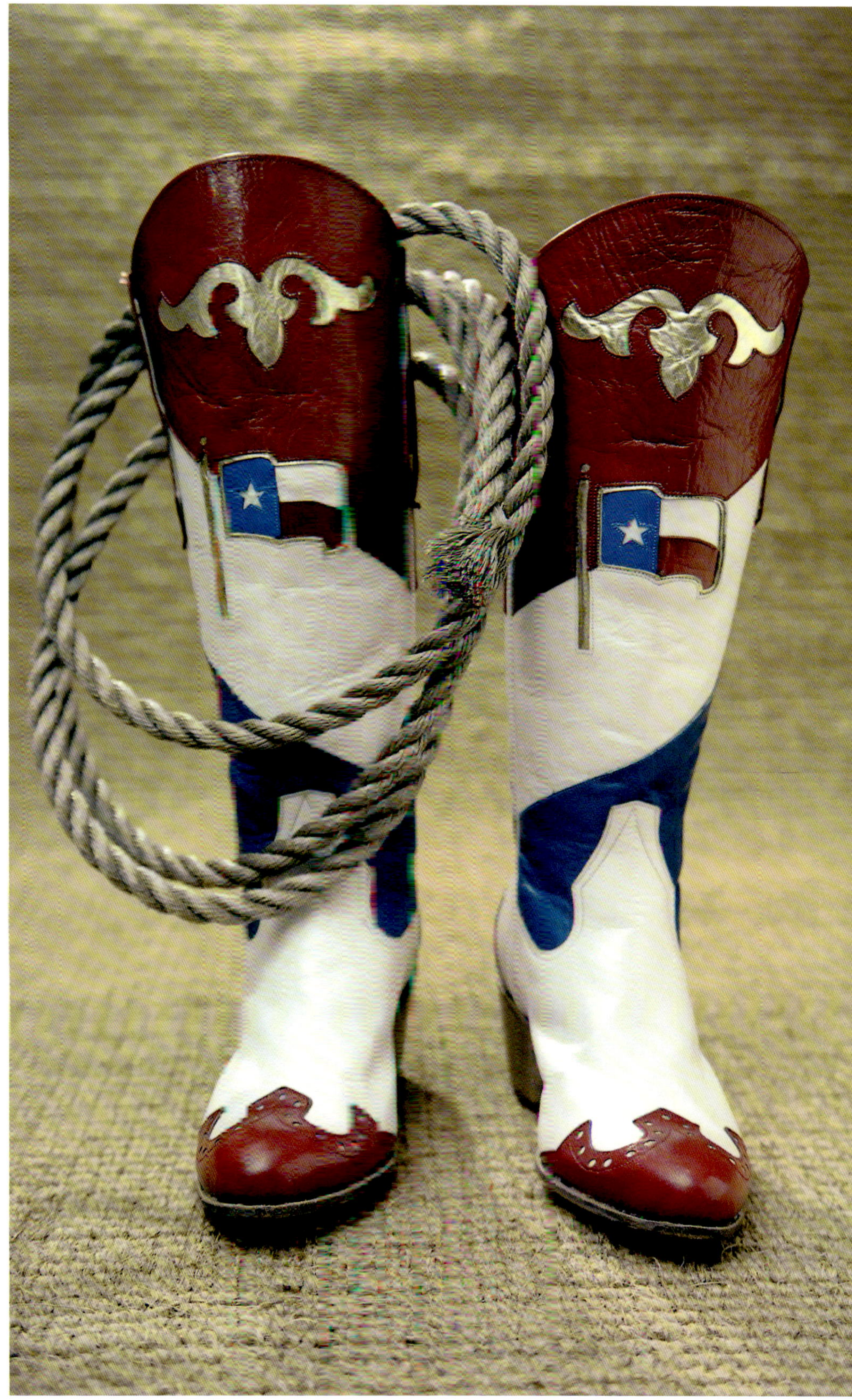

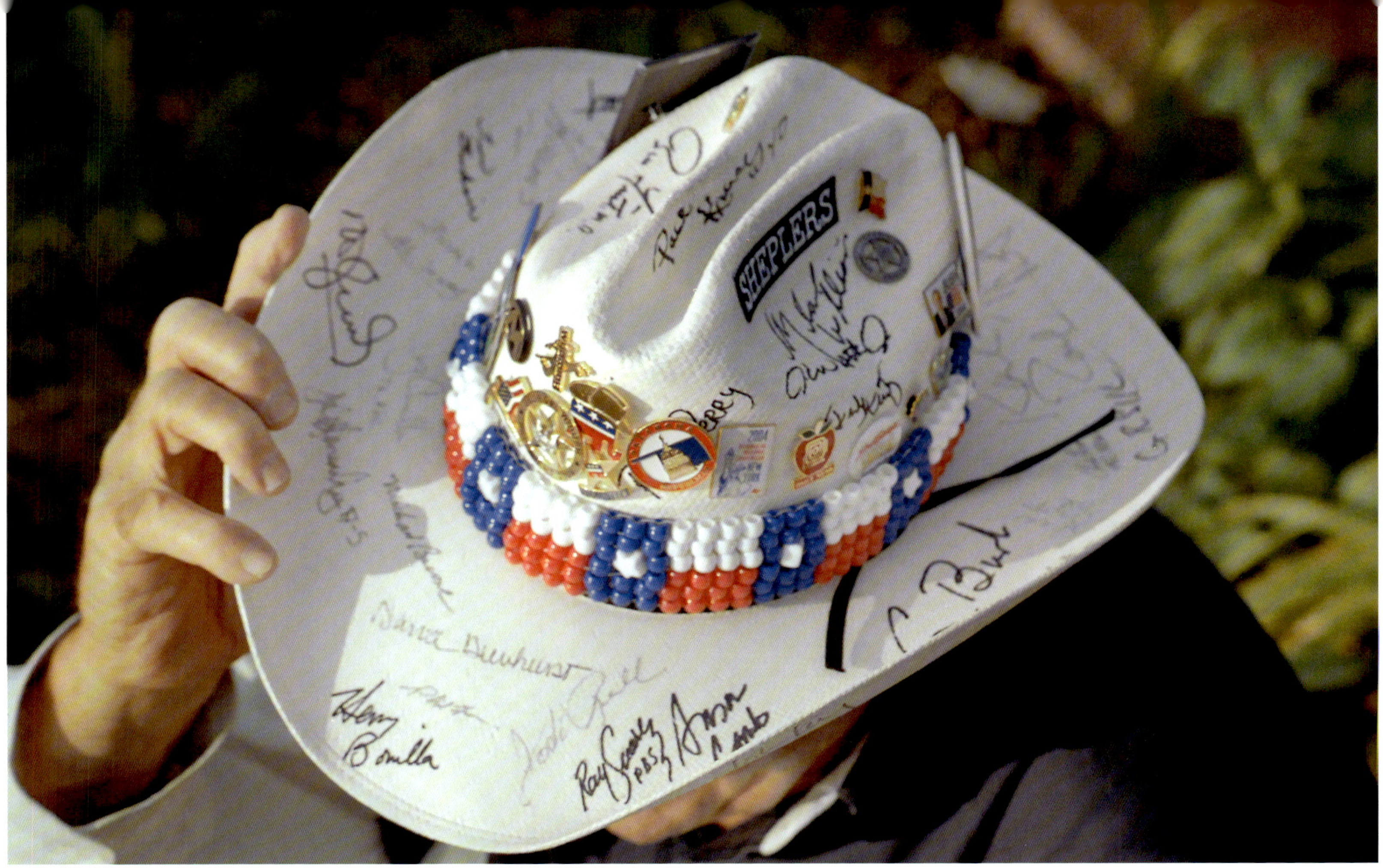

"Delegate" (Wayne Turner, Waxahachie), 2005

Wayne Turner of Waxahachie was an Alternate Delegate to the 2004 Republican National Convention for District 6, where his cowboy hat with the Lone Star flag band was signed by former President George W. Bush and other dignitaries.

"Camp Chairs" (Johnny Camp, Athens), 2003

Johnny Camp of Athens makes his Lone Star outdoor furniture in his workshop in the back of his home on State Highway 31 north of the city. Pull up a chair. ▶

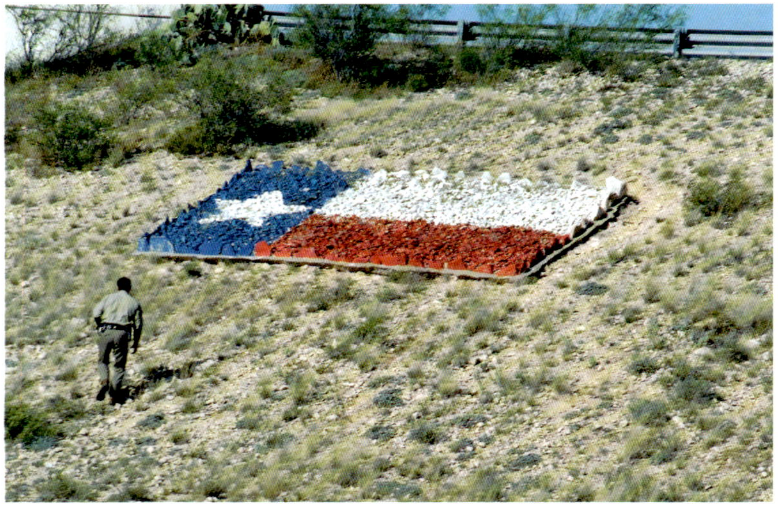

"Stone Symbol" (Fort Stockton), 2004

Game Warden Billy Lucio checks out the flag at a rest stop on Interstate 10 just east of Fort Stockton. Carefully placed on the hillside, this stone Lone Star flag is part of the state's effort to keep the pride alive. Rest a bit.

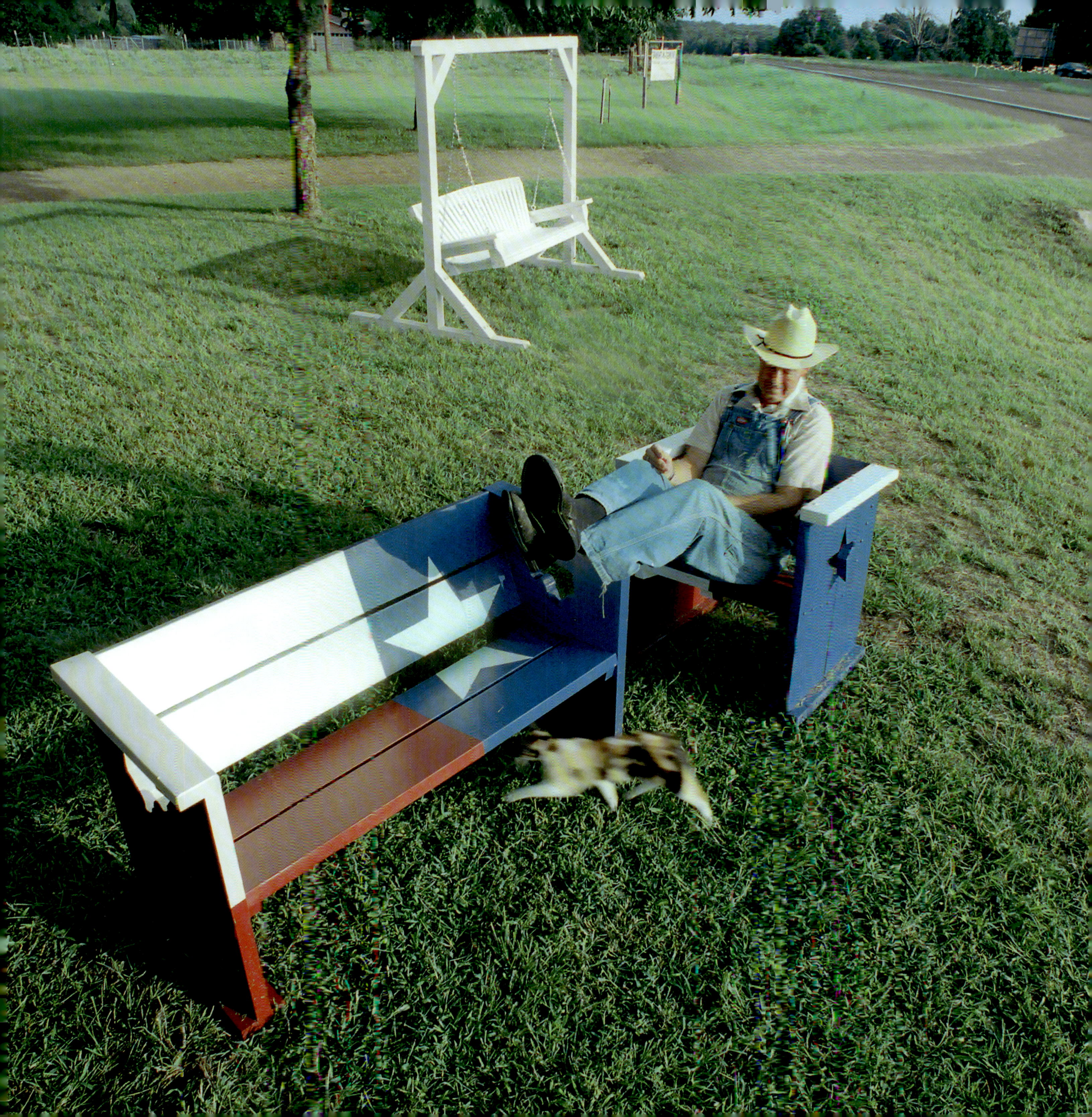

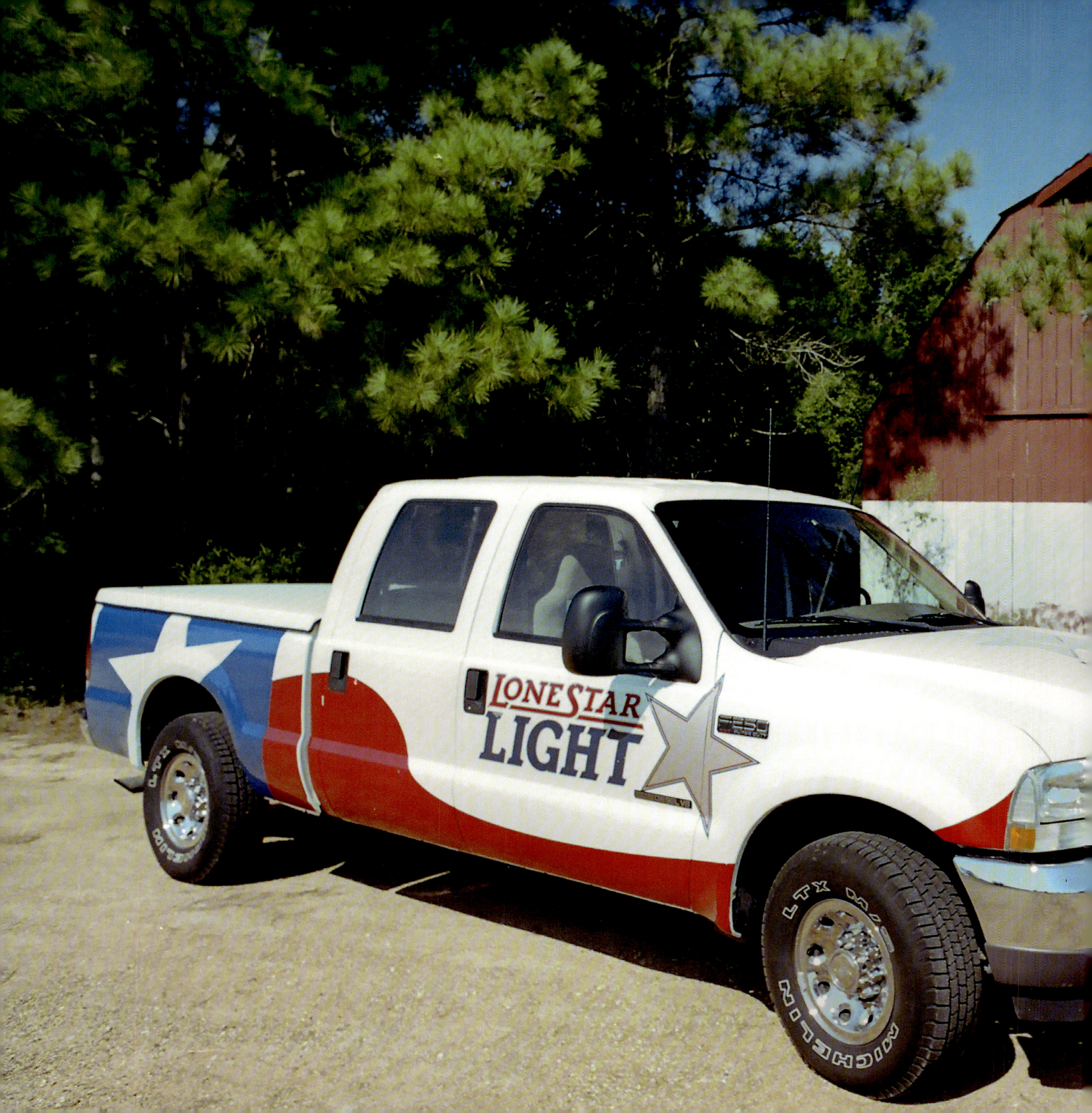
LoneStar
LIGHT

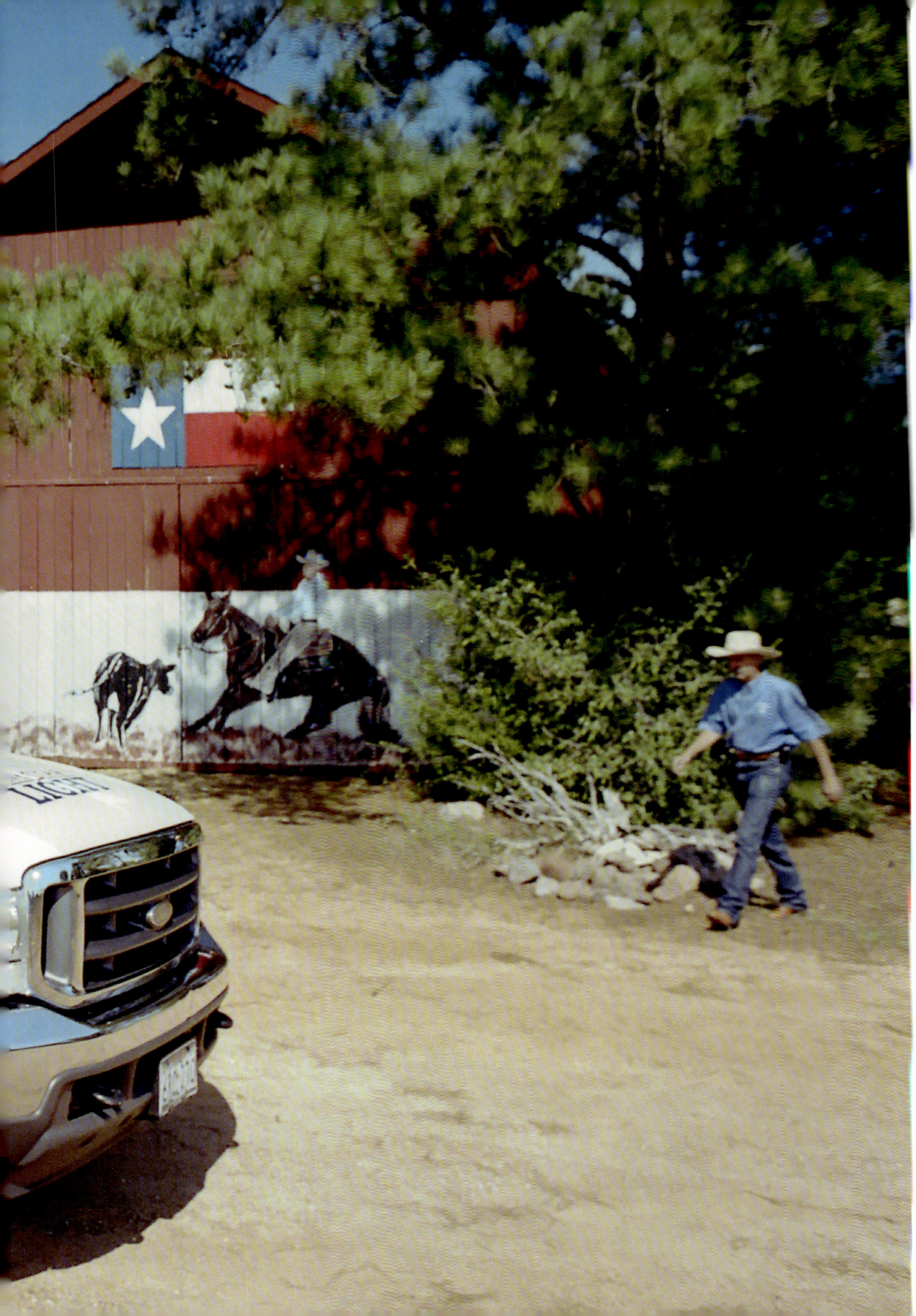

"Beer Wagon"
(Kristen Distributing Co., Bryan) 2004

Making his rounds. Jody Giese heads for his beer wagon (truck). Jody works for Kristen Distributing Company in Bryan, distributing Lone Star pride.

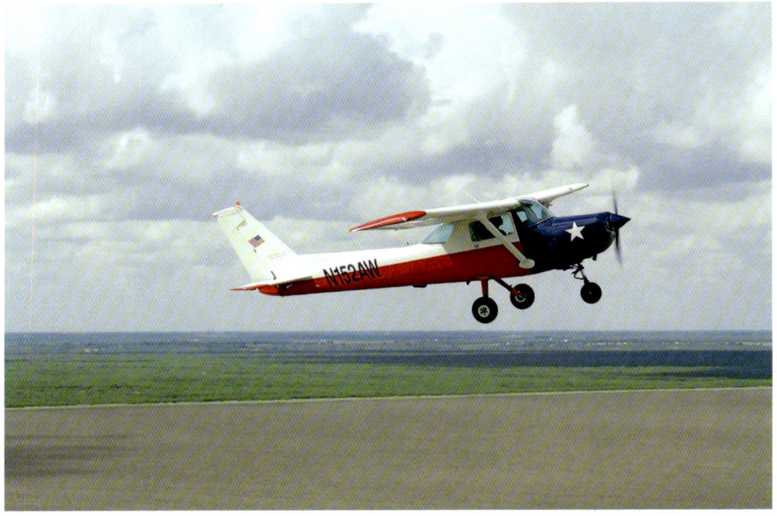

"Take-Off" (Pilot Anse Windham, Kingsville), 2004

Pilot Anse Windham takes off from a Kingsville area airport. Anse is well known for his charity work and his airplane painted Lone Star proud. In 2003 Anse and grandson Brealon Ashworth flew around the United States. Up, up, and away.

"Resale" (Dewayne Walling, Devers), 2004

Auctioneer Dewayne Walling is the owner of the D & L Resale Shop on old Highway 90 in Devers. Dewayne can be seen out front greeting passers-by. Sold.

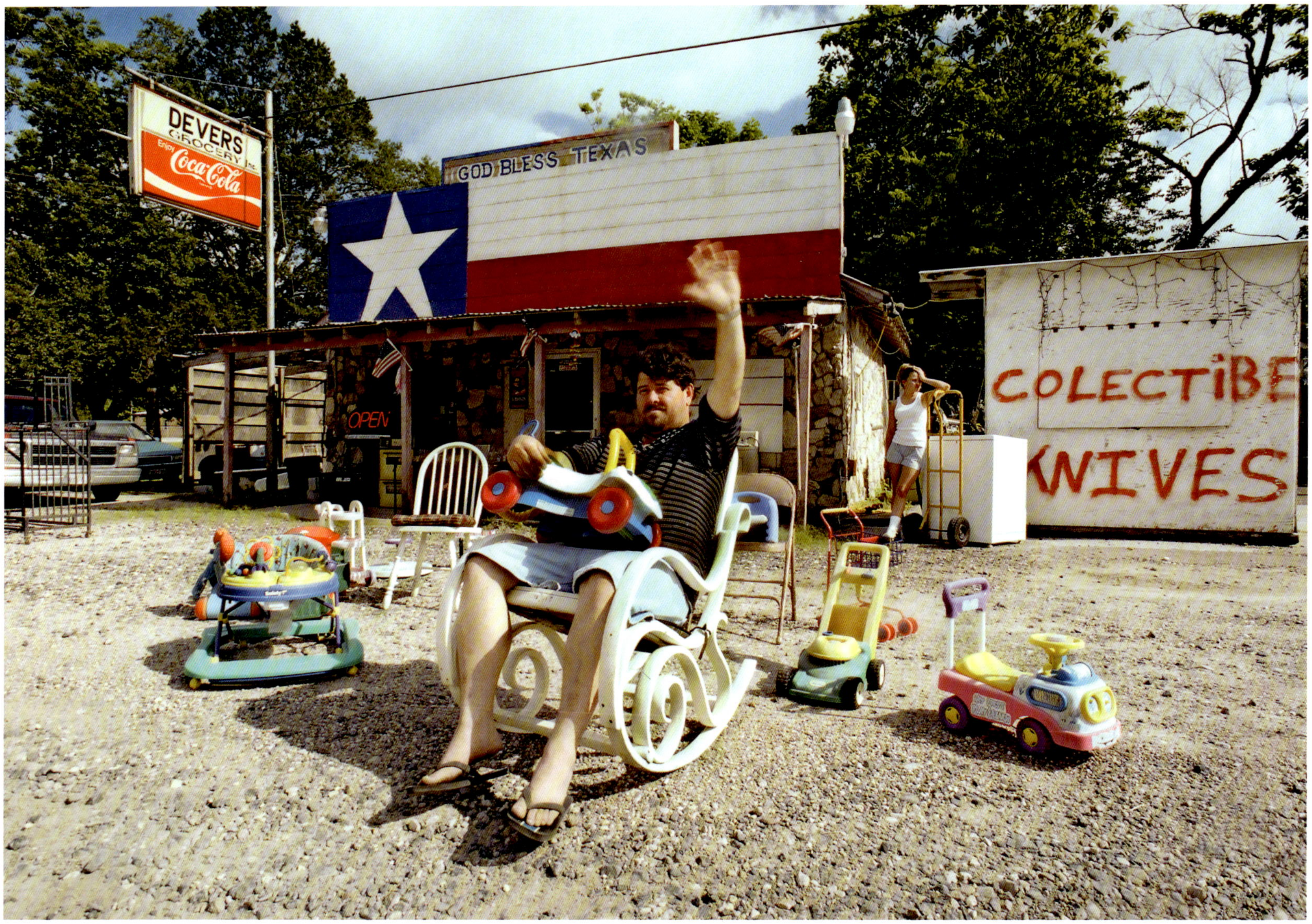

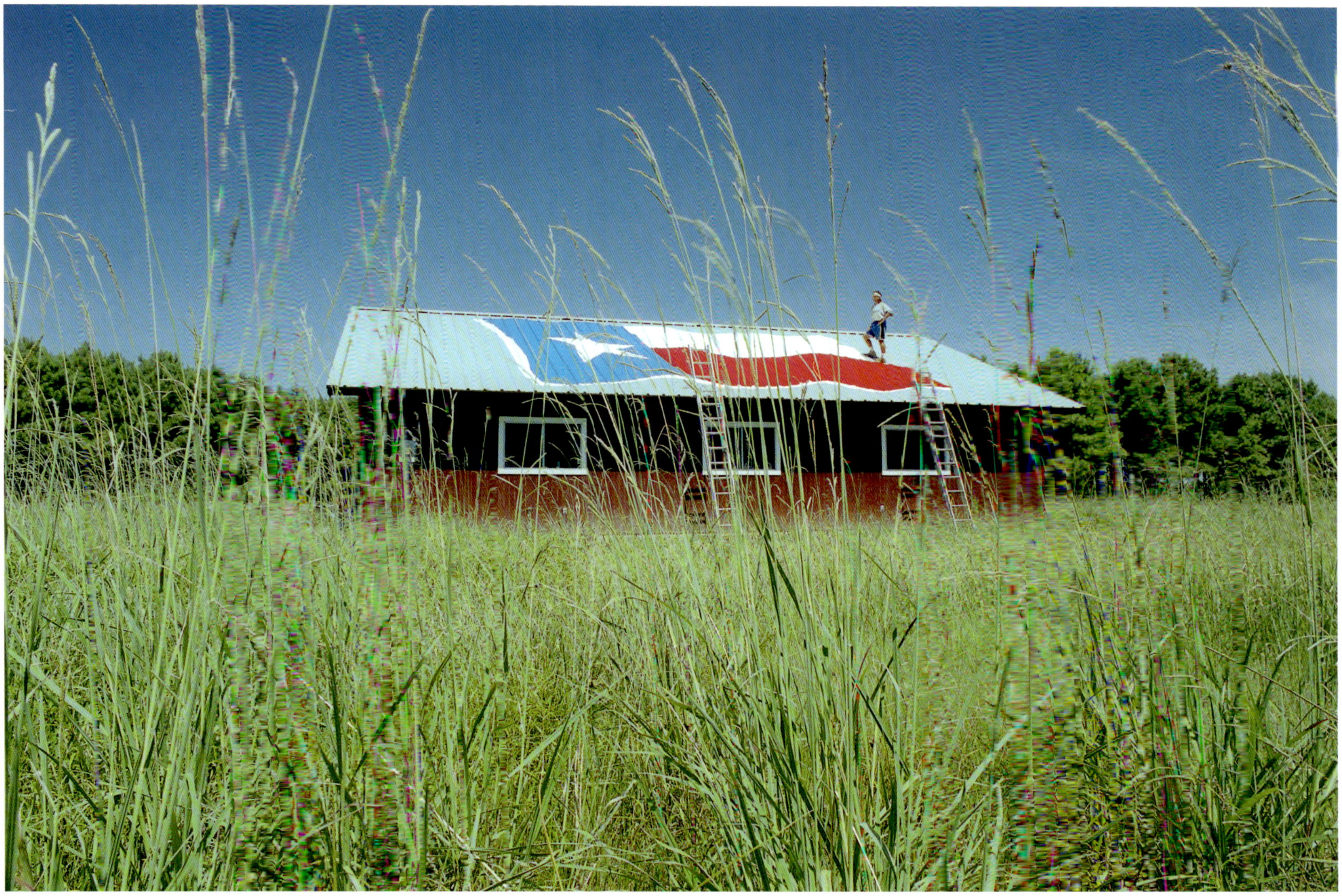

"Wavy House" (Robert Fife Equipment House, Hempstead), 2005

Standing on his equipment house, Robert Fife checks out the progress of his Lone Star flag. Located on Highway 6 on the way to College Station from Houston, Robert's flag is painted in a wave, as if waving to passers-by. Drive by and wave.

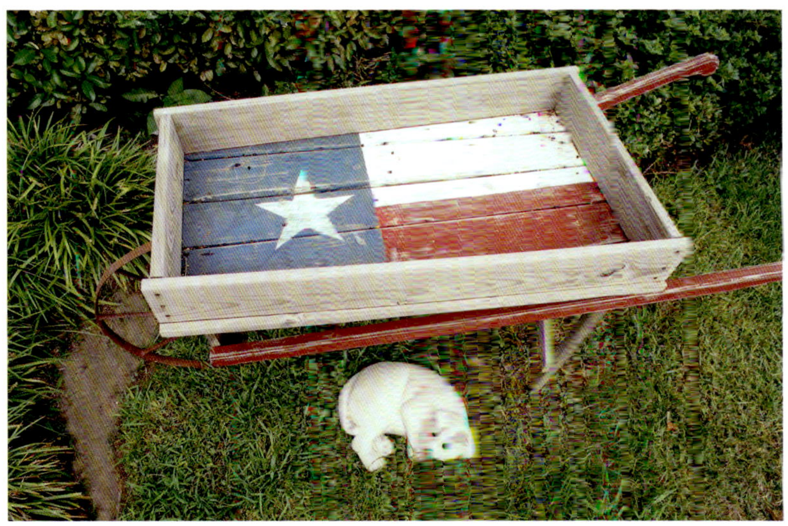

"No Small Load" (Eagles' Nest Gallery, Kemah), 2005

The Eagles' Nest Gallery is located in Kemah, a small fishing, tourist, and boating town just south of Houston. At the gallery everyone is greeted with Lone Star pride. The cat's meow.

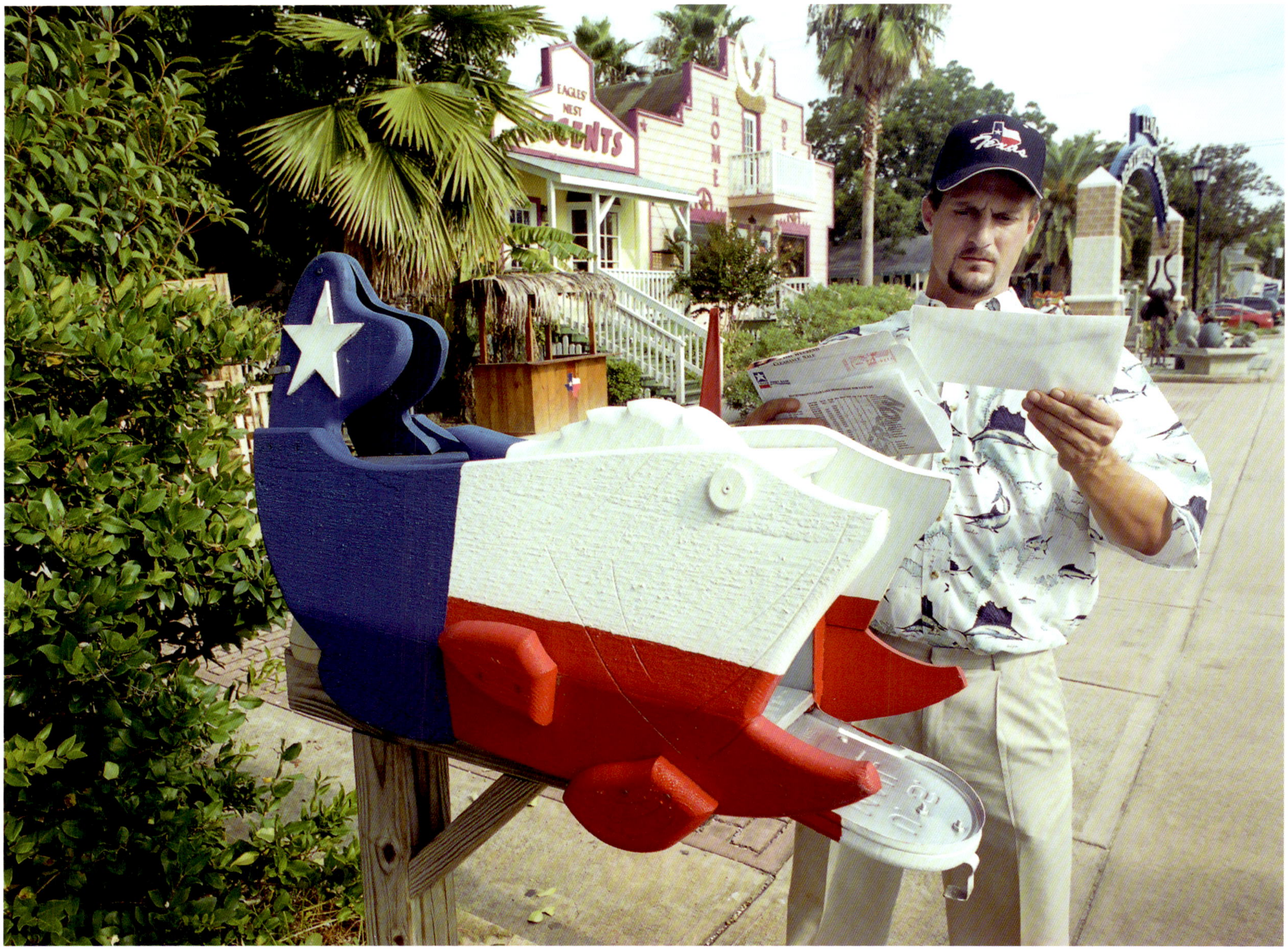

"Bass Mail" (Mick O'Brien, Eagle's Nest Gallery, Kemah), 2005

Mick O'Brien, general manager of the Eagles' Nest Gallery in Kemah on Galveston Bay, reels in the morning mail.

"Tex-Mill" (Welcome windmill, Texas City), 2004

Located between Galveston and Houston, Texas City greets visitors with a western welcome area.

"Lone Star Pacers" (John and Esther Ellis, Memorial Park, Houston), 2002

Sporting their Lone Star shorts, John and Esther Ellis set off on their daily run at Houston's Memorial Park, one of the city's premier spots for runners.

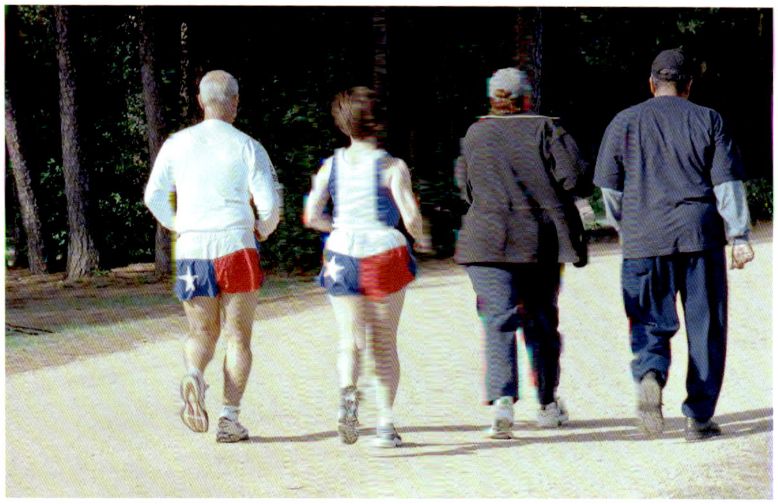

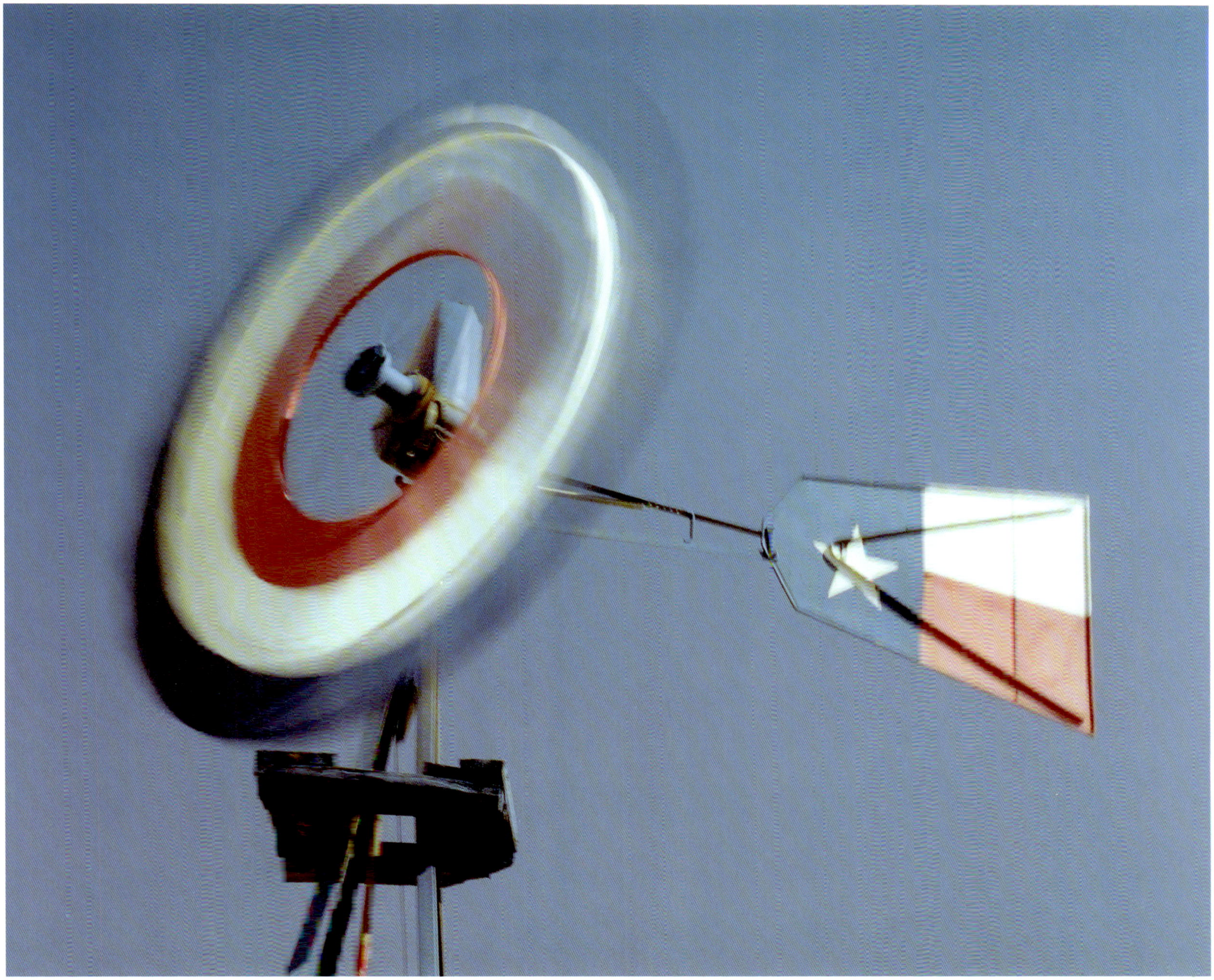

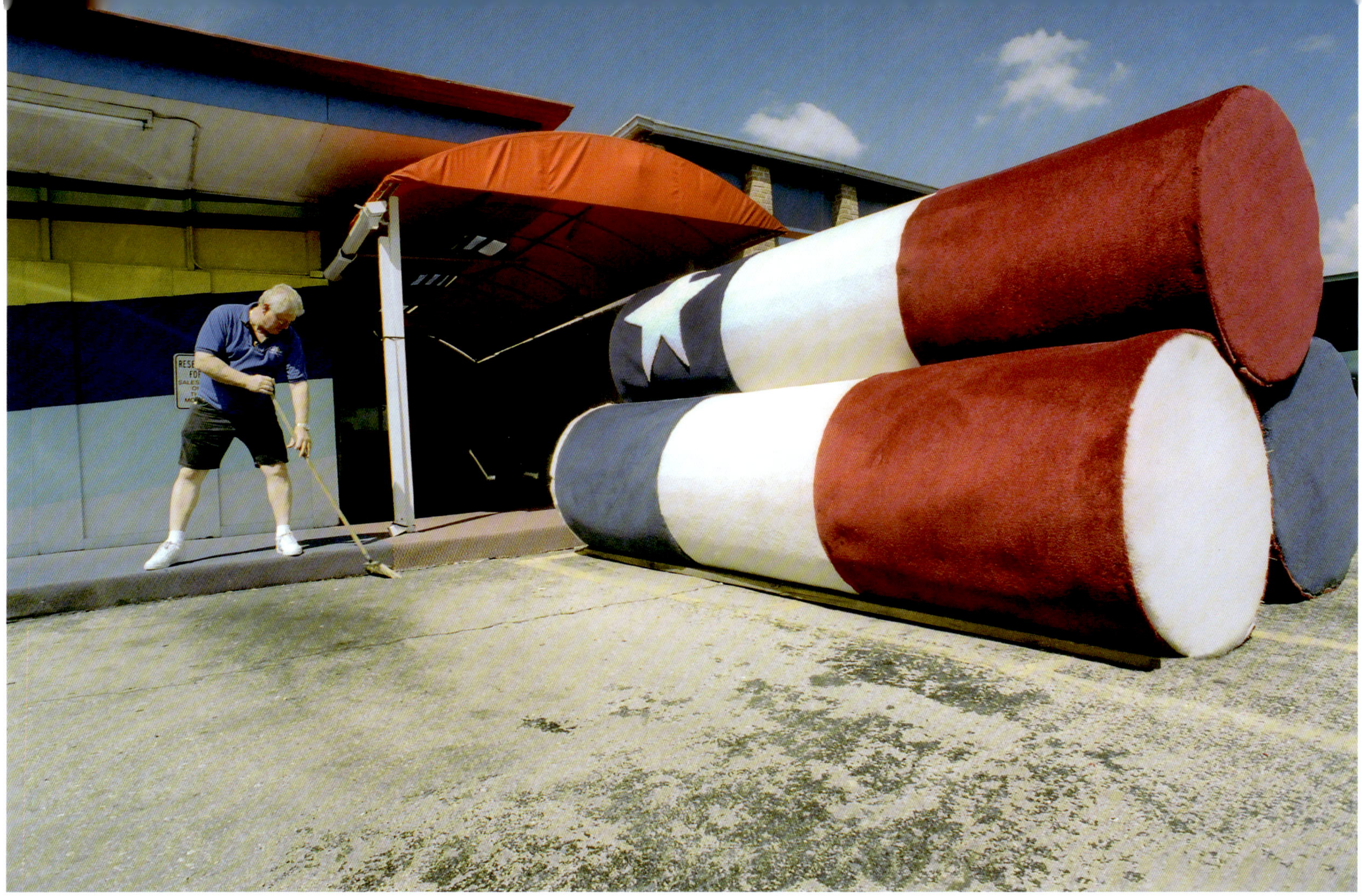

"Carpet Roll" (Butch Coleman, Carpet Giant, Houston), 2002

Butch Coleman of Carpet Giant in Houston sweeps and cleans before he rolls out the Lone Star carpet for customers. Texas pride will floor you.

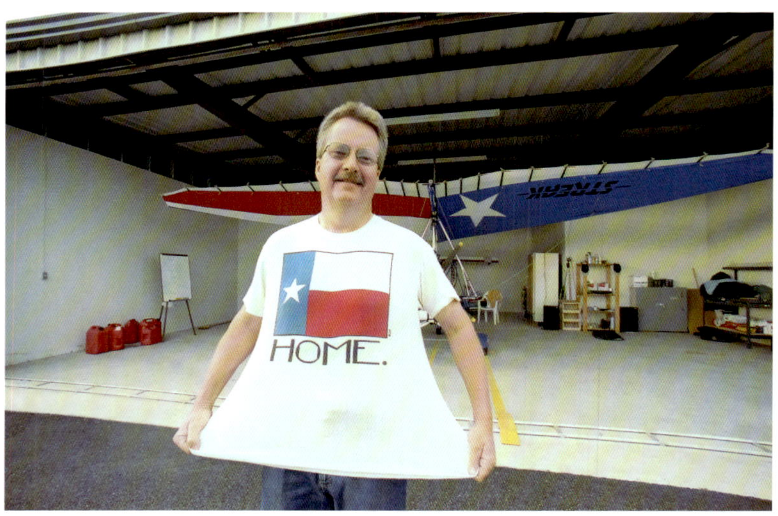

"Home Boy" (Aaron Kliem, Corpus Christi), 2004

In Brookshire, Aaron Kliem stands in front of his Lone Star Hang Glider. Make no mistake about which state he is all up in the air about. Aaron is a native of Corpus Christi now living in Houston.

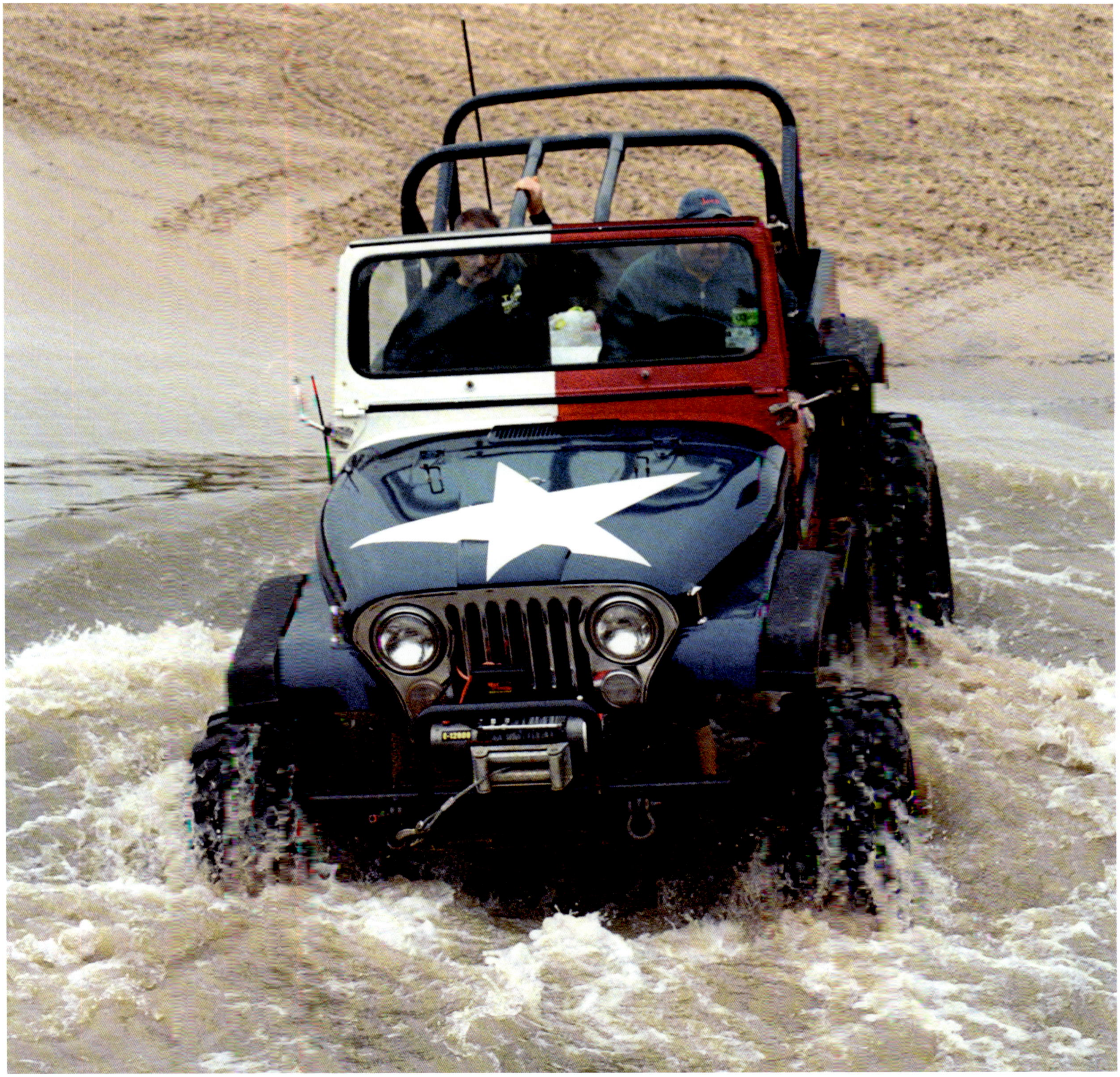

"Rugged Crossing" (Ray Kuhn, Crosby), 2003

Ray Kuhn and friend Neil Pierce give his Lone Star Jeep a workout at the Soggy Bottom ATV park in Crosby.

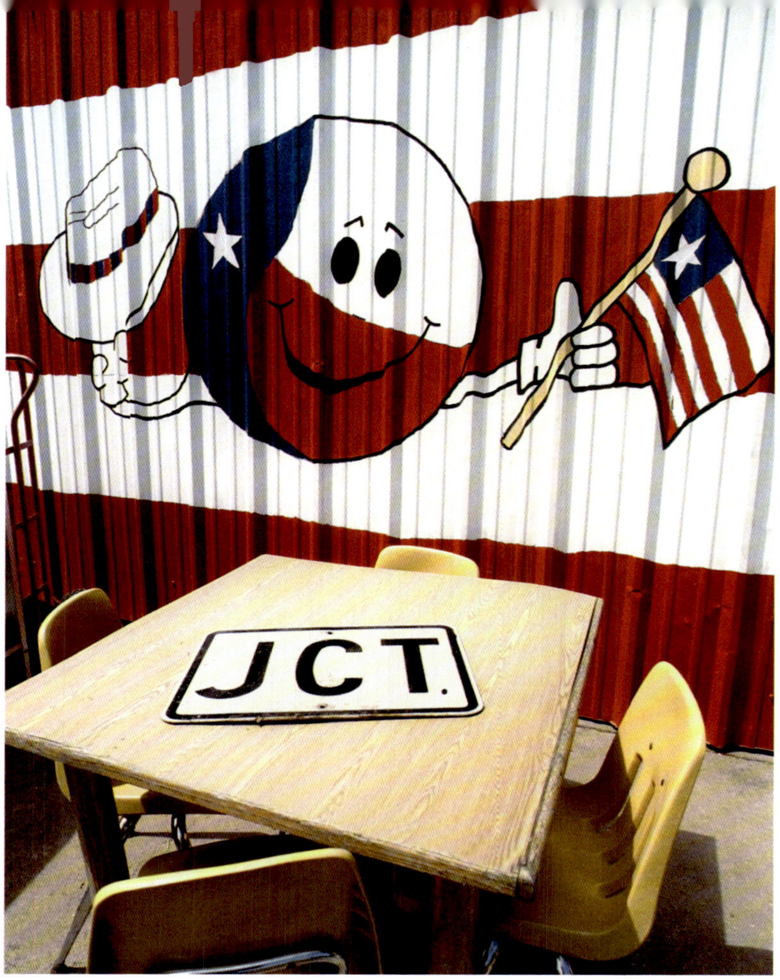

"Crack-a-Smile" (Sack Ice House, Lake Somerville), 2002

Located near Lake Somerville, the former Sack Ice House is all smiles over the Lone Star flag.

"Rearview" (Sweet Pea Café, Navasota), 2004

The former Sweet Pea Café in Navasota was known for its great breakfast and homemade pies. Looking back, it was just one great place to eat. A mirror image.

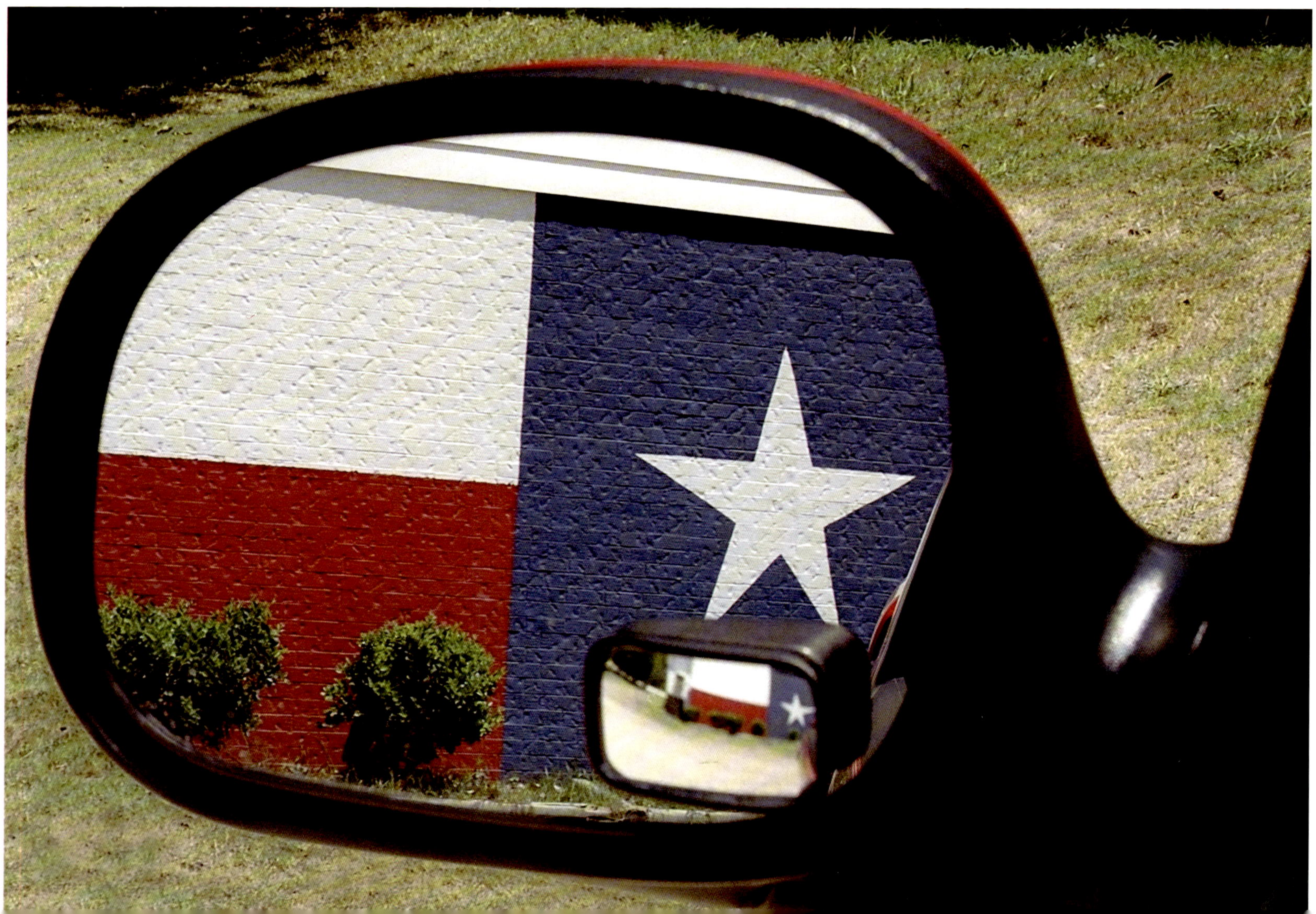

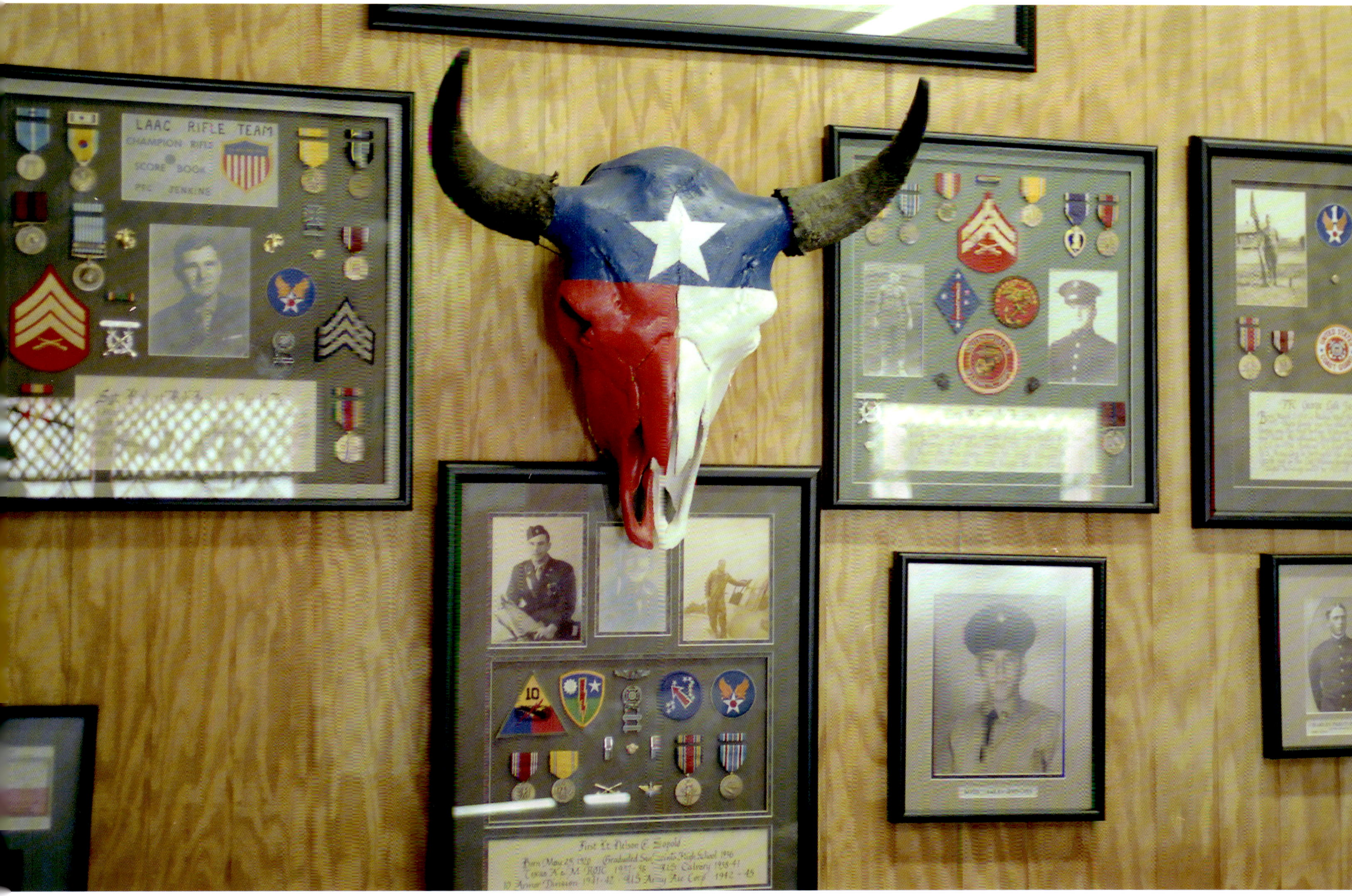

"Buffalo Awards" (Scott's BBQ, West Columbia), 2004

Scott's BBQ and Catering in West Columbia has been run by the Leopold family since 1940. Five generations of Scott Leopold's family have faithfully served their country in the armed forces. No bull.

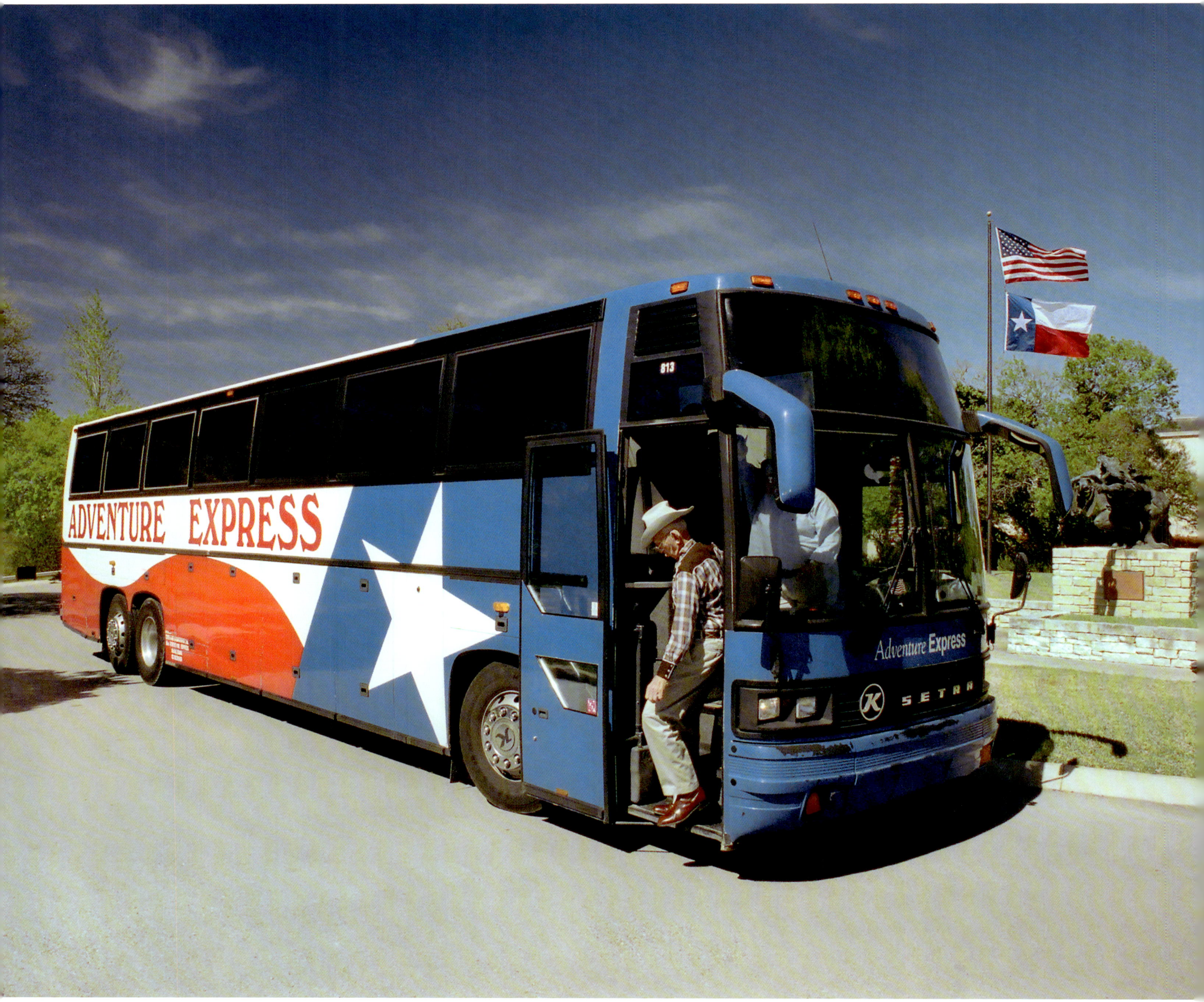
ADVENTURE EXPRESS
813
Adventure Express
SETRA

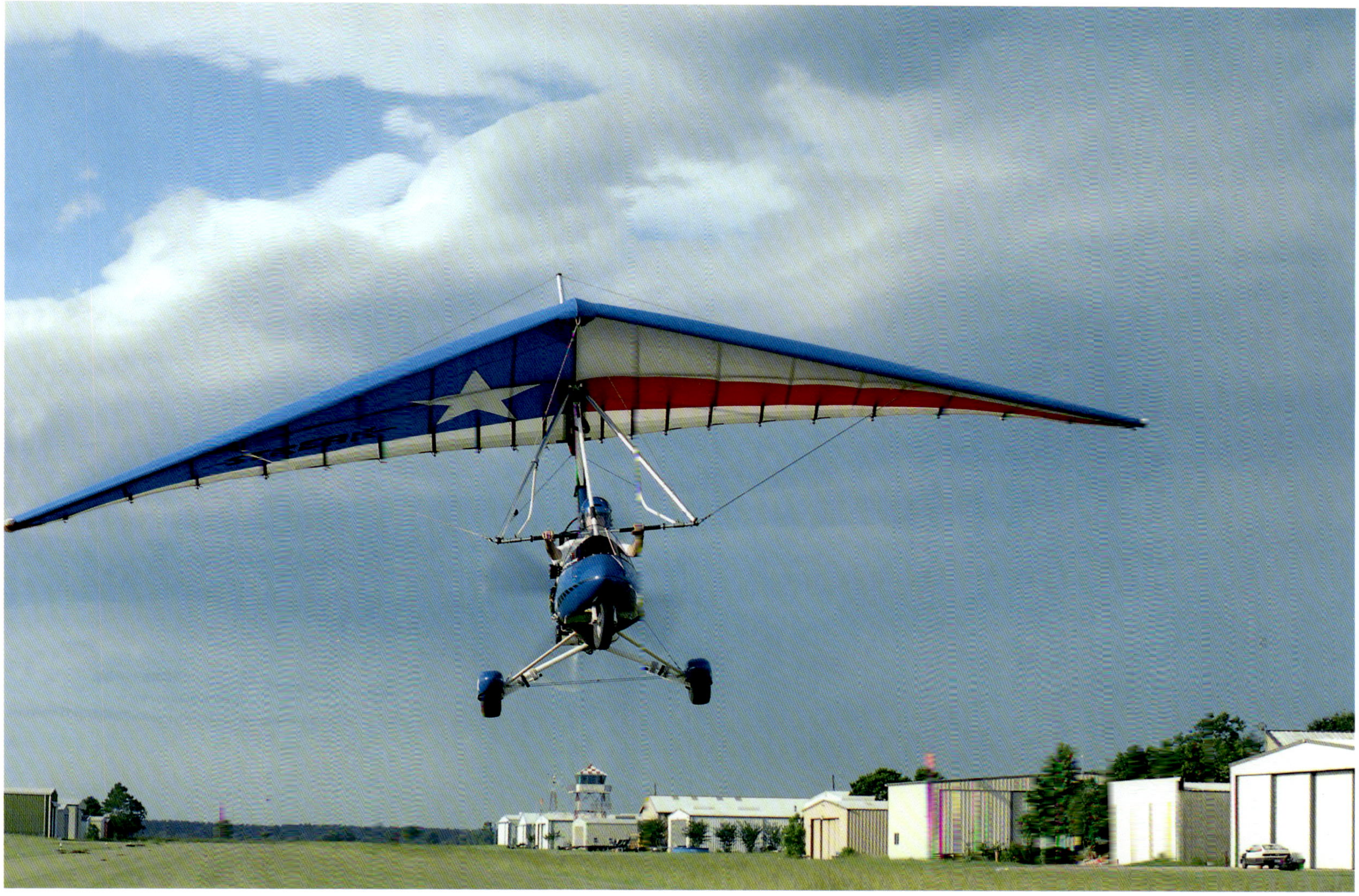

"Feather Light" (John Listi, Brookshire), 200[illegible]

John Listi of Houston, flying his Lone Star Air Borne 2000 Edge X, comes in for a landing at Brookshire Sports Flyers Field.

"Go West" (Cowboy Artists of America Museum, Kerrville), 2003

Howard Stallsmith walks off a Lone Star–painted Adventure Express bus in front of the Cowboy Artists of America Museum in Kerrville.

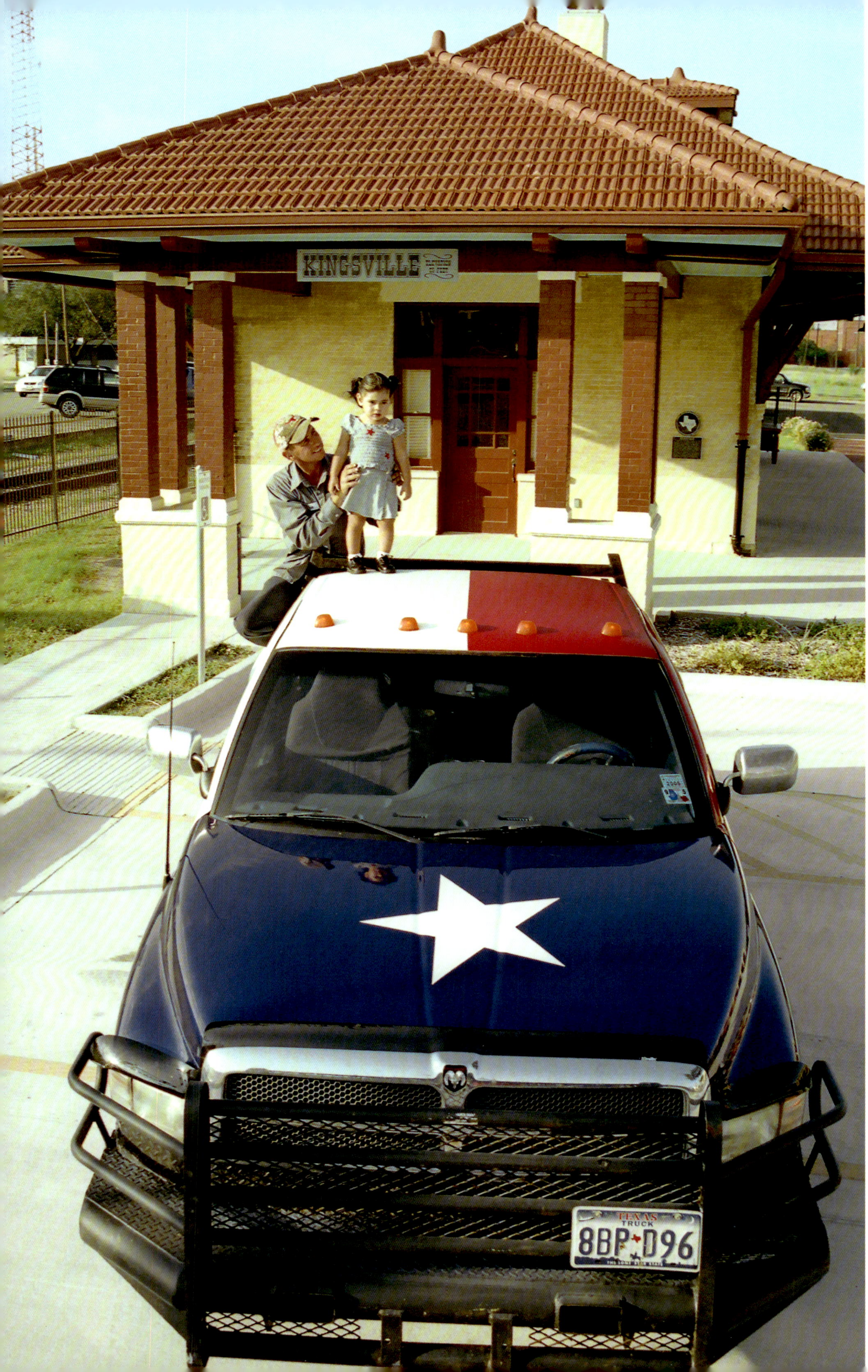

"King Truck" (Jacob Pankratz, Kingsville), 2004

Jacob Pankratz of Kingsville proudly shows his Lone Star truck to Emili Paige Villarreal in front of the historical railroad station. Blow your whistle.

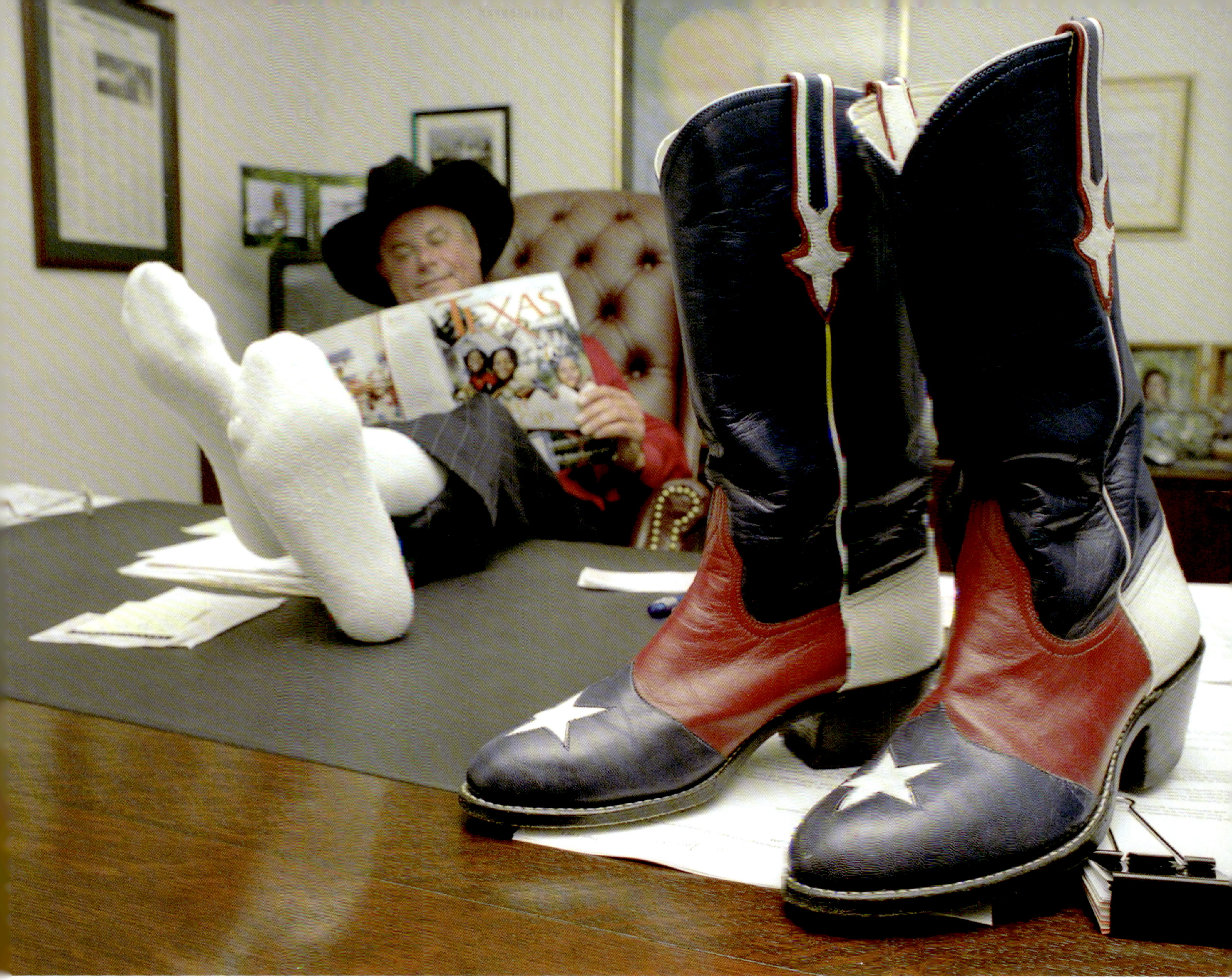

"City Boots" (Jordy Tollett, Houston Visitors Bureau president), 2002

Jordy Tollett, president of the Greater Houston Convention and Visitors Bureau, is Lone Star proud, toe to toe. These boots are made for walking.

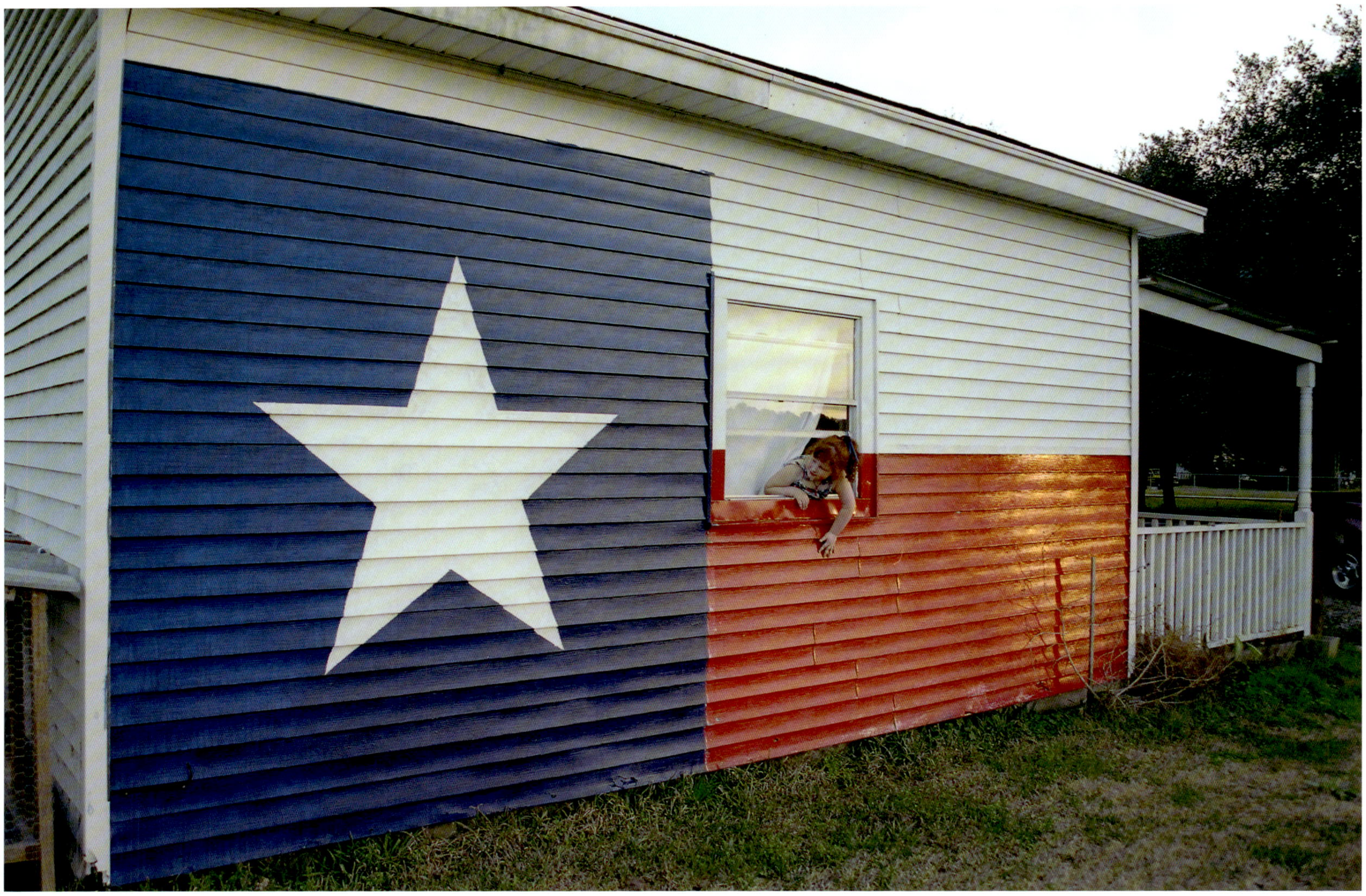

"Side Window" (Dani Crowder, Shepherd), 2004

Randy and Mary Crowder's daughter Dani looks out the guesthouse window on their farm in Cleveland. The Crowders painted the Lone Star flag themselves.

"Butter" (Rolando De La Garza, Houston), 2003

Houston ice sculptor Rolando De La Garza's motto is, "Remember, anyone can carve ice . . . not everyone can sculpt it." Butter (his nickname) can be seen creating his work wearing his Lone Star western hat. Cool.

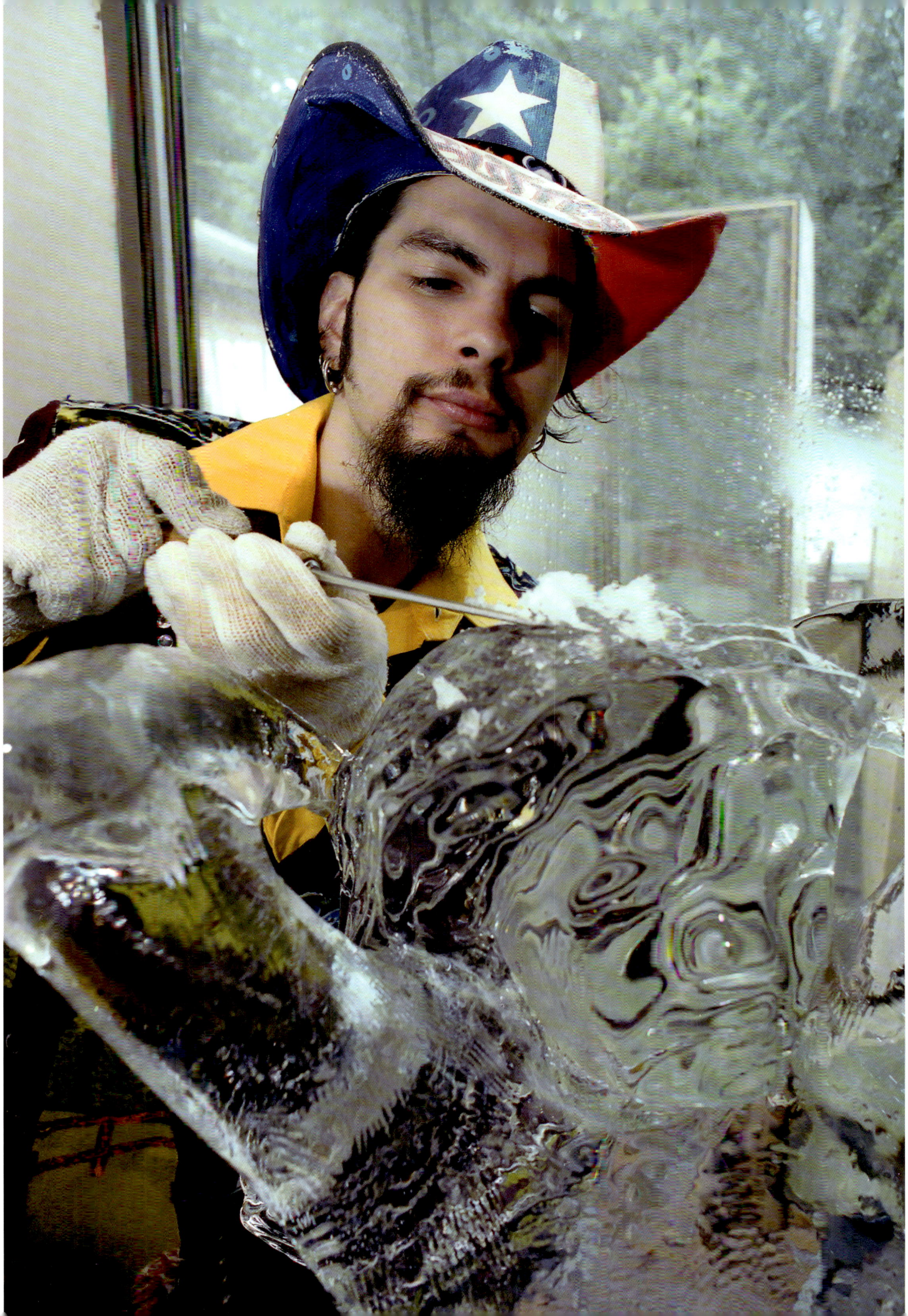

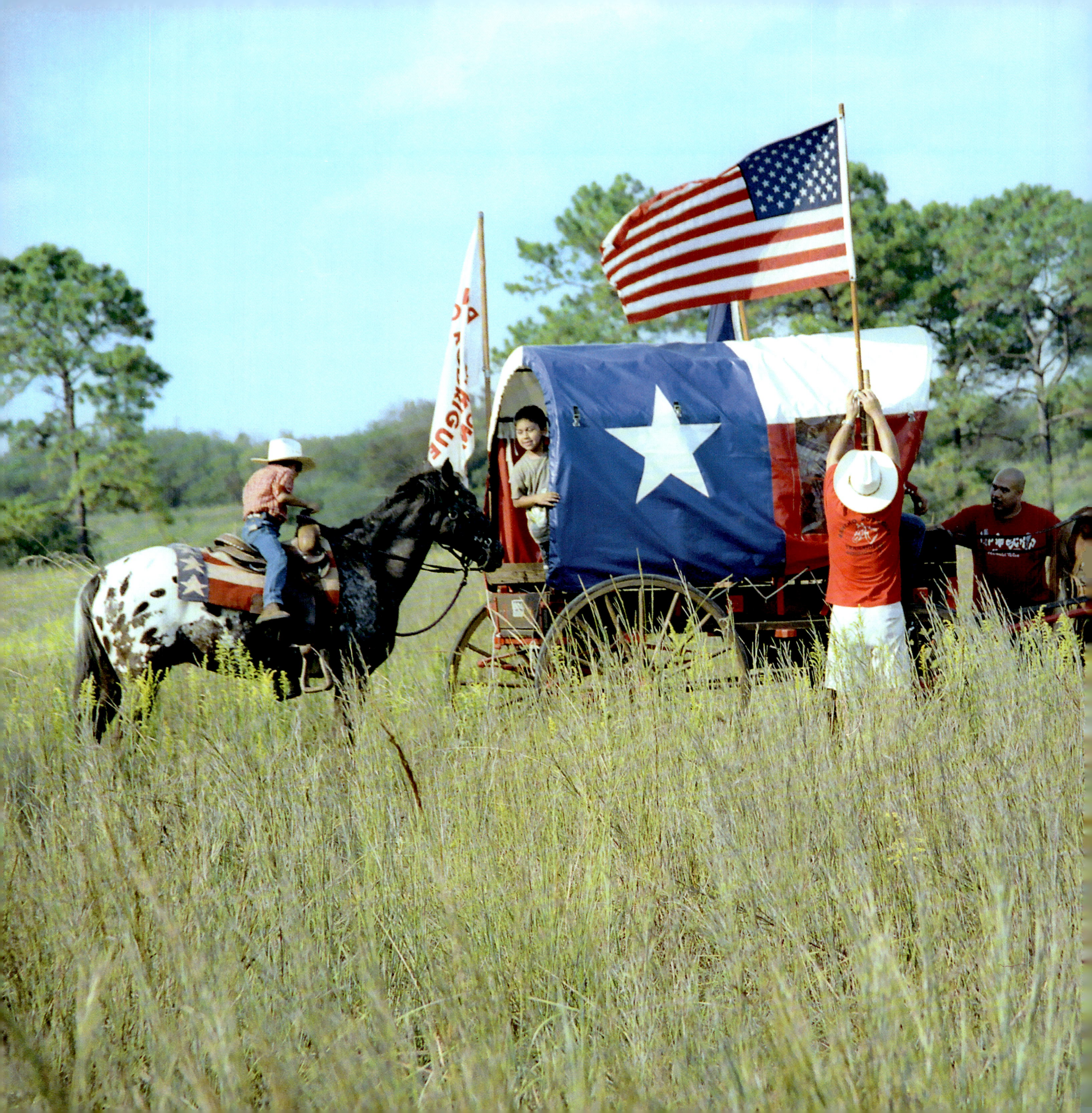

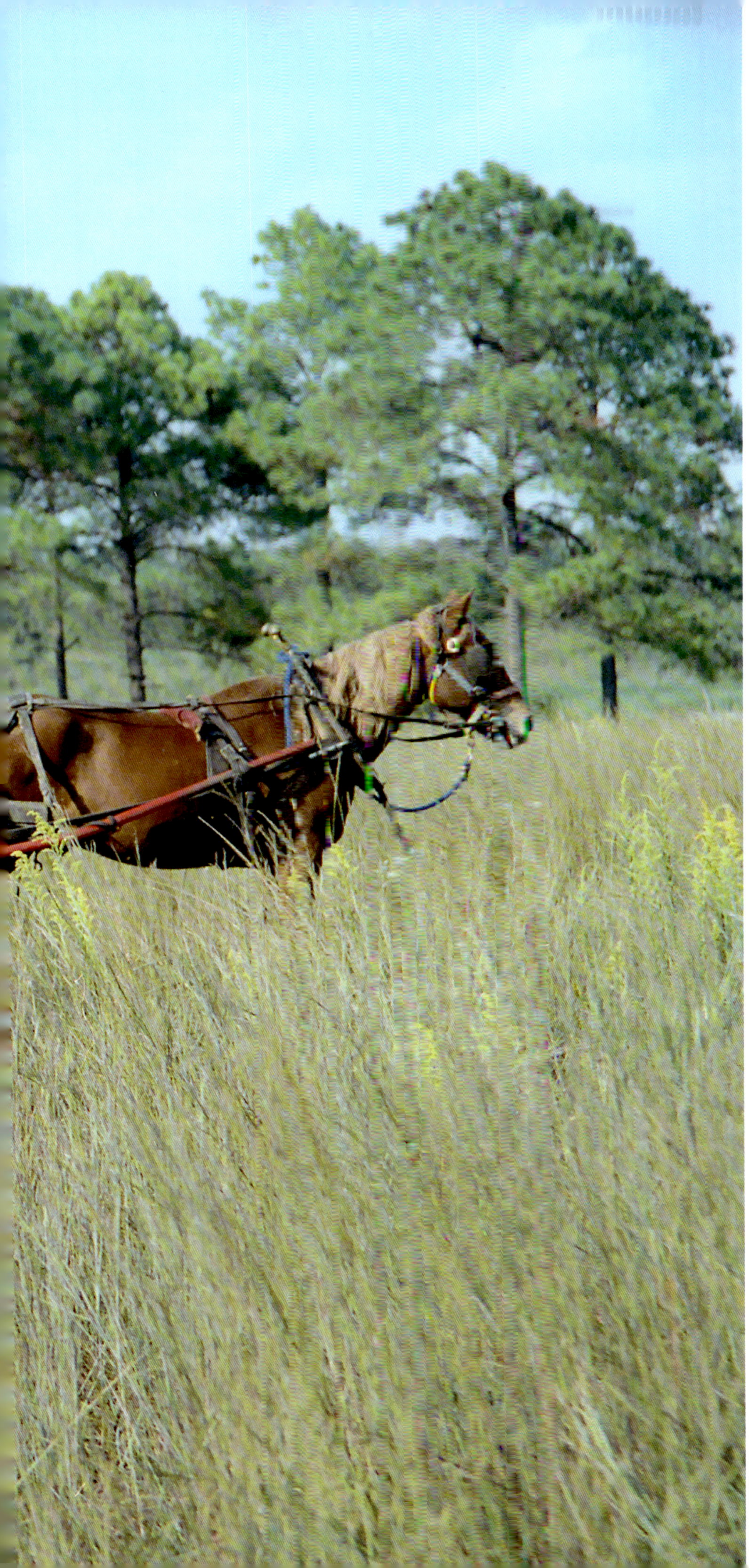

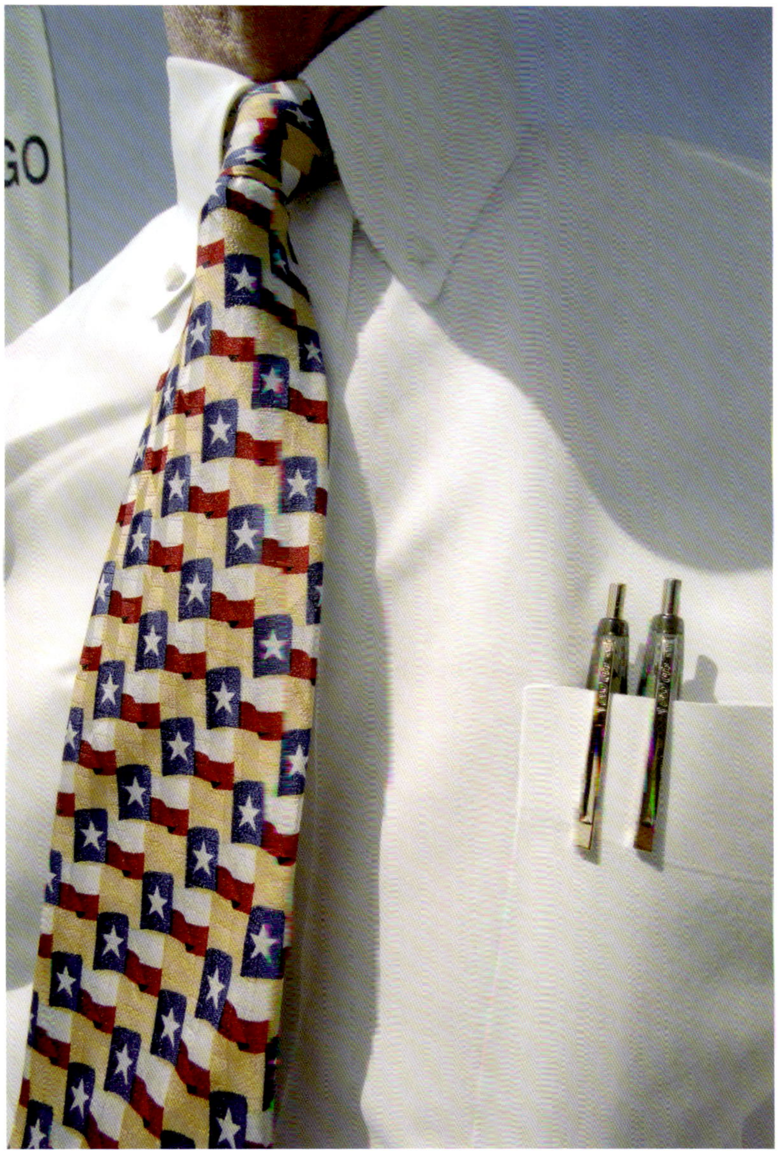

"Tie Up" (Jerry Patterson, Texas Land Commissioner, Freeport), 2003

Making a political visit to Freeport, Texas, Land Commissioner Jerry Patterson was spotted wearing his Lone Star State tie while overseeing the new water treatment equipment along the Gulf Coast.

"Wagon West" (Rancho Rodriquez Trailriders, Houston), 2004

Ruben Rodriguez Sr., president of the Rancho Rodriguez Trailriders from Houston, sets up the flags on their Lone Star covered wagon at the start of a ride. The Ranchos travel the state to participate in trail rides and parades. Giddy up.

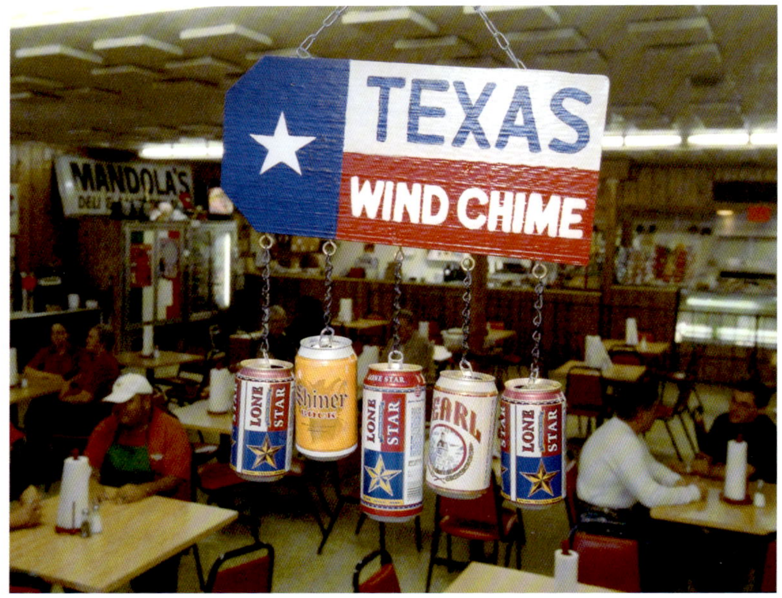

"Chiming Buzzzzz" (Frank Mandola's deli, Houston), 2005

Walking into Frank Mandola's deli on the south side of Houston, you'll be greeted by a Texas wind chime that may bring music to you ears. Drink too many and you'll get a buzz.

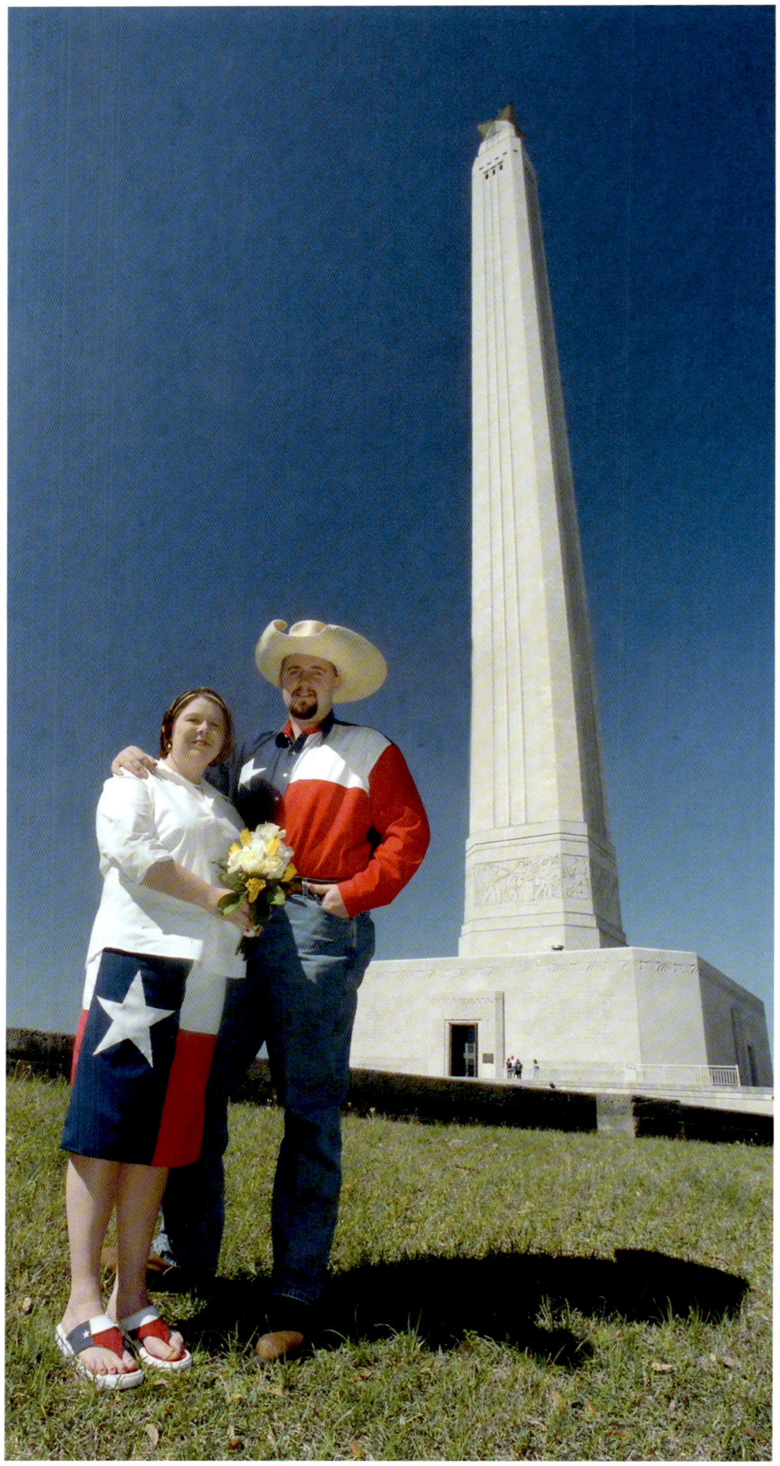

"San Jac" (Newlyweds Kenneth & Joanna Armstrong, Timpson), 2005

Dressed in the state colors, Kenneth Armstrong and Joanna Crenshaw (Mr. and Mrs. Armstrong), were married in front of the San Jacinto Monument—"Where Texas won its independence and Kenny lost his," says Joanna.

"18-Wheeler" (Fred Morefield, Somerville), 2005

Truck driver Fred Morefield proudly stands on his 18-wheeler, protected by a Lone Star bug screen. Fred drives for the Blaschke trucking company.

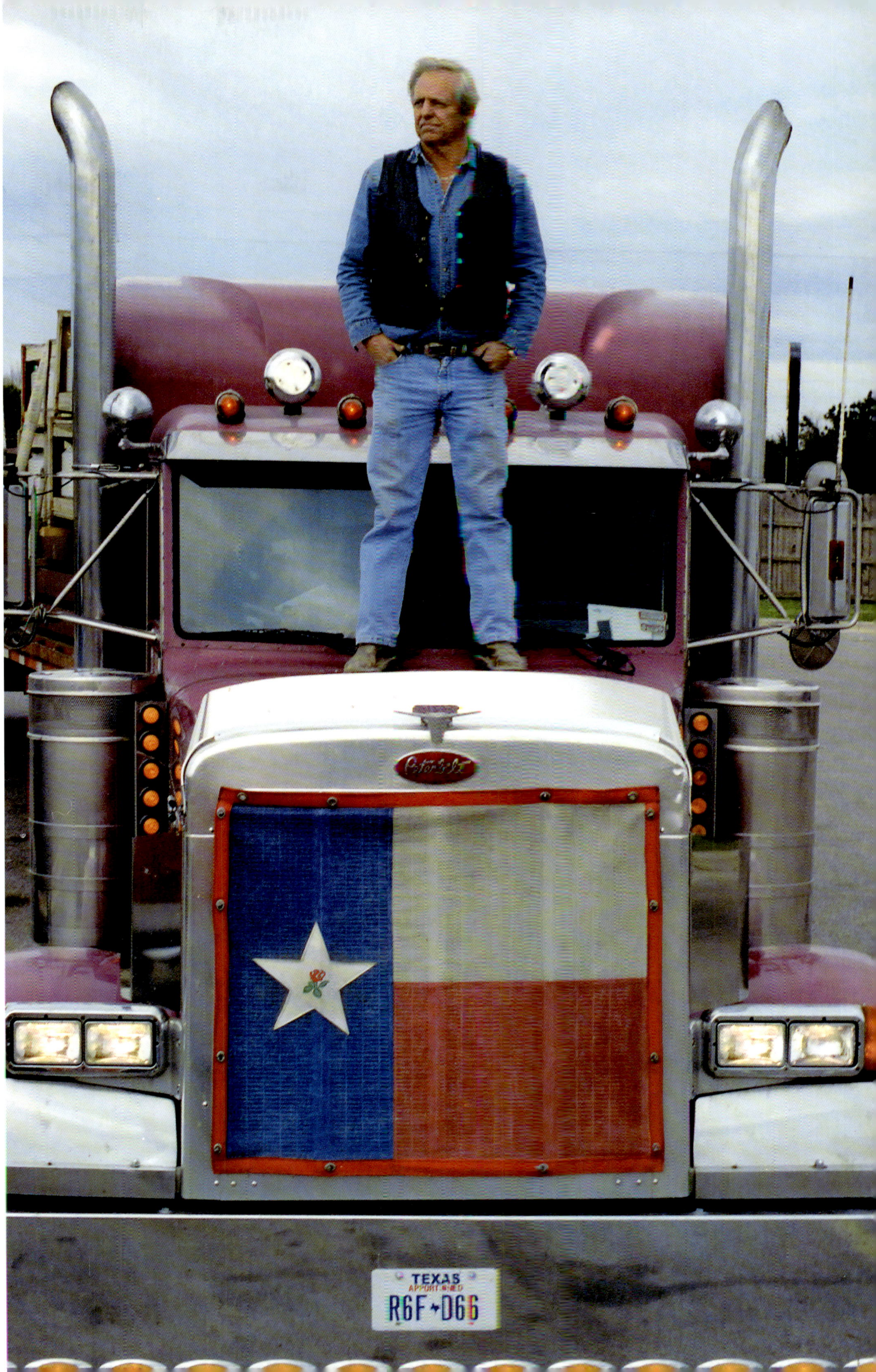

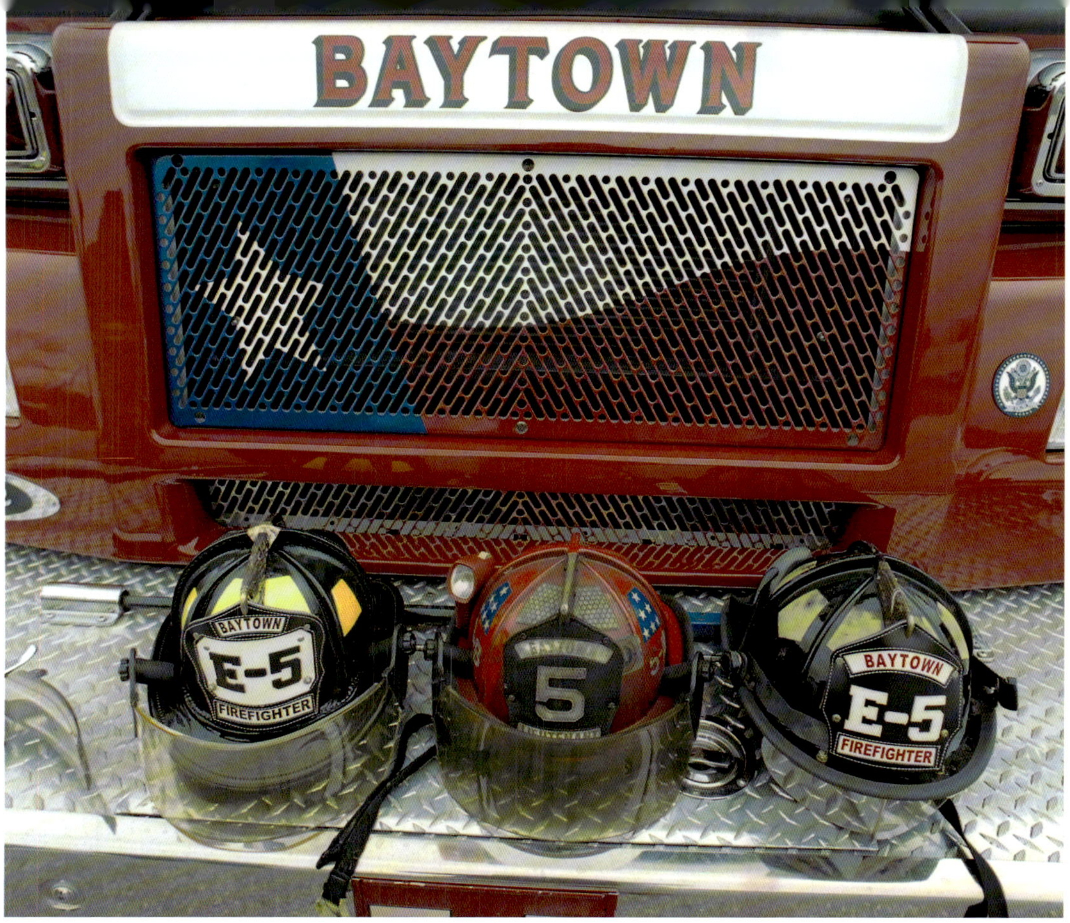

"Fire Helmets" (Fire Station #5, Baytown), 2005

A-Shift members' helmets sit on the Baytown Fire Department Pierce pumper fire truck that proudly displays the Lone Star flag. All fired up.

"Firefighters" (Fire Station #5 A-Shift, Baytown), 2005

Craig Contreras, David Mendisabal, and Gaston Gagne, members of the Baytown Fire Department A-Shift, flank their Lone Star flag Pierce pumper fire truck. Rough and ready.

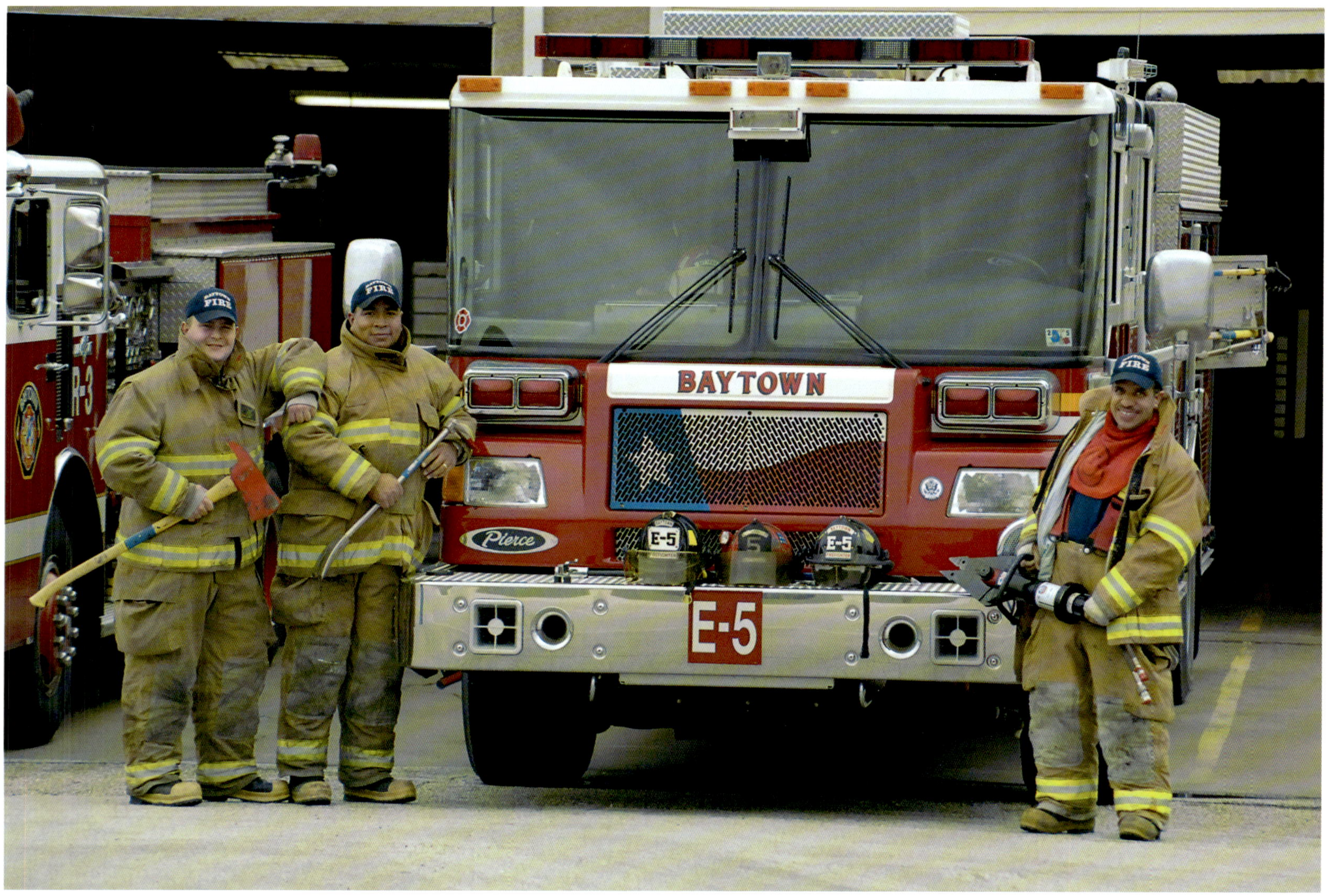

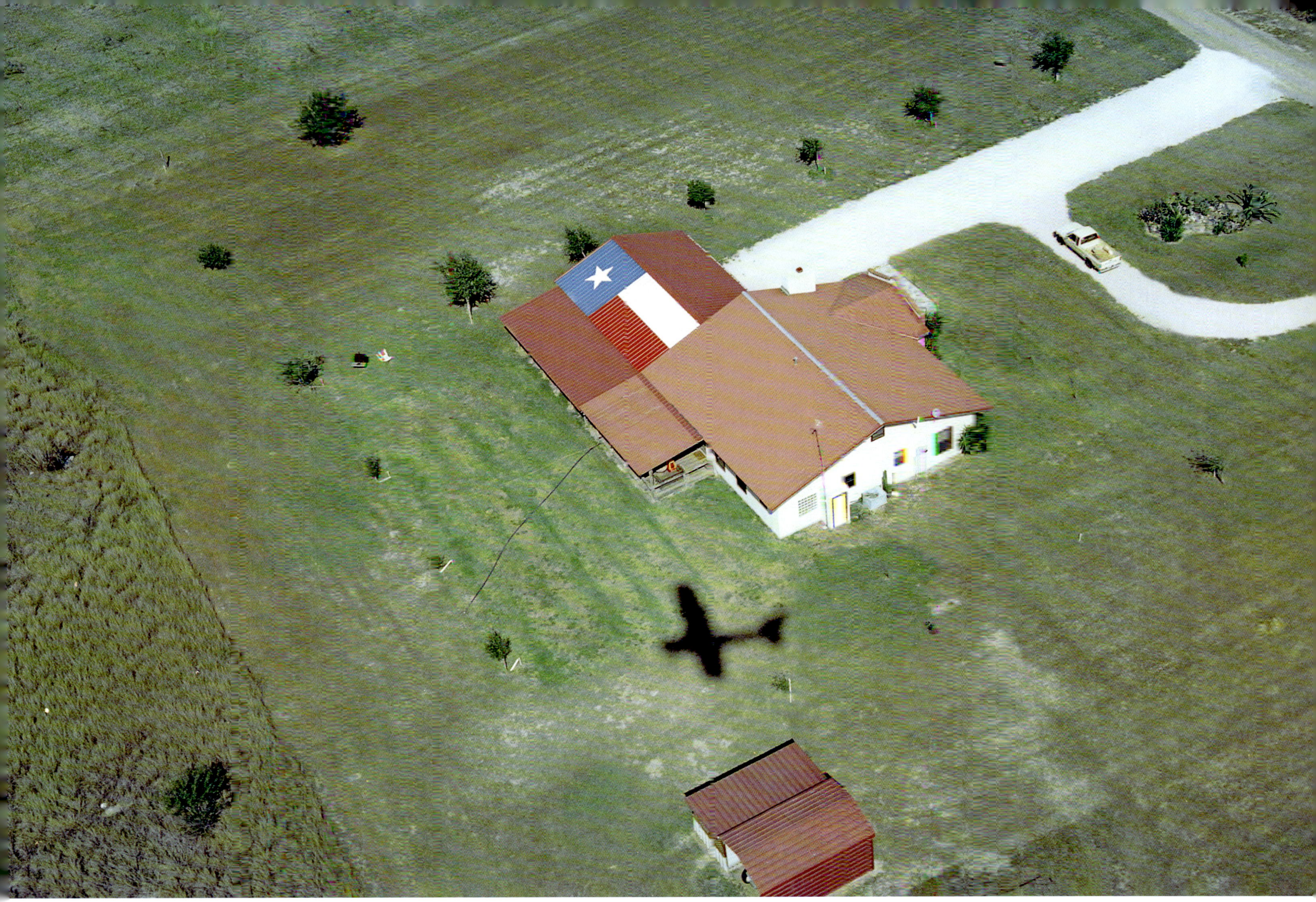

"Plane Farm" (Miller's family farm, Ricardo) 2004

A single-engine plane's shadow passes over the Miller family farm, just south of Kingsville. Miller's roof lets all who fly over know they are in Lone Star country.

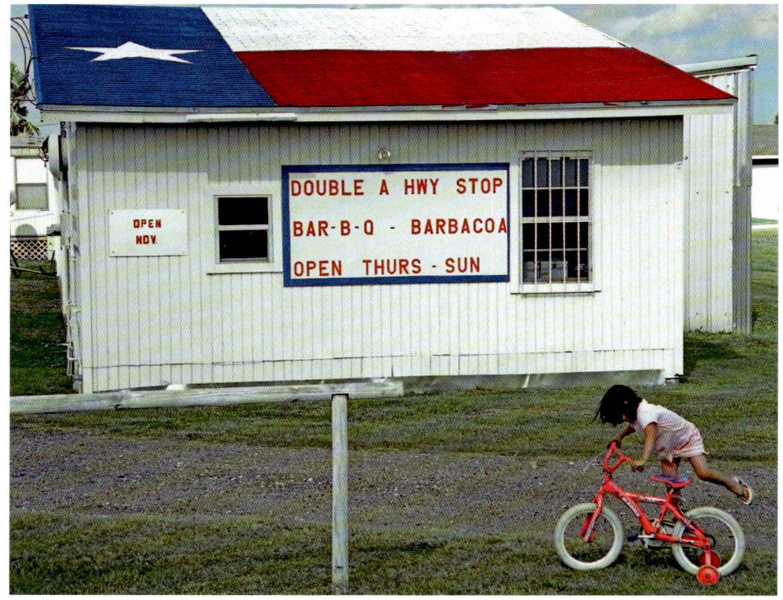

"In the Pink" (Meronda Arrellano, Bishop), 2004

Meronda Arrellano practices riding her bicycle in front of the family BBQ house in Bishop. The restaurant with its Lone Star roof is located on State Highway 77. Peddle in.

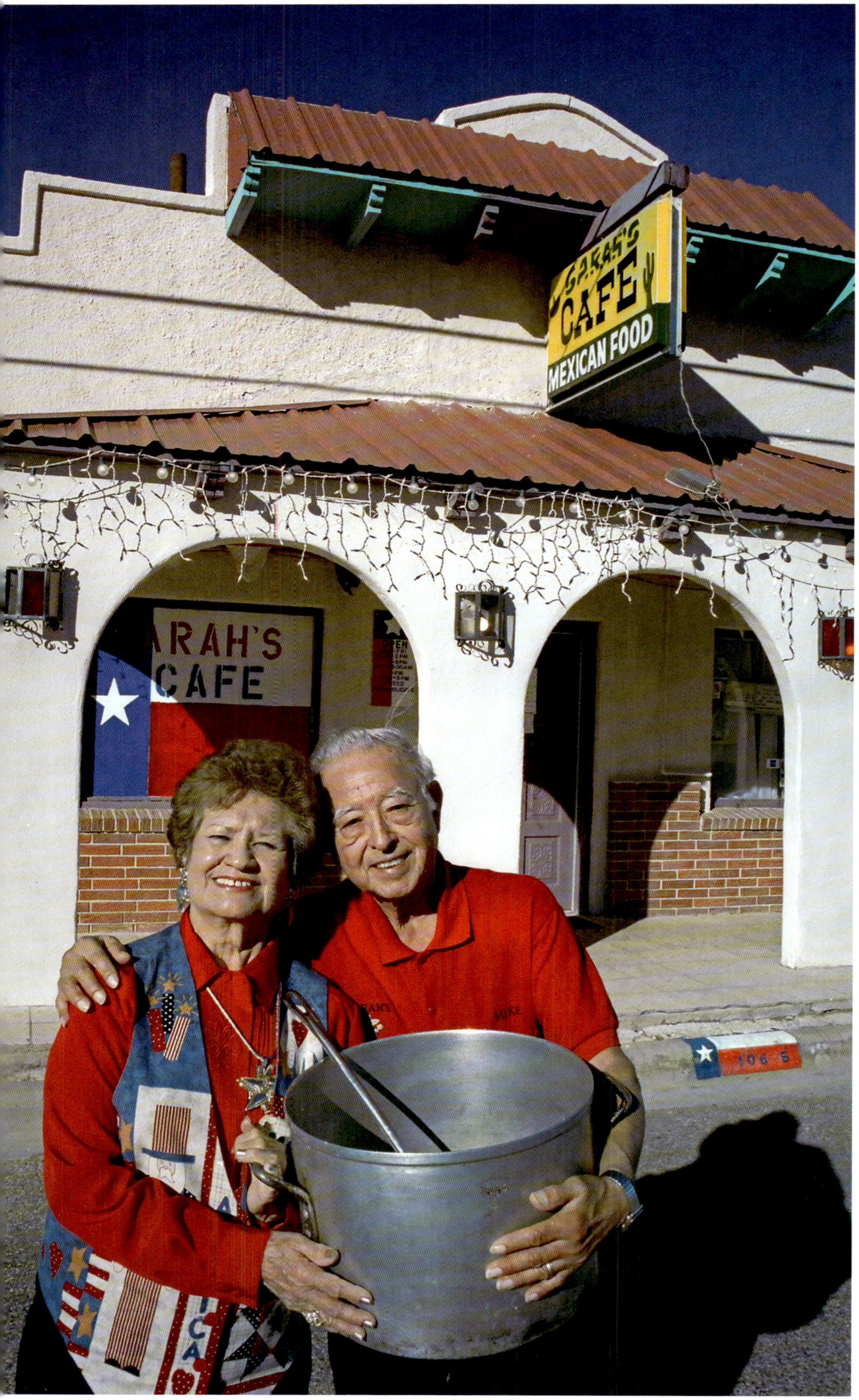

"Sarah's" (Mike & Cleo Castelo, Sarah's Café, Fort Stockton), 2004

Sarah's Café, the oldest restaurant in Fort Stockton, has been operated by the same family in the same location since 1929. Owners Mike and Cleo Castelo's motto is "A chili a day keeps the doctor away." Hot peppers.

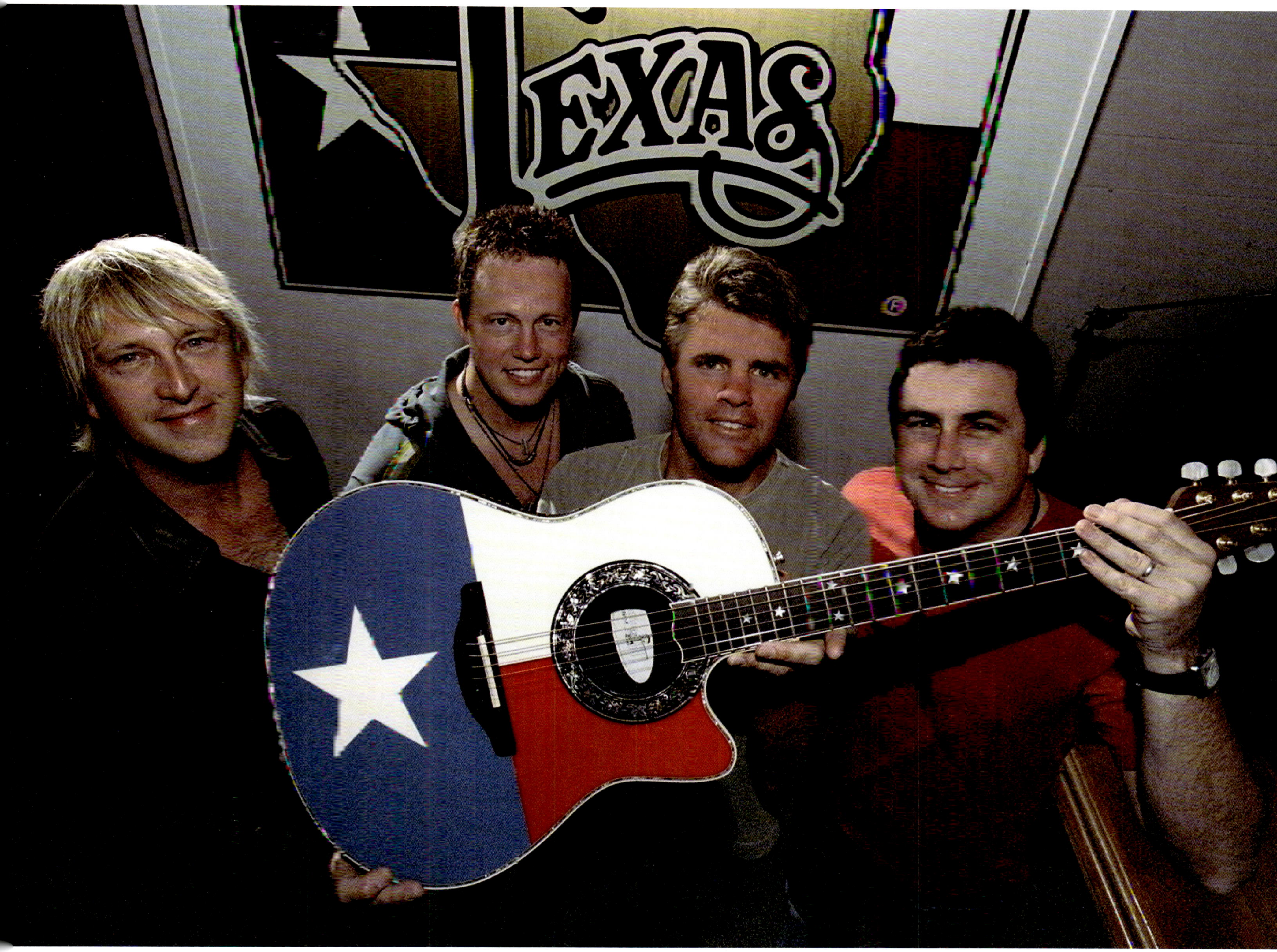

"Guitar Boys" (Lonestar at Billy Bob's, Fort Worth), 2005

The four original members of the band Lonestar—Keech Rainwater, Dean Sams, Richie McDonald, and Michael Britt—hold their signature Lone Star flag guitar backstage at Billy Bob's in Fort Worth.

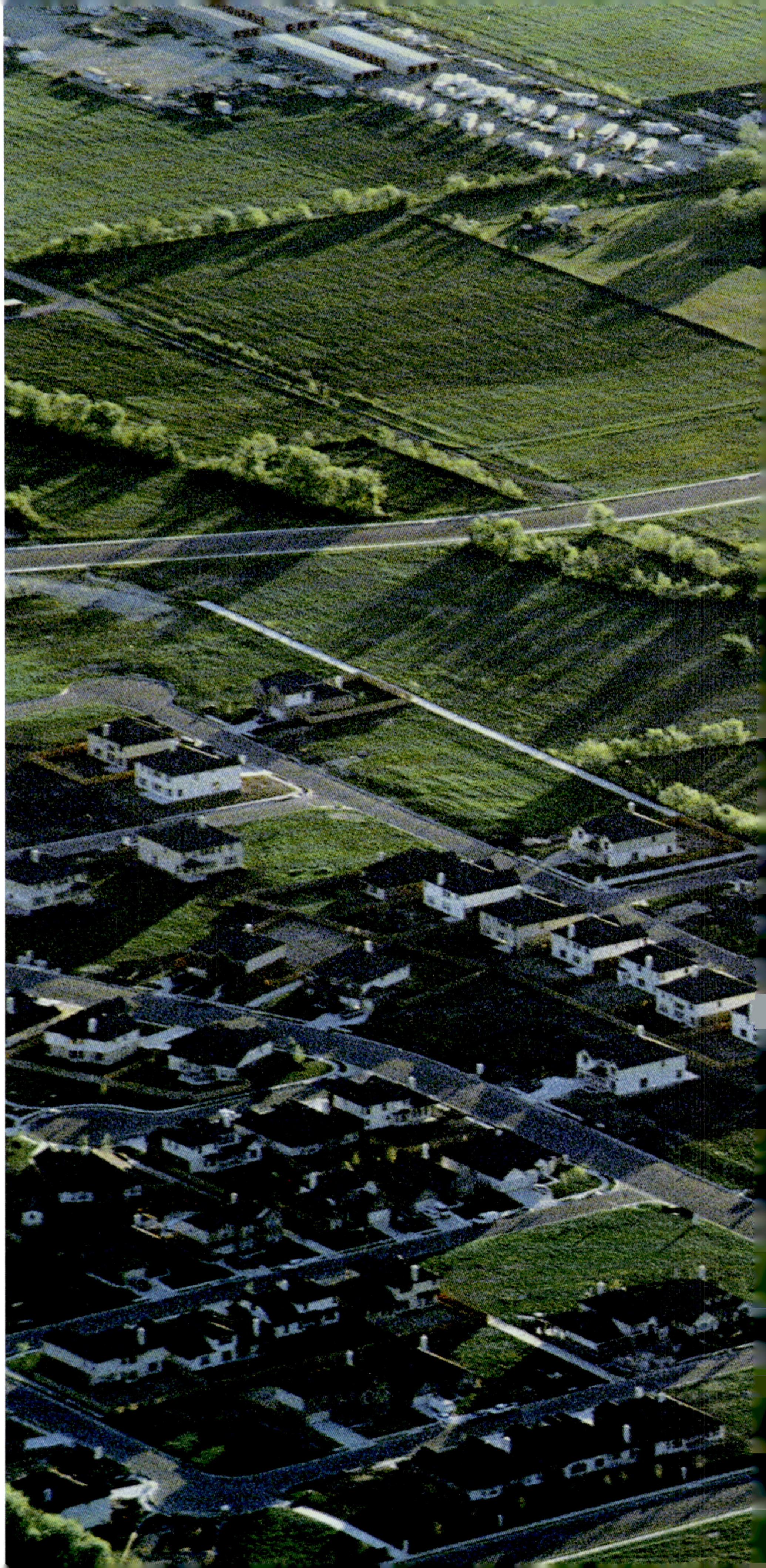

"Aerodactyl" (Bruce Lavorgna, balloon pilot, Austin), 2005

The Aerodactyl (the Texas Lone Star balloon), drifts over the city of Austin in early morning, piloted by Bruce Lavorgna. Bruce, who has been flying for over twenty years, is high on Texas. No hot air.

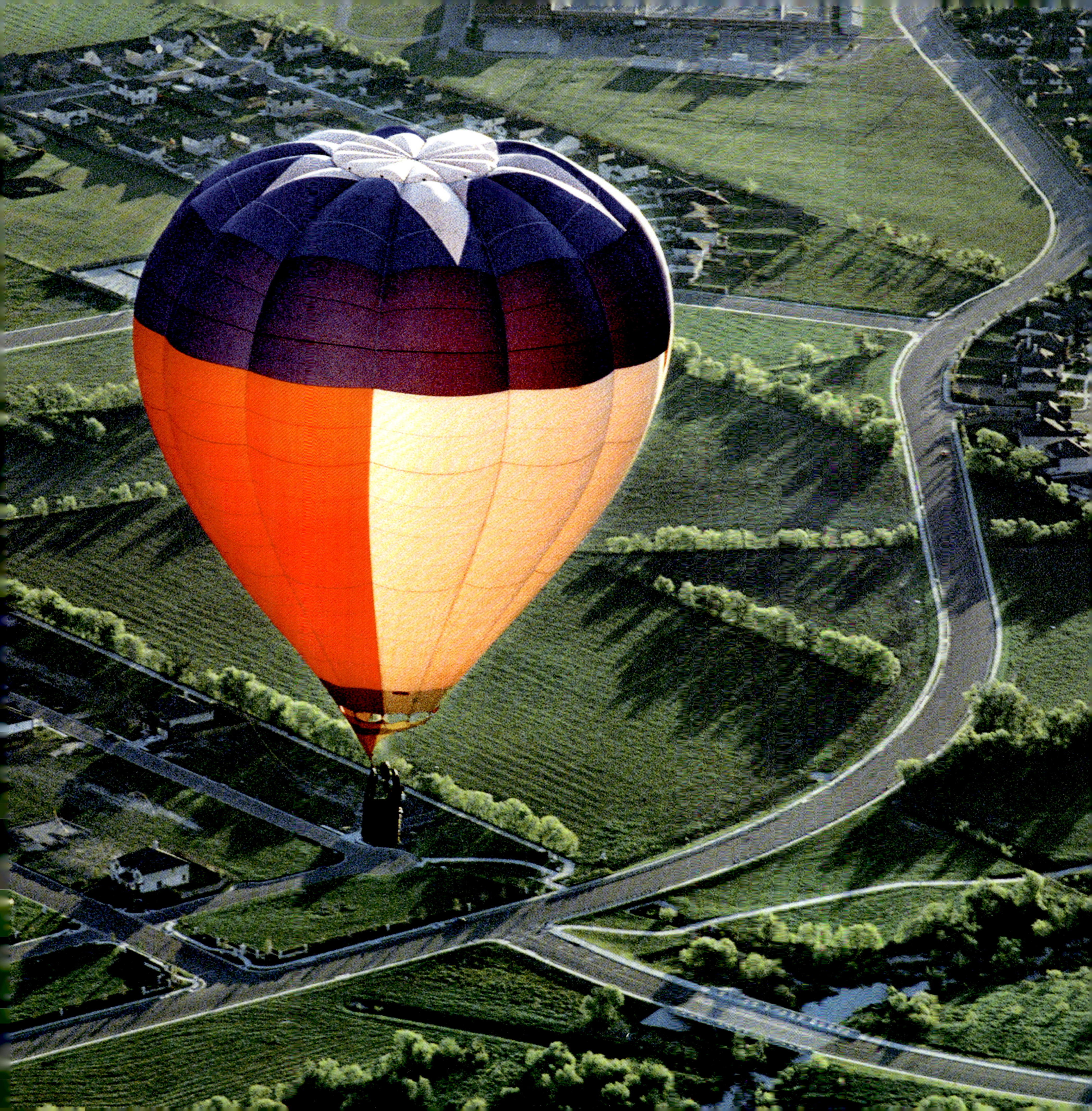

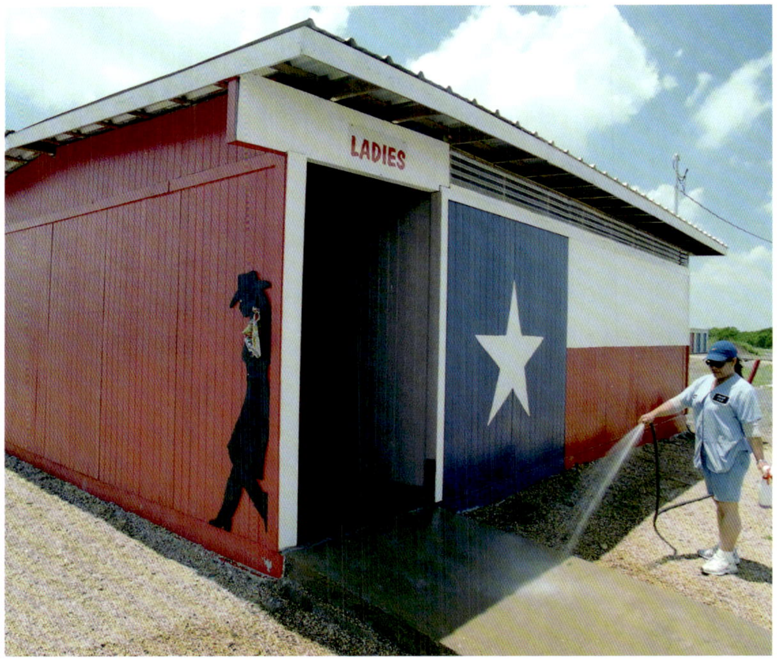

"Ladies Only" (Maria Gonzales, Jarrell Flea Market), 2005

Maria Gonzales, a worker at the Jarrell Flea Market in Jarrell, makes sure everything is Lone Star clean. The Flea Market is located on Highway 35 between Austin and Temple.

"Splish Splash" (Scott Walker, San Marcos), 2007

Don't worry, Scott Walker isn't all wet. This signature antique tub proudly painted like the Lone Star flag perches on the rooftop of his business, Clawfoot Bathtub Warehouse. Throw him a towel!

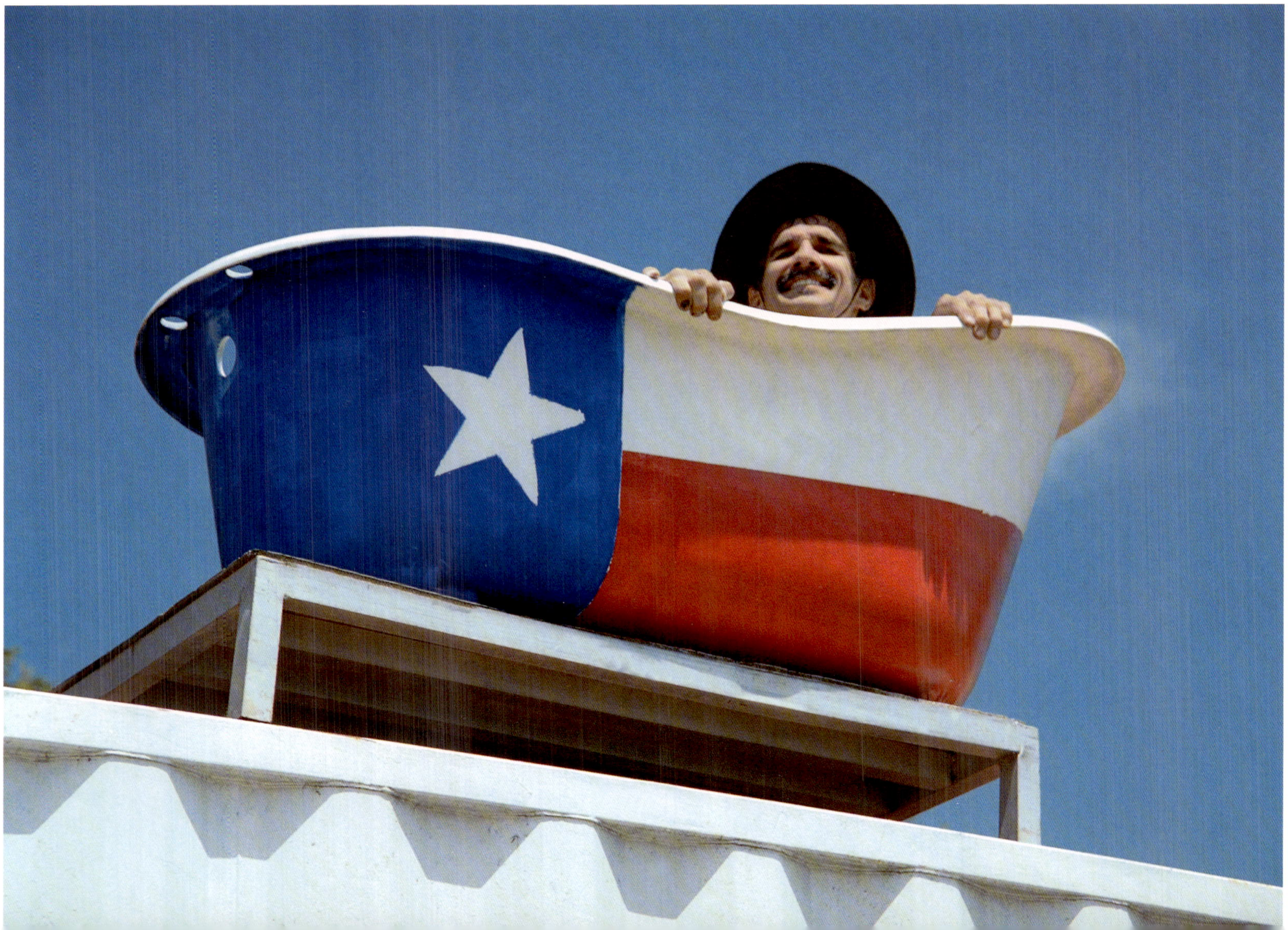

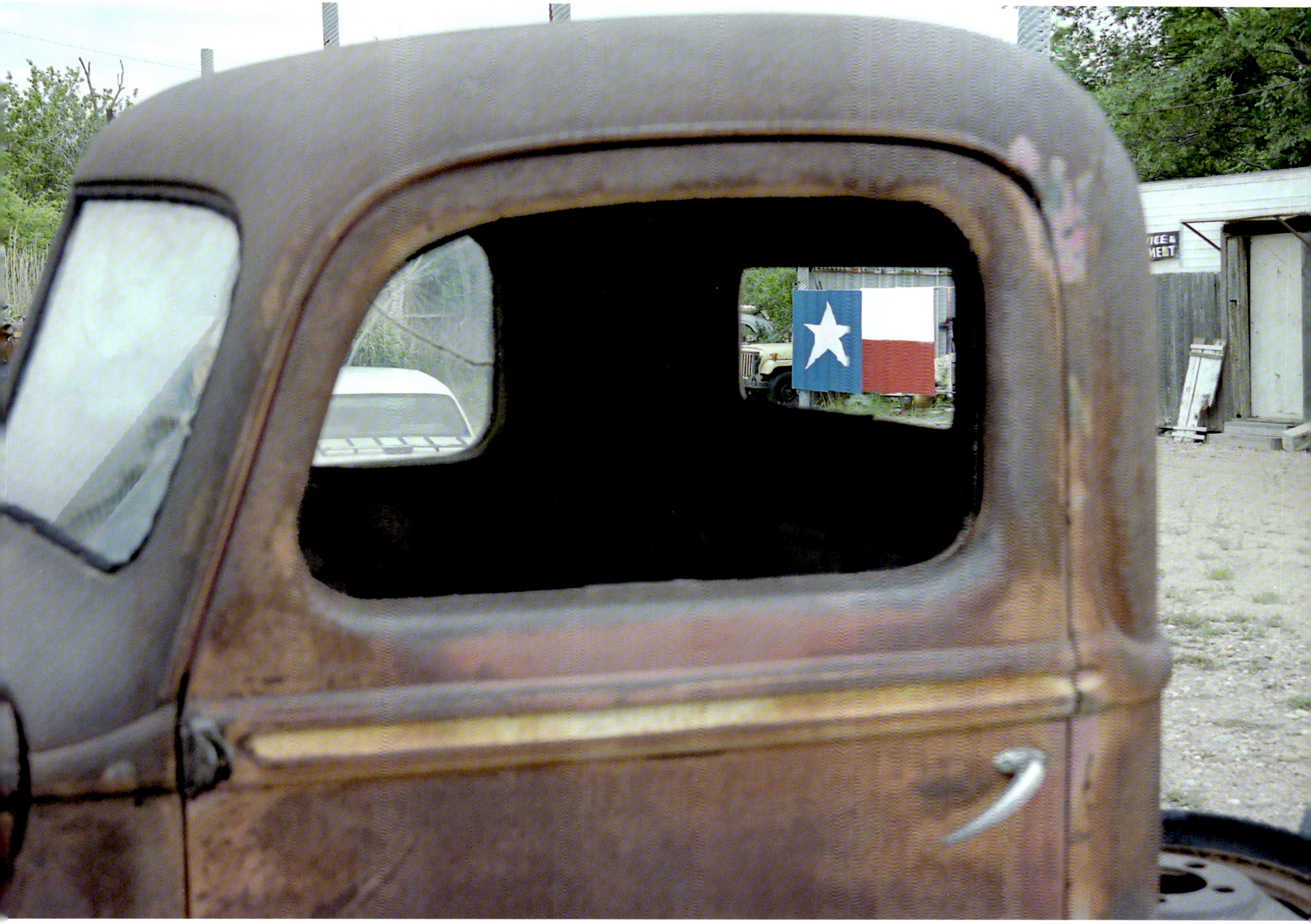

"Looking Backward" (Bright's Arts & Crafts, Clarendon), 2005

An antique Ford pickup truck frames a painted tin Lone Star flag at Bright's Arts & Crafts in the small Texas Panhandle town of Clarendon. One man's junk. . . .

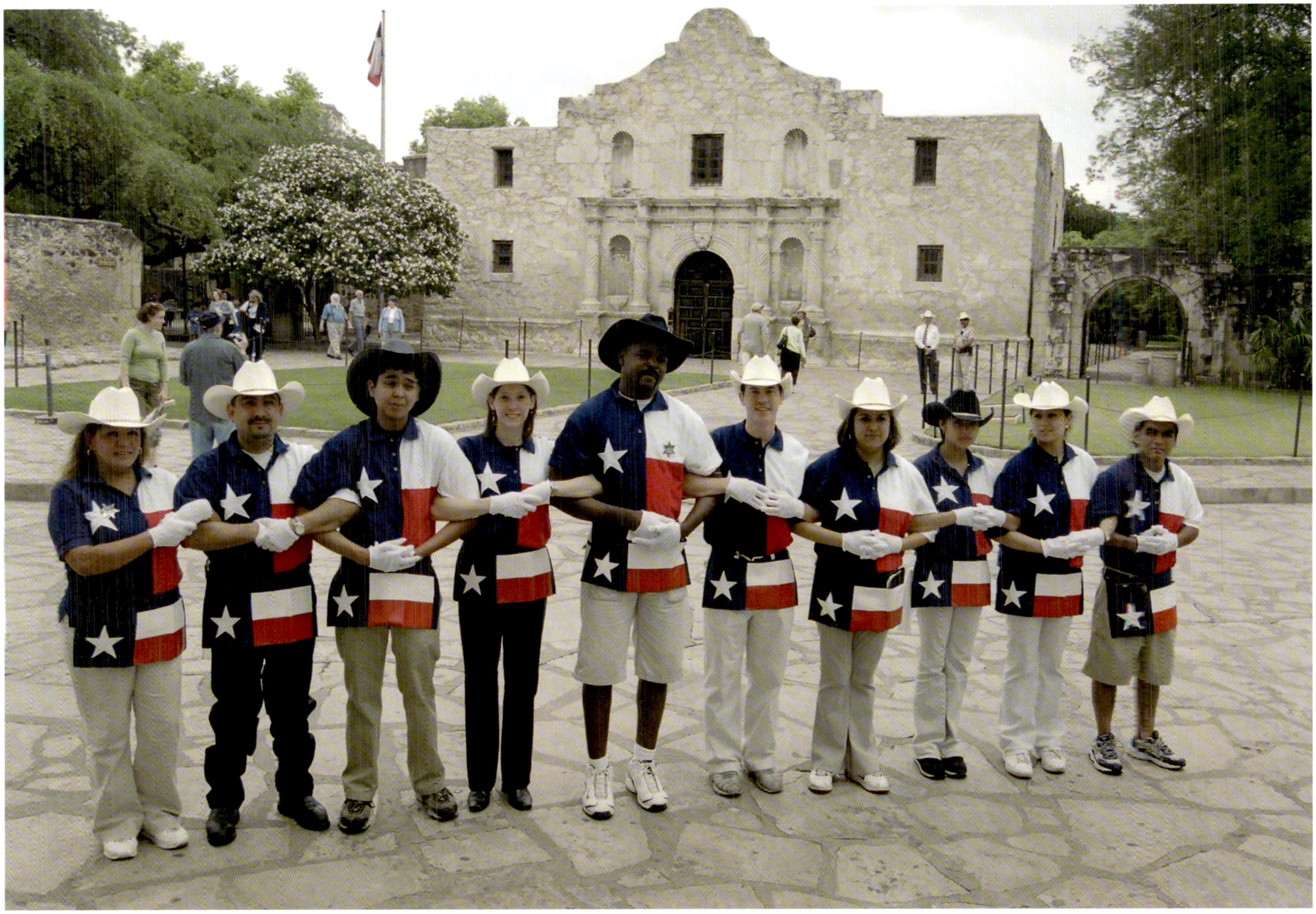

"The Alamo" (The Republic of Texas Restaurant staff, San Antonio), 2005

A few members of the staff of the Republic of Texas Restaurant, located on the River Walk in San Antonio, stand with their Lone Star uniforms, looking like defenders of the Alamo.

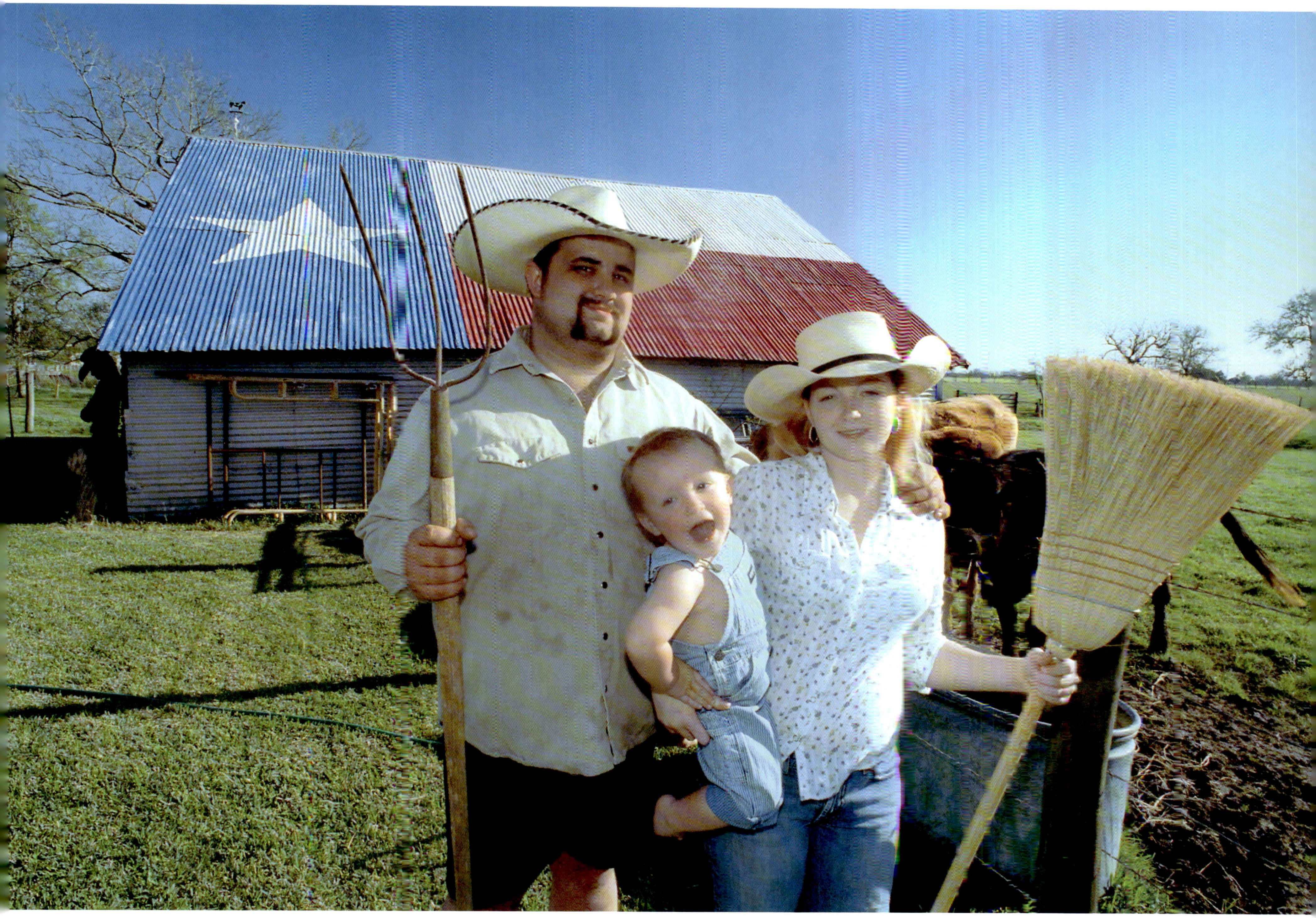

Family Farm" (The Loessin family, East Bernard), 2005

Zach and Cassie Loessin with their son Logan, owners of the Diamond R Ranch, stand in front of their Lone Star barn in East Bernard. Zach painted the barn himself. Texas gothic.

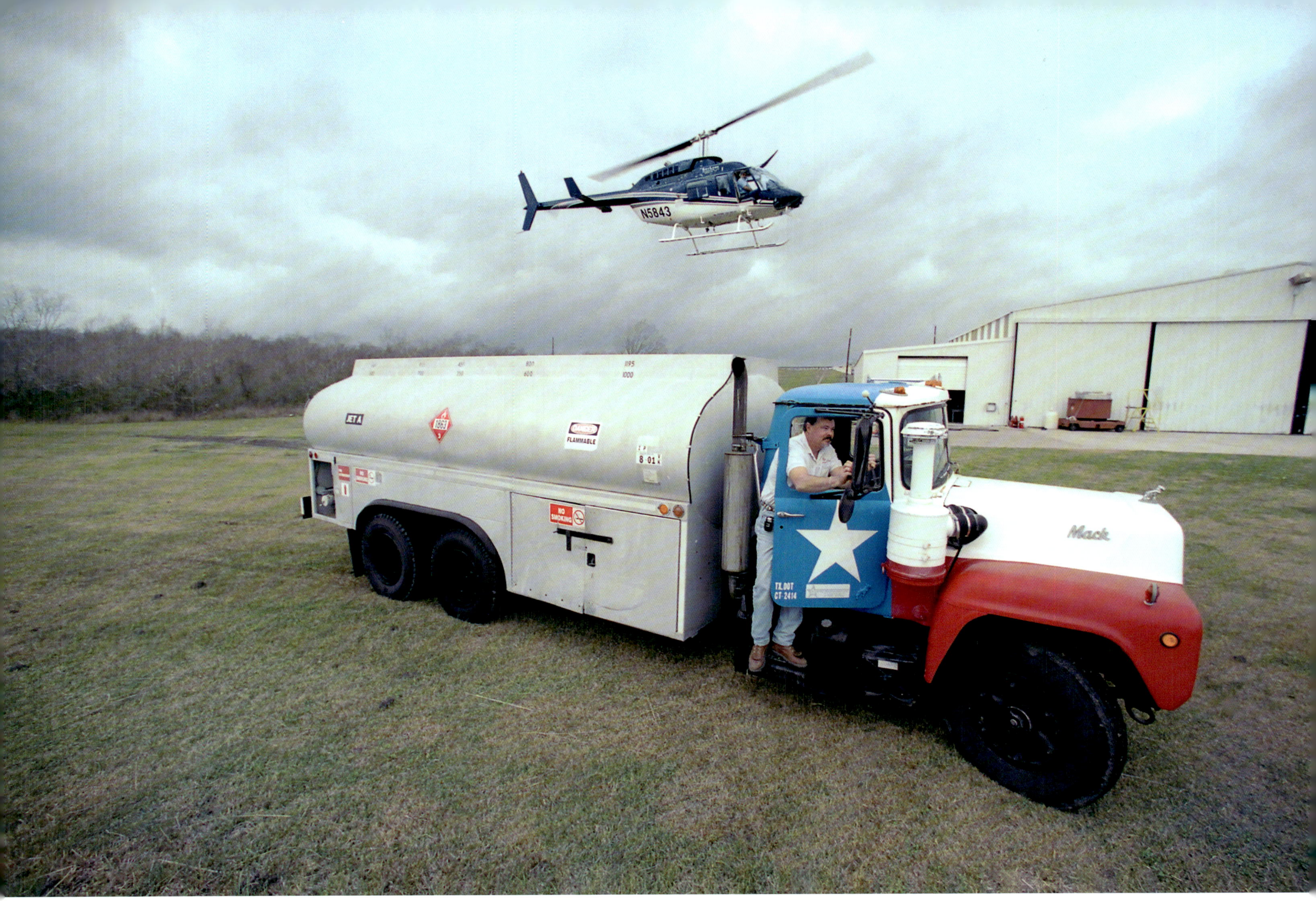

"Tanker-Cop" (Go Helitrans, Manvel), 2005

Owner Greg Obert of Go Helitrans in Manvel and pilot/safety instructor Steve Rayburn maneuver their helicopter in a test run using their Lone Star fuel truck. Treetop flyer.

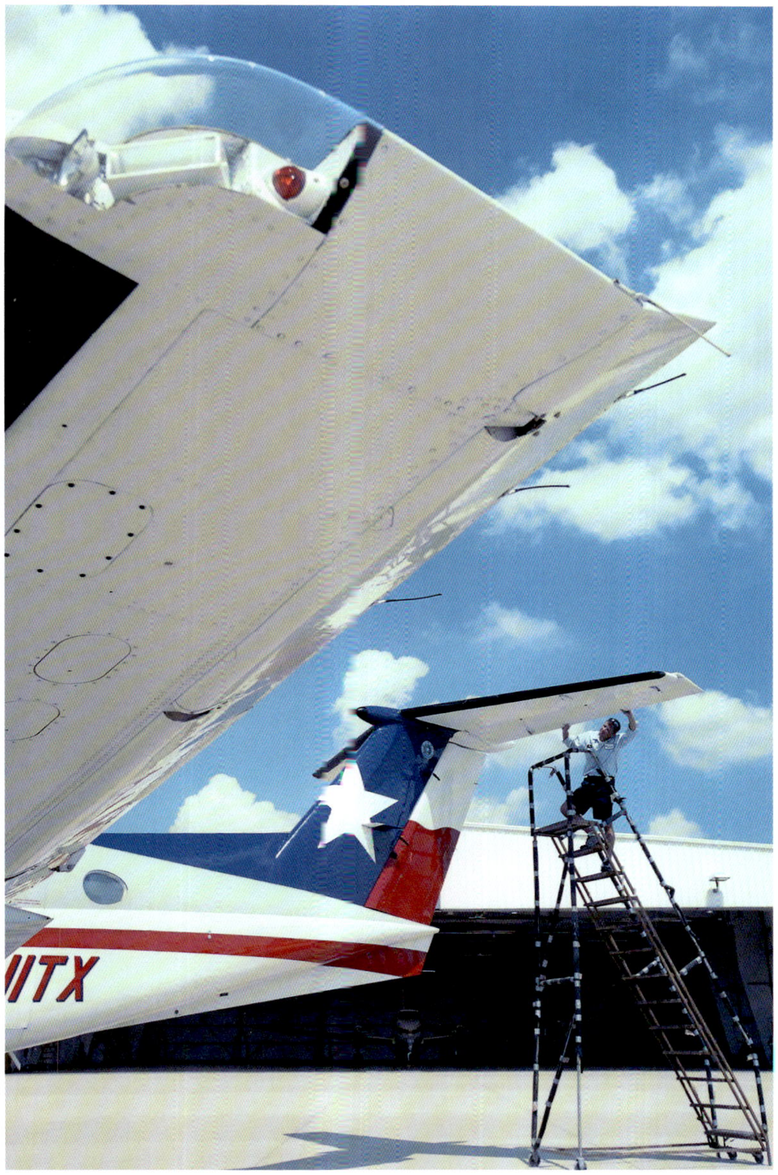

"State Plane" (The state's airplane, Austin), 2005

In Austin, Texas Department of Transportation Aviation Division flight line specialist Phil Anderson makes his safety checks on the state's Lone Star aircraft, a Beechcraft Super King Air 200. Fasten your seat belt.

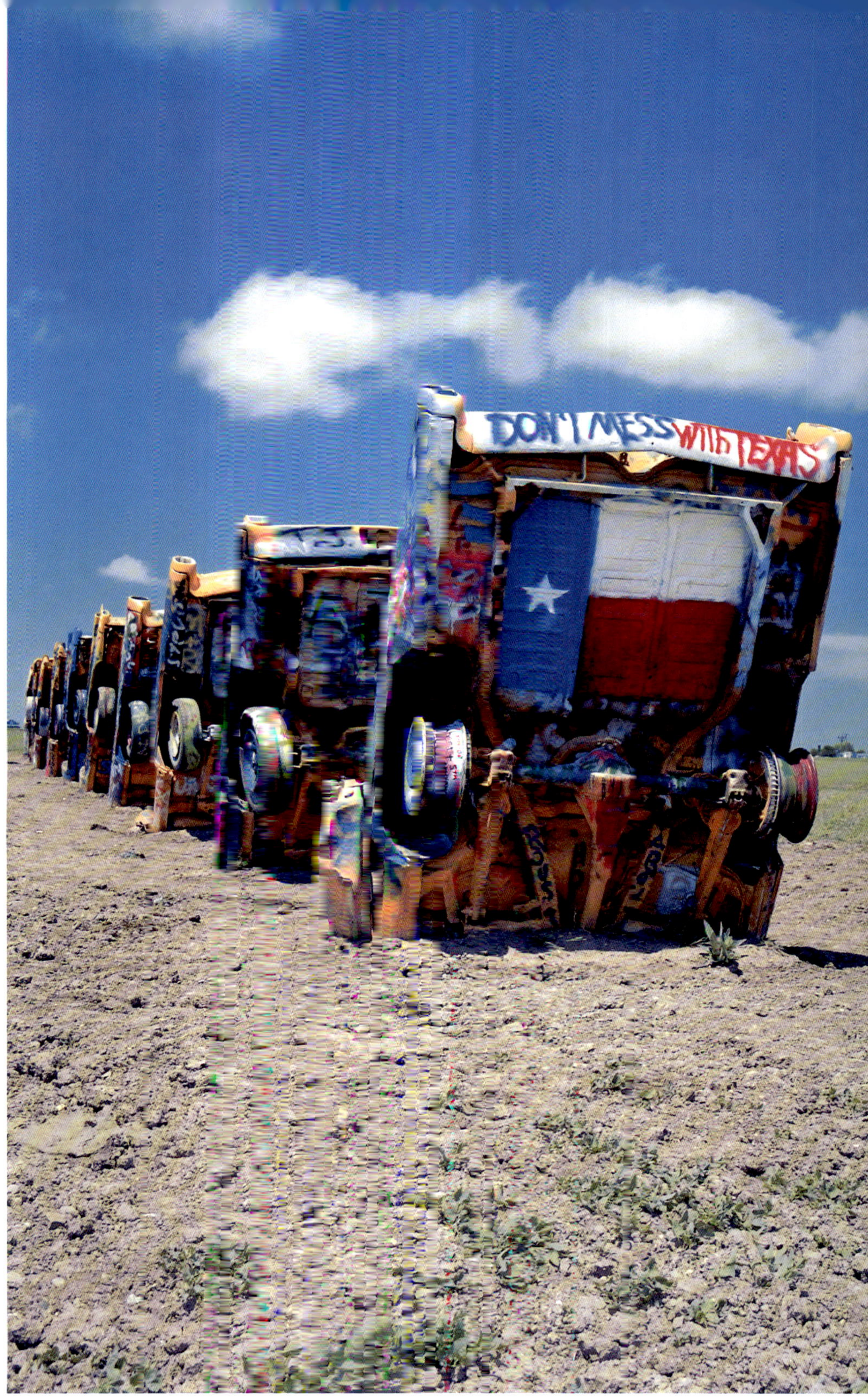

"Grounded Wheels" (Cadillac Ranch, Amarillo), 2005

The Cadillac Ranch, located west of Amarillo on Interstate 40, is the brainchild of Stanley Marsh 3, former mayor of Amarillo. Ten cars planted at the exact angles of the Great Pyramid display their famous tail fins. Panhandle fantasy.

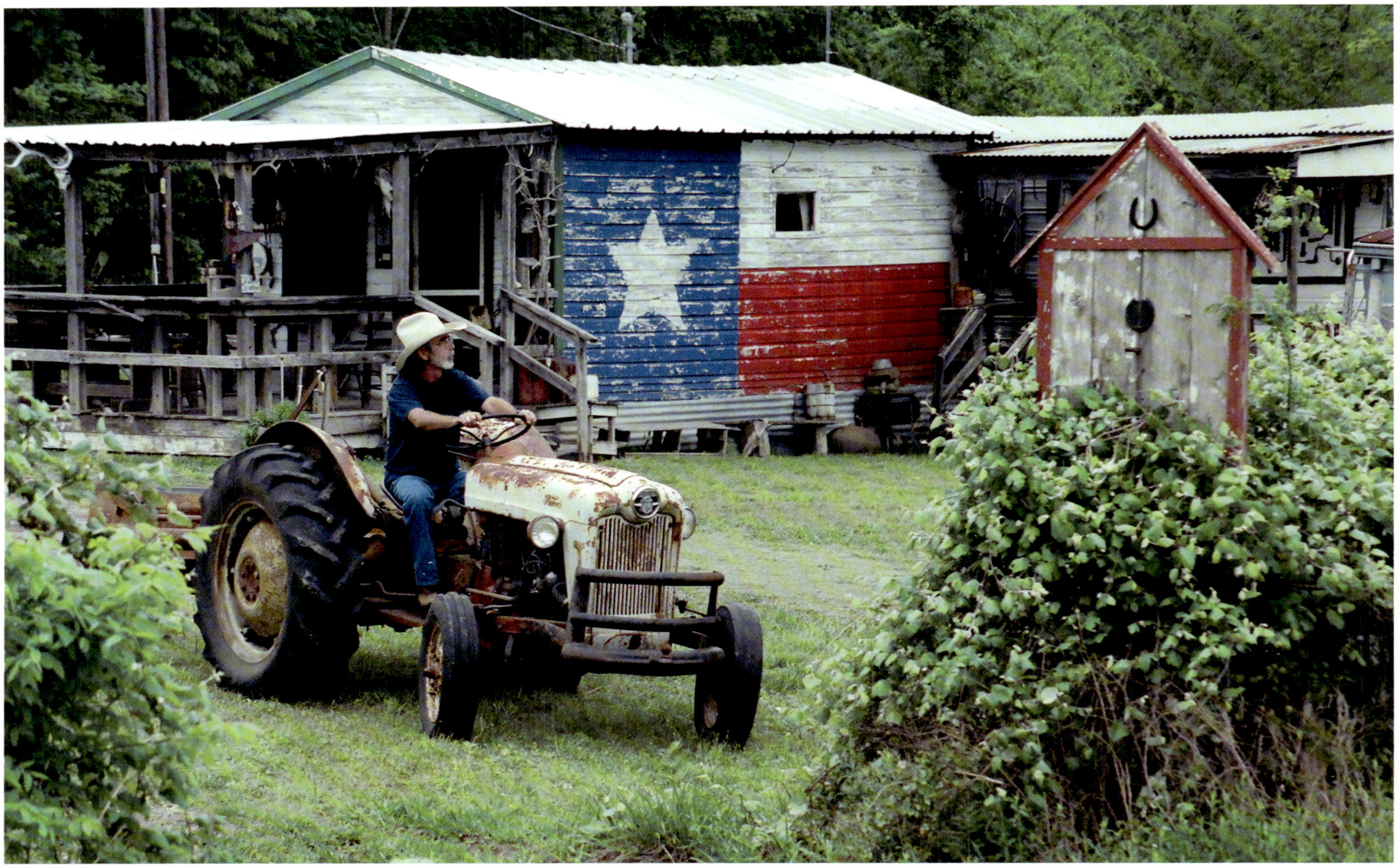

"Tractor Peel" (Andy McGinty, Washington County), 2005

Andy McGinty looks after his family's place in Washington County, used for special occasions. "It's just a fun old place to gather."

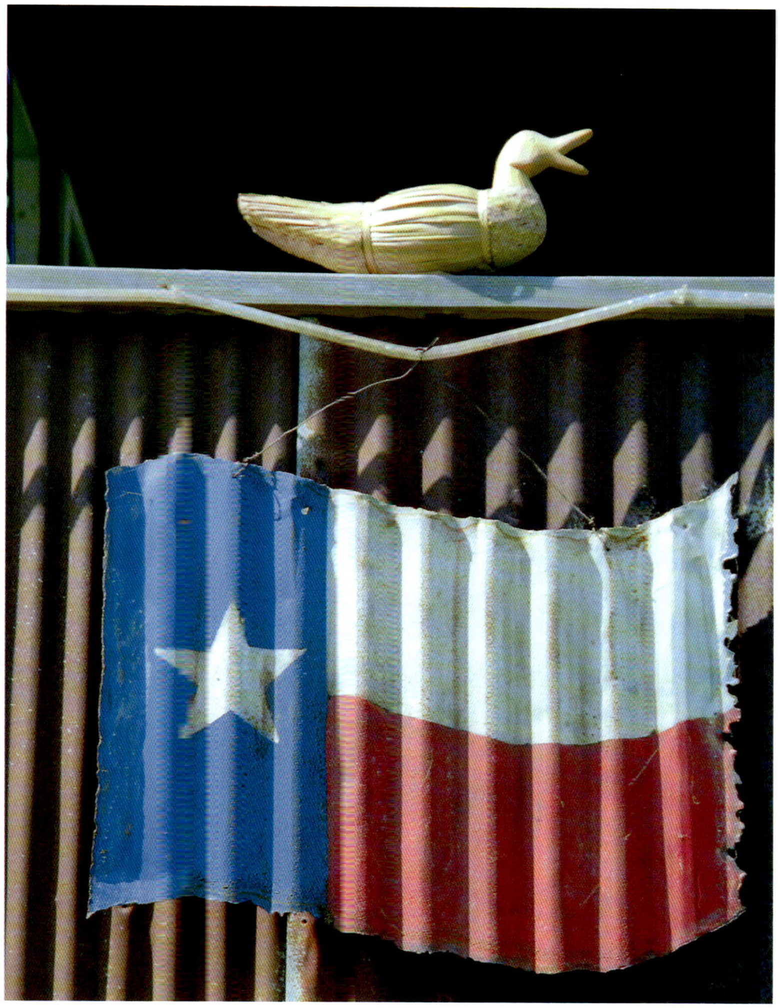

"Duck Call" (Branding Iron Bar-B-Q, Goliad), 2004

Johnny Ripps, owner of the Branding Iron Bar-B-Q in Goliad, says his motto is "I found the beef." This duck and sign give the call to his Lone Star customers. Just ducky.

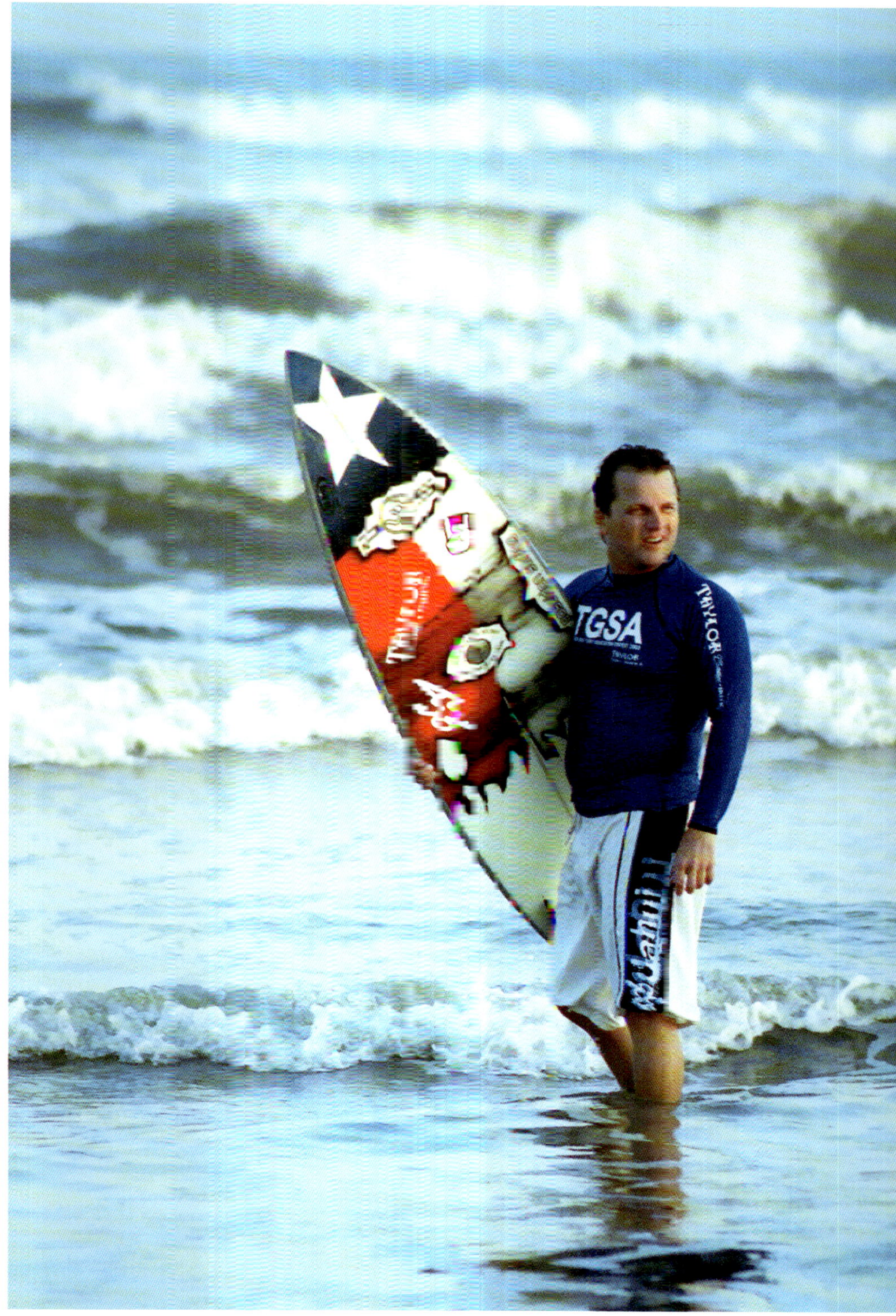

"Surfer Boy" (Bronson Hilliard, Galveston), 2005

Bronson Hilliard of Houston was one of the state's standout surfers in the '90s. Bronson has traveled the world, loving the surf and his Lone Star State. Hang ten.

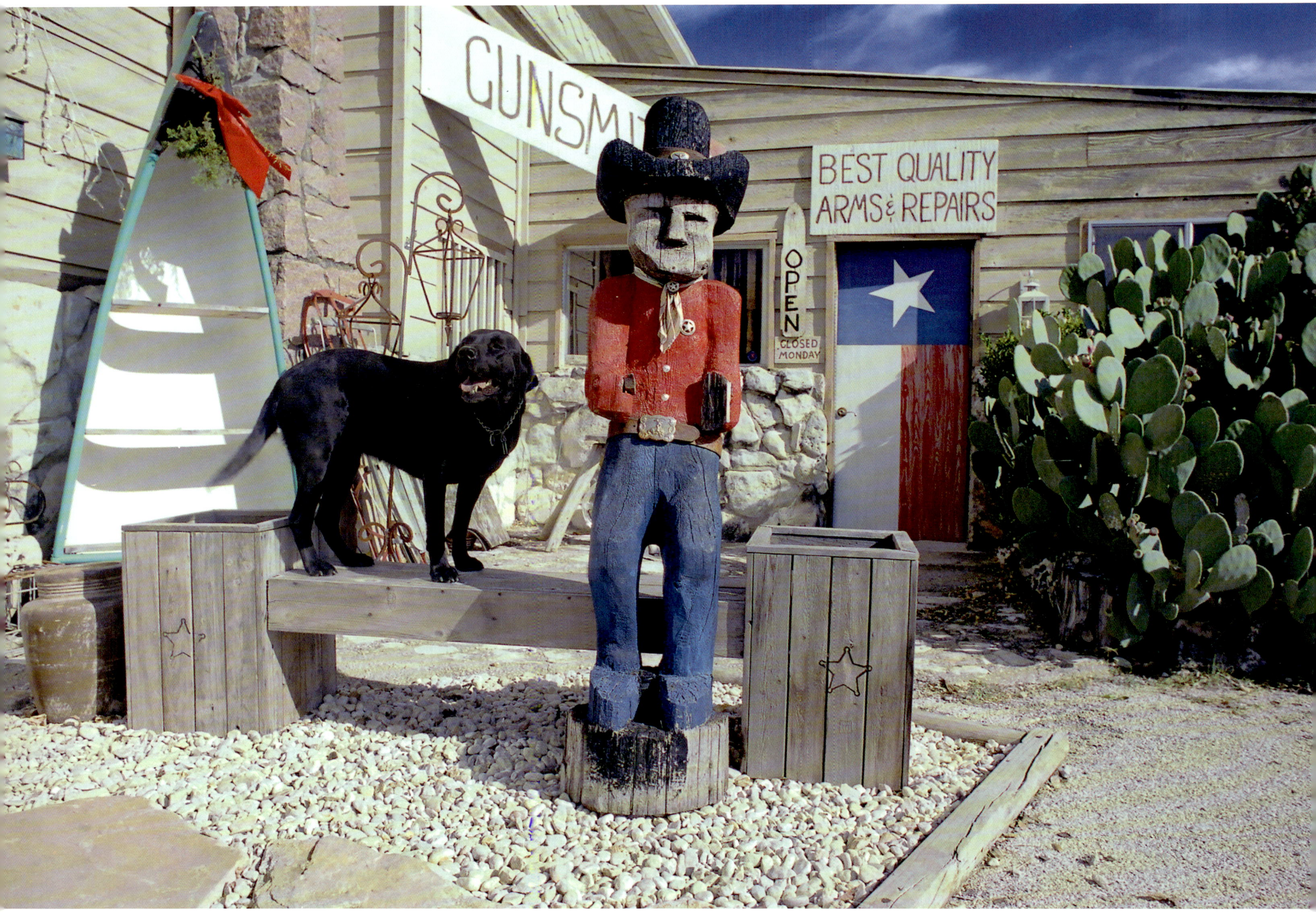

"Gunsmith" (Corner Stone Gunsmith Shop, Ingram), 2004

Located on Old Ingram Loop in Ingram, the Don Schultz's Corner Stone Gunsmith Shop specializes in arms, stocks, and fancy woods. Open the Lone Star door and Whoopie, Schultz's black lab, will greet you.

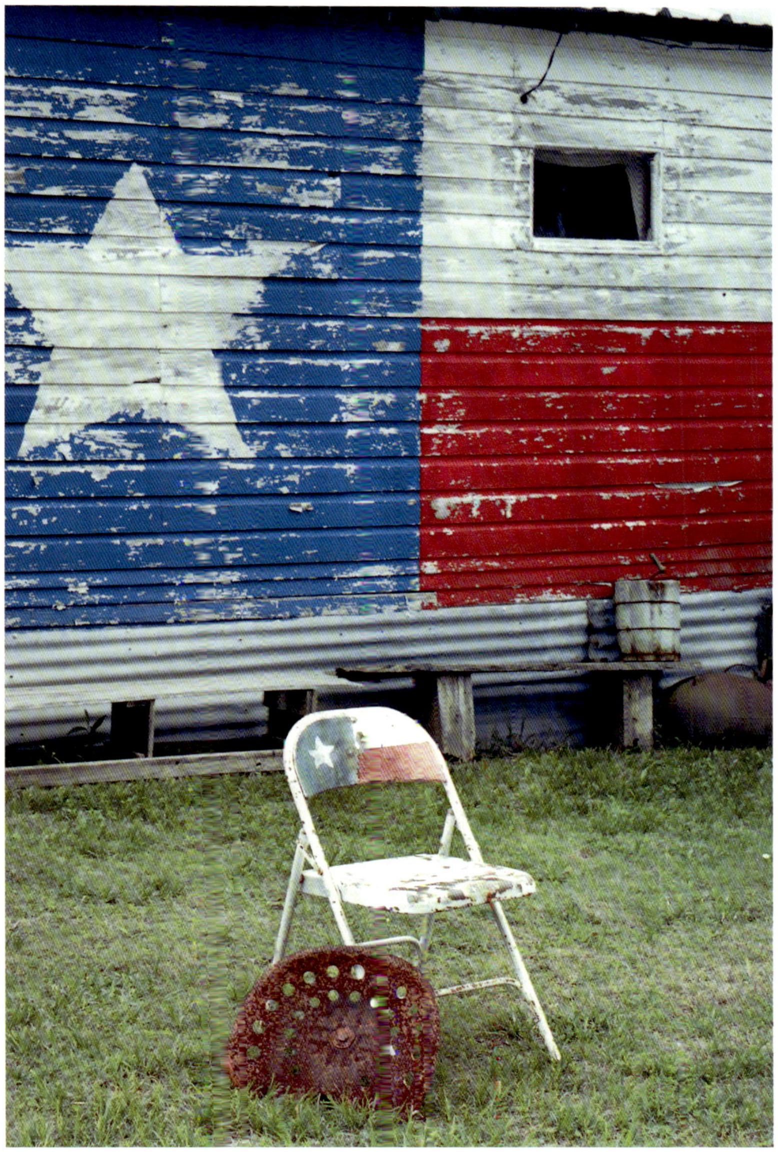

"Have-a-Seat" (McGinty family's country place, Washington County), 2005

The McGinty family may fight over the Lone Star folding chair at gatherings held on their Washington County place, just for the love of the state. Pull up a chair.

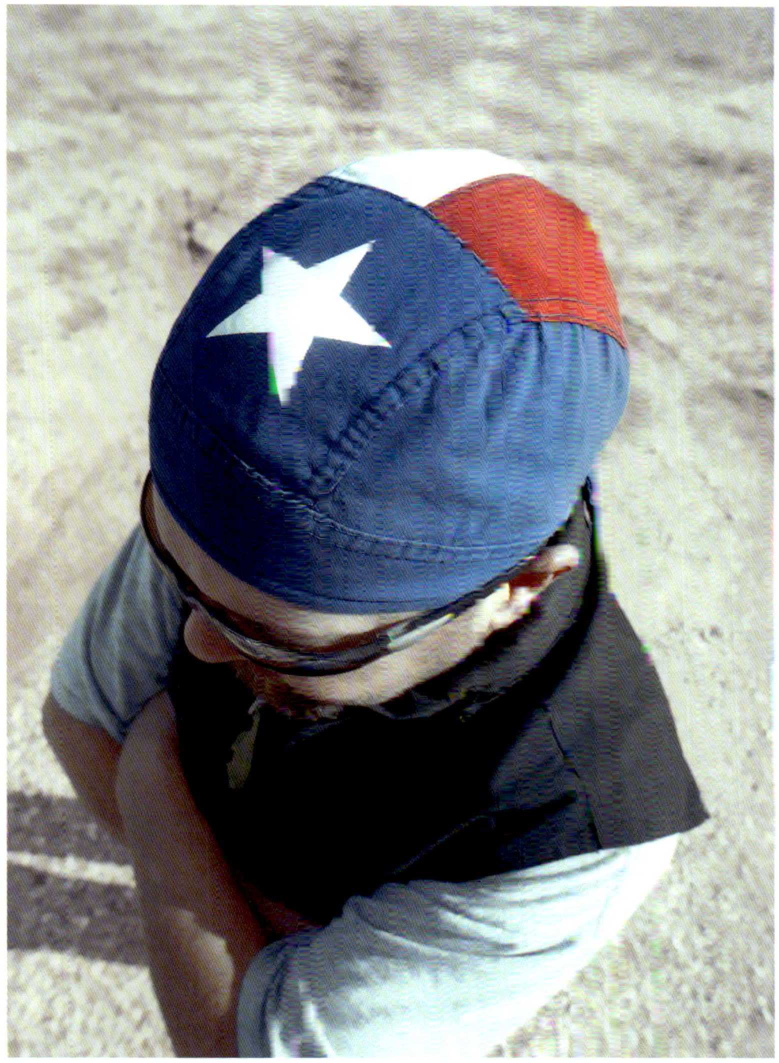

"Work Cap" (Denney Moss, Buna), 2002

Born in the Texas Panhandle and now living in the East Texas town of Buna, Denney Moss always has his Lone Star thinking cap on when at work. That's using your head.

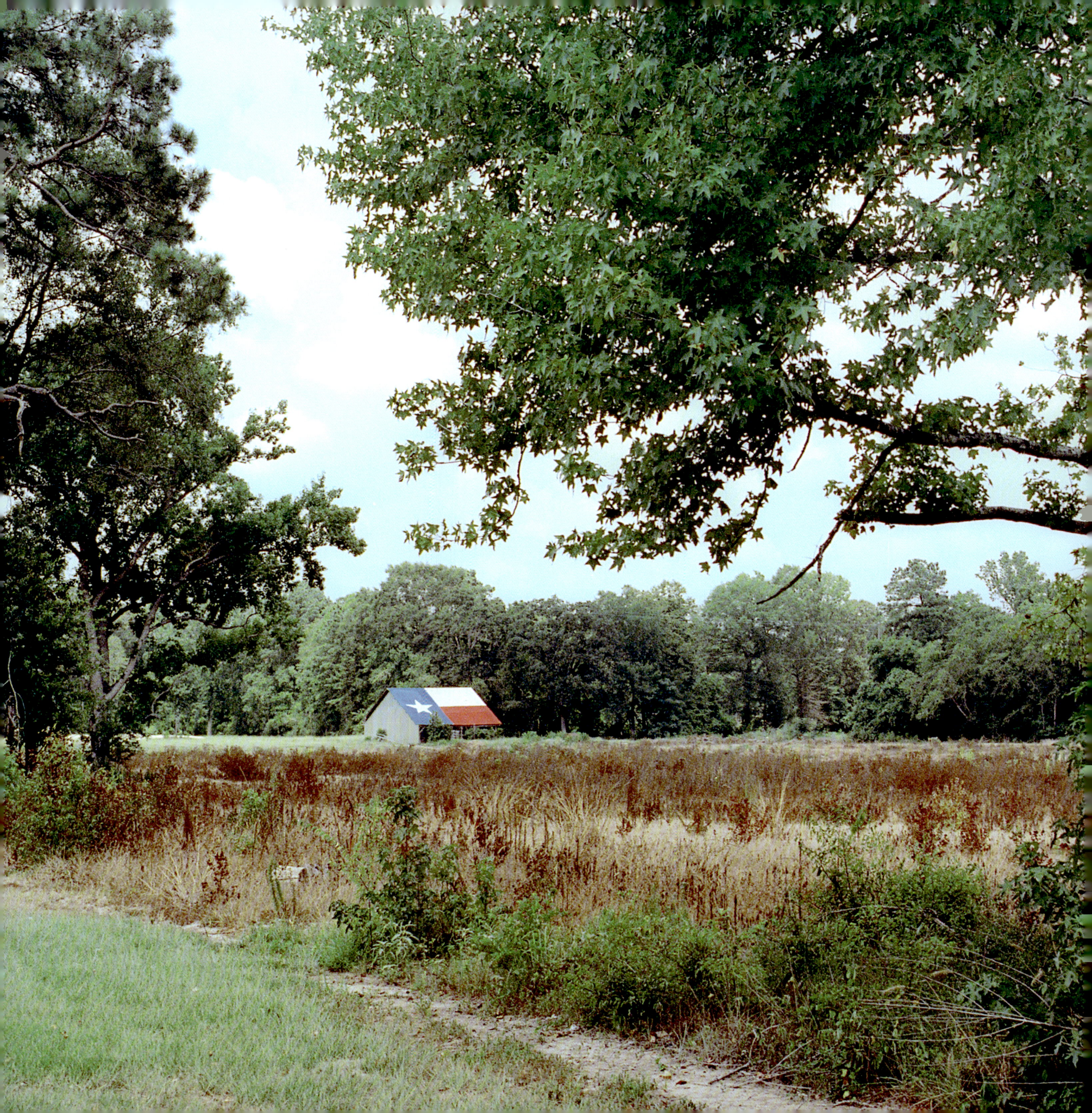

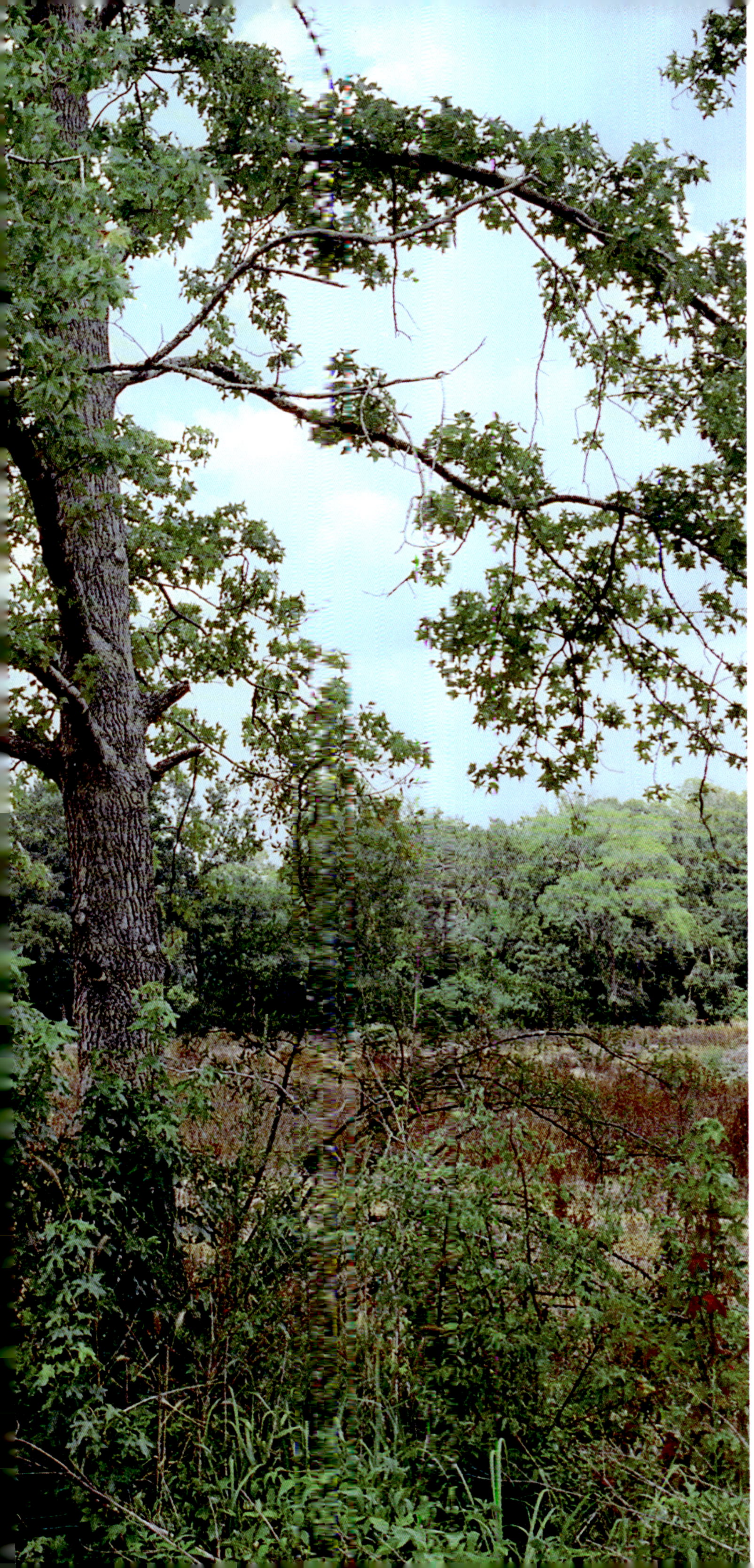

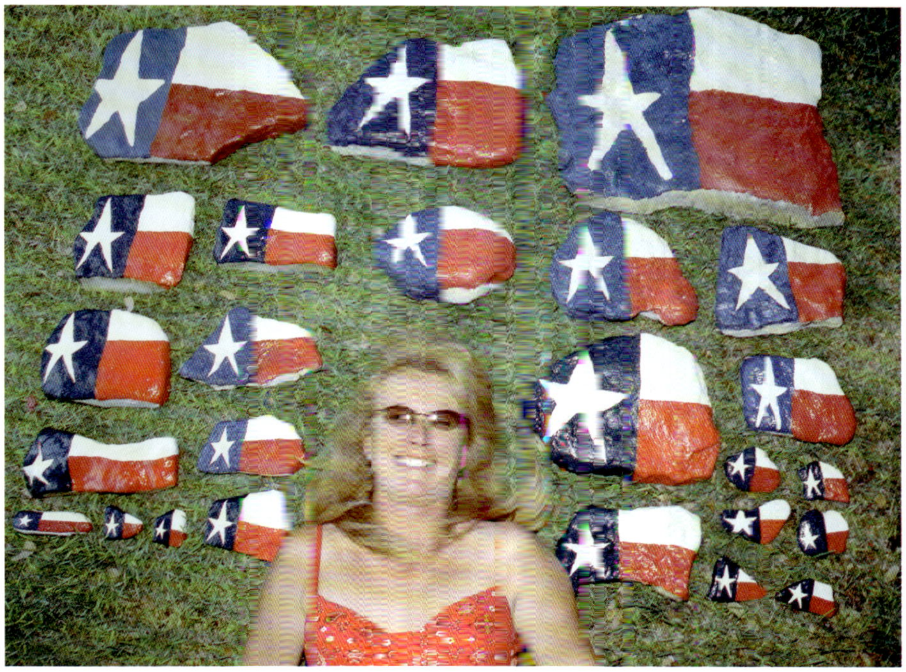

"Rock Solid" (Barbara Colom, Medina), 2005

Hill Country artist Barbara Colom, owner of Sassy Texas Custom Design, fashions her Lone Star flags from water-smoothed Medina River stones. On the rocks.

"Small Barn" (John Ralph Pouland barn, Diboll), 2002

Located in the small East Texas town of Diboll on State Highway 59, the Pouland family's Lone Star–proud barn, nestled in the trees, can be seen back in the field.

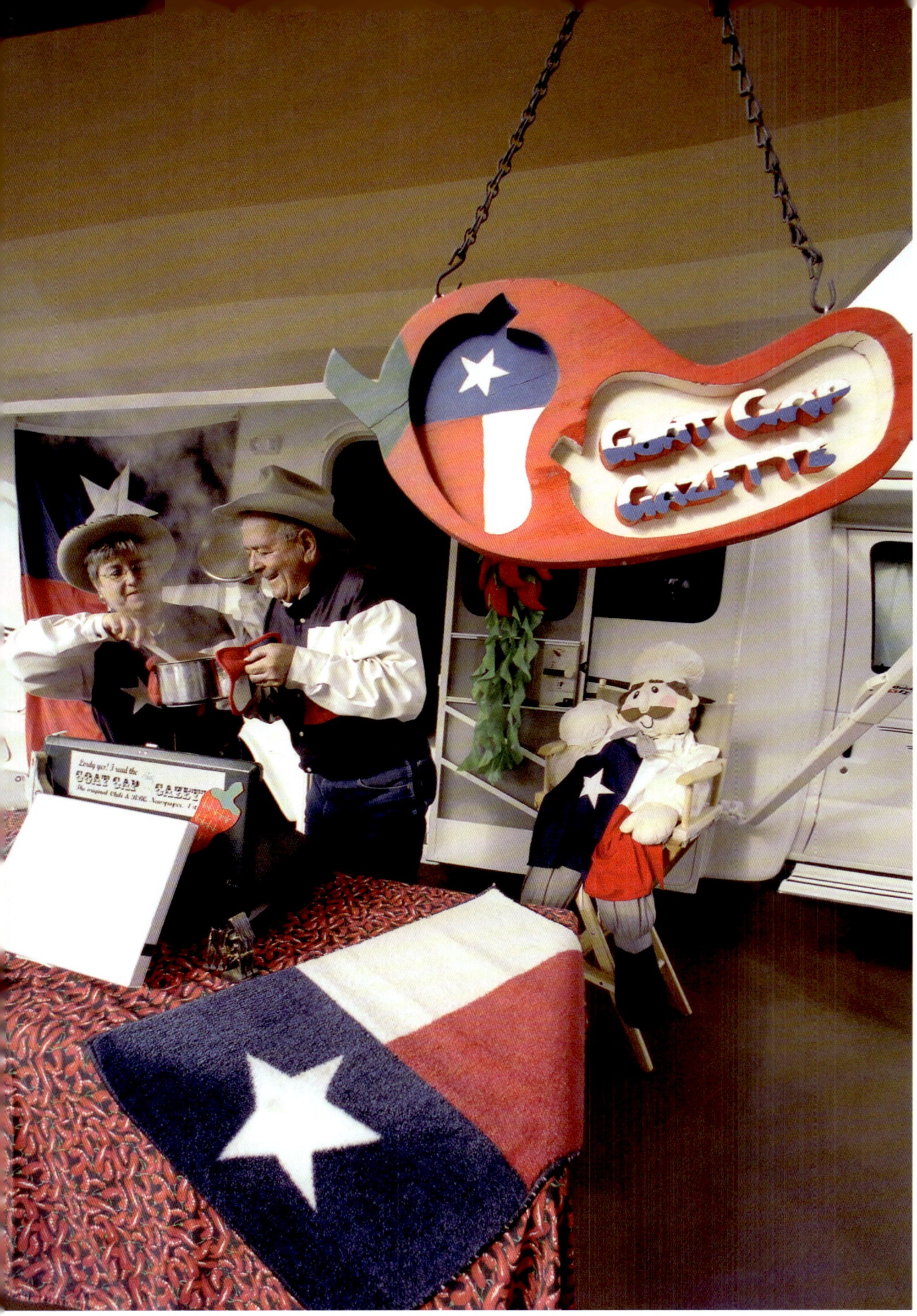

"Cook-Off" (Wayne and Debbie Turner, Waxahachie), 2004

Wayne and Debbie Eiland Turner of Waxahachie have toured the country, cooking chili and promoting Texas pride along the way. Debbie publishes the *Goat Gap Gazette*, the original chili newspaper, and Wayne decorates their cook site with Lone Star and chili items. Overlooking the couple is their Master Chili Chef, who travels with the couple. Too many cooks spoil the broth.

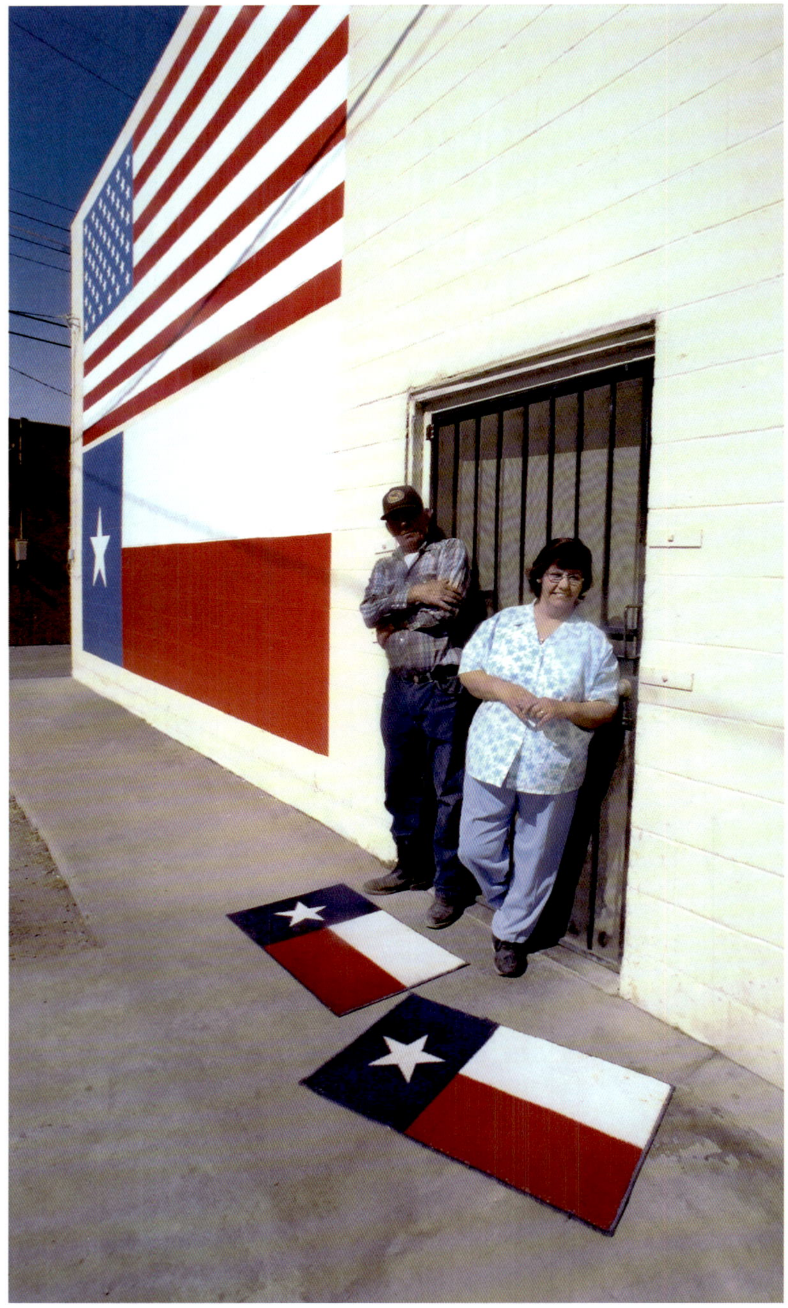

"Welcome Mat" (Vernie and Mary Ford, Clarendon Steakhouse, Clarendon), 2002

Vernie and Mary Ford, owners of the Clarendon Steakhouse in the small Texas Panhandle town of Clarendon, always have their Lone Star welcome mats out for customers. Bon appetit.

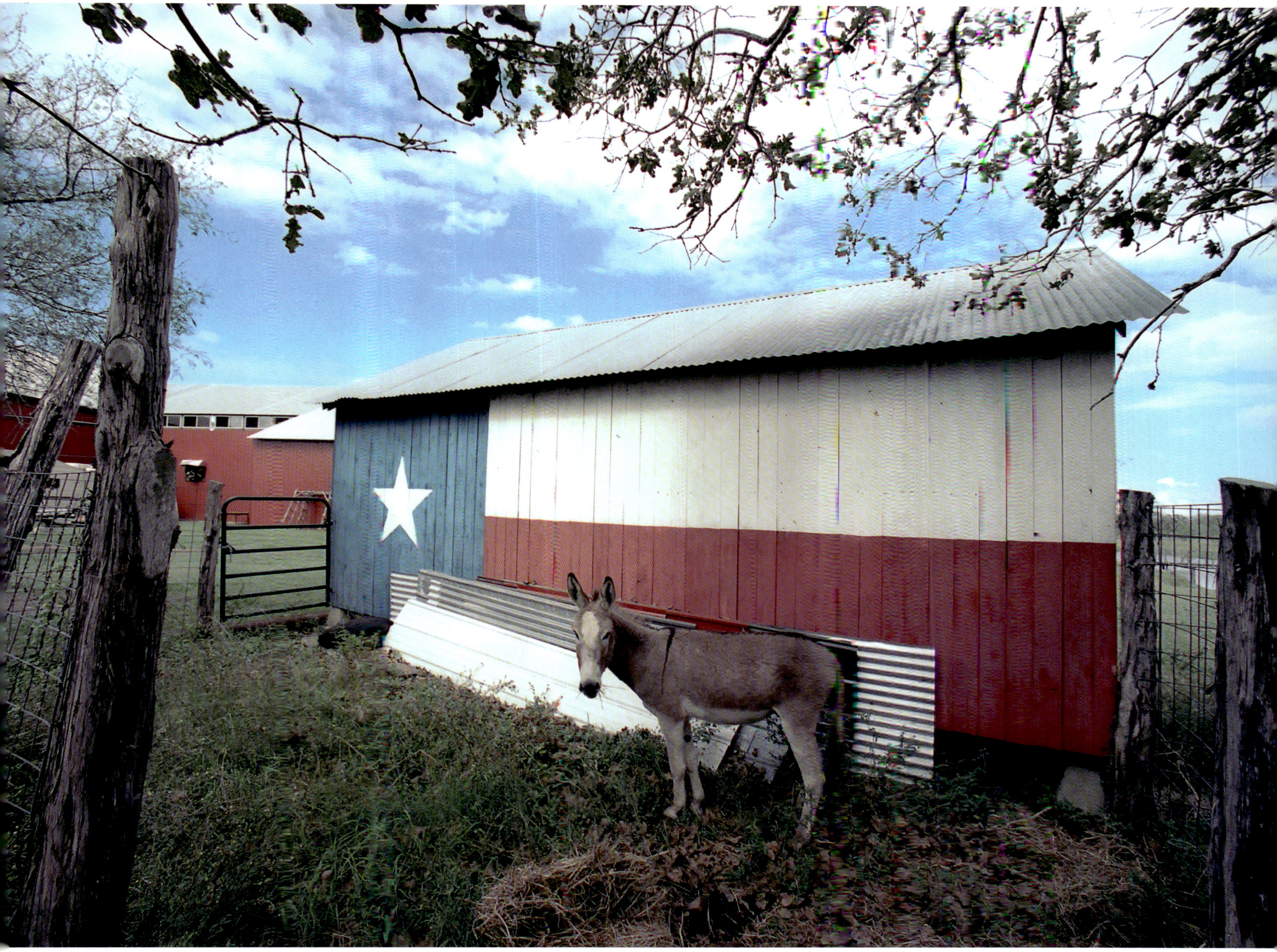

"Bethlehem Donkey" ("Willie," Raisin L Ranch, Raisin), 2004

Willie, a Bethlehem donkey, walks past one of many Lone Star barns on George and Lynette Migl's Raisin L Ranch and Country Club, "Registered Breeder of Special Events" in Raisin, Texas. Don't be stubborn.

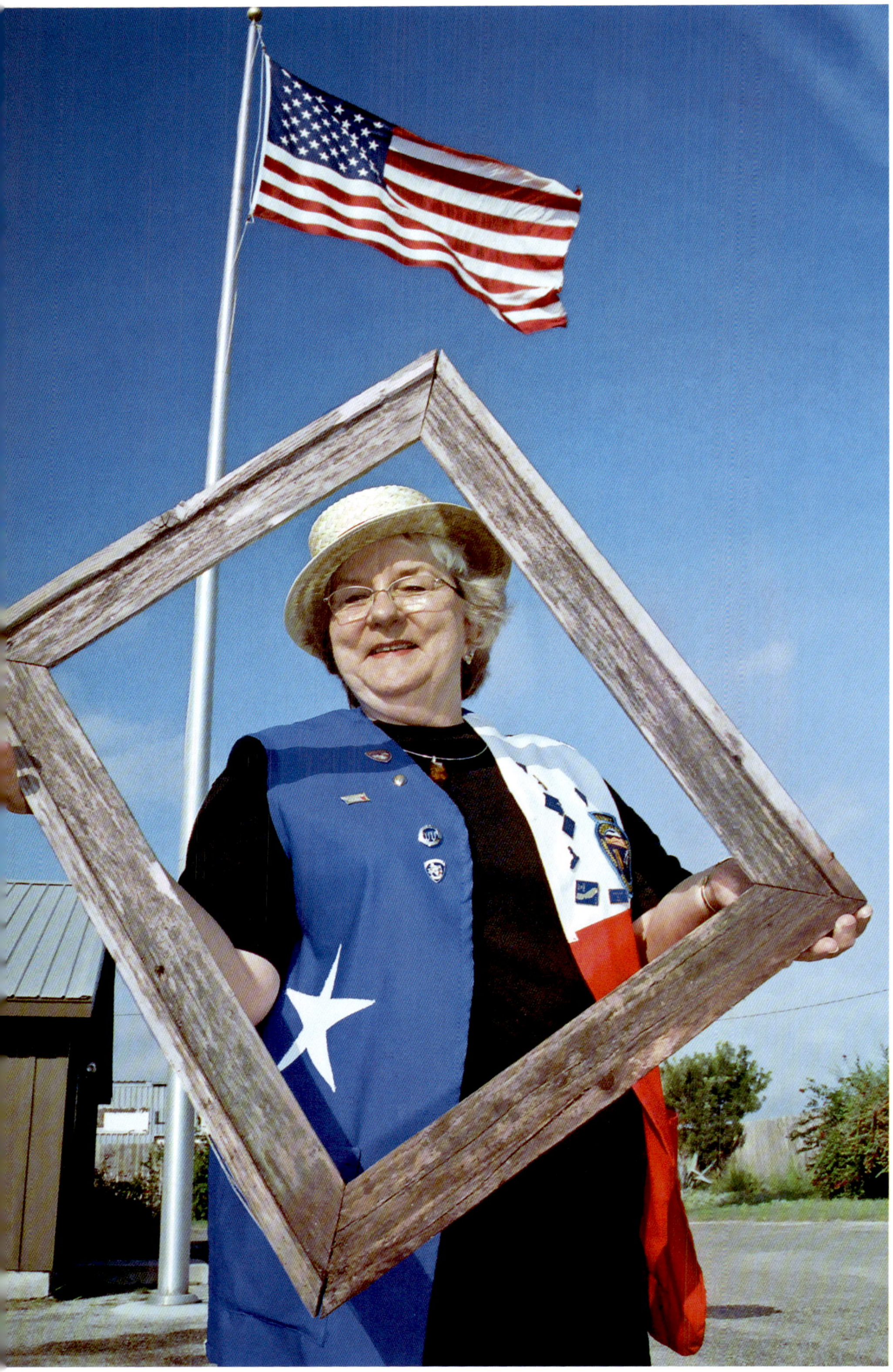

"Frame Work" (Mary Windham, Kingsville), 2004

Mary Windham of Kingsville loves the colors and flag of the Lone Star State. She frames a vest she made for her husband Anse. Vested interest.

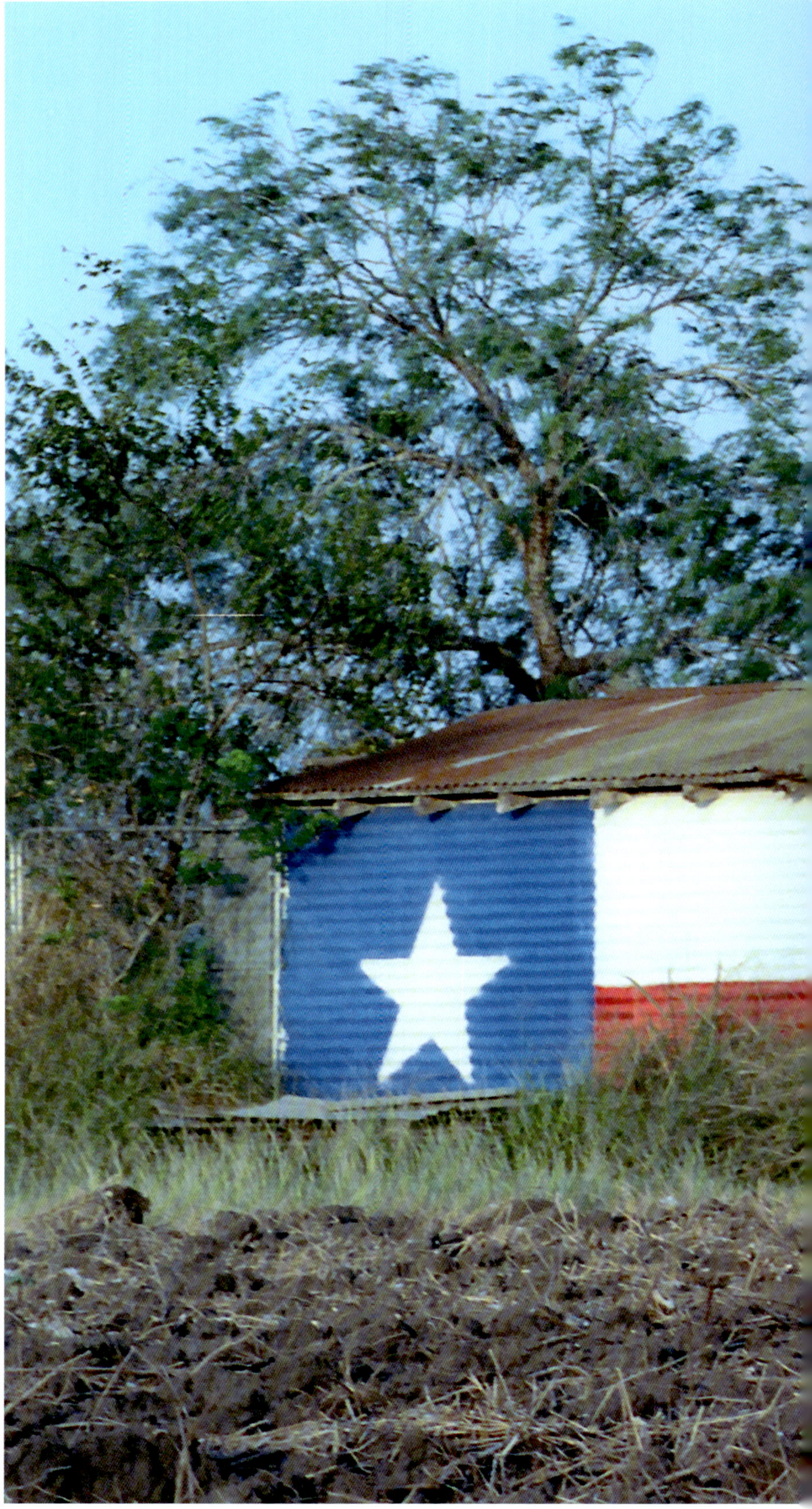

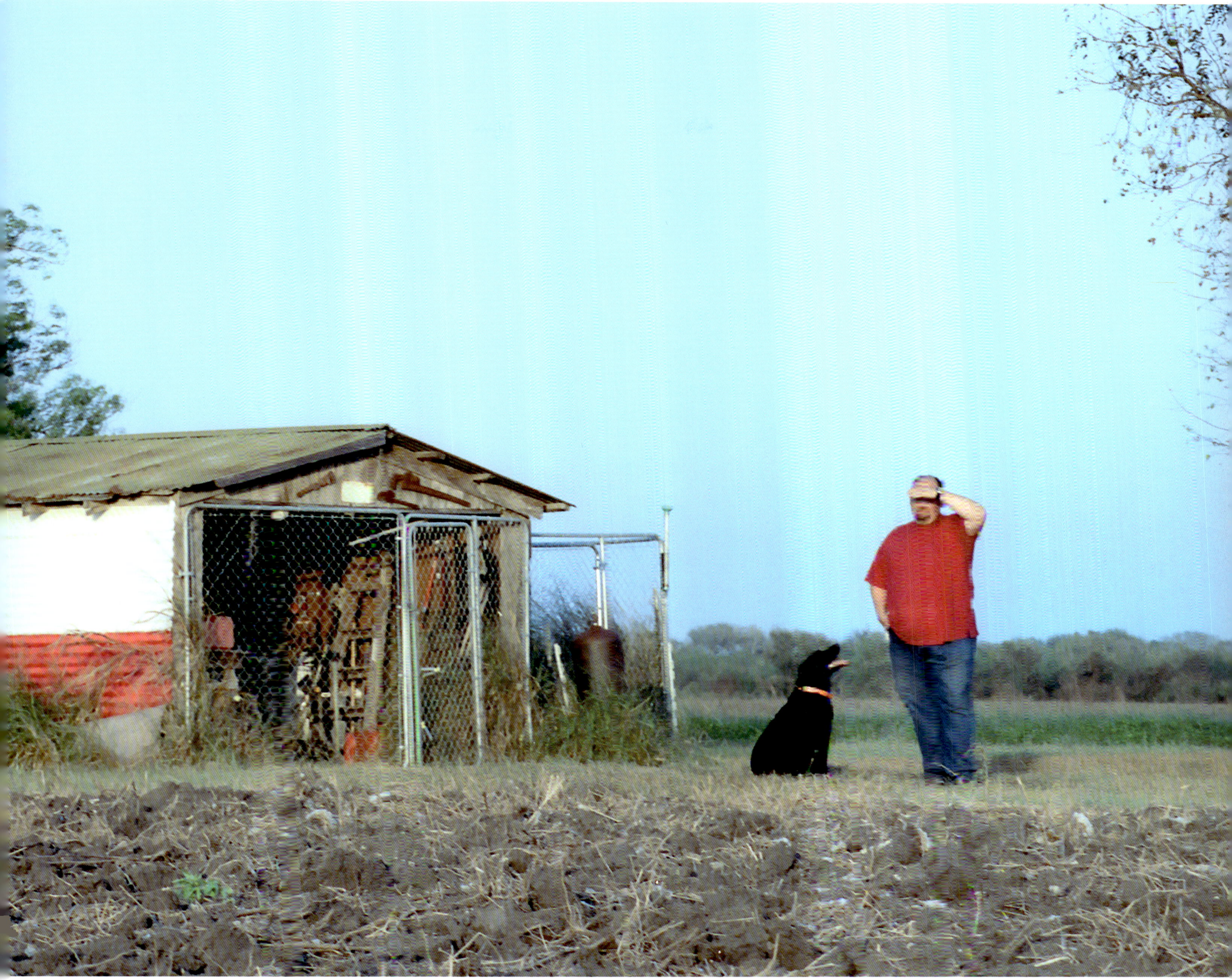

"Man's Best Friend" (Glenn Scholz with his dog Asia, Driscoll), 2004

Glenn Scholz, with his black lab Asia by his side, looks out over his land in Driscoll. The little Lone Star equipment barn was painted by Glen and overseen by Asia. Teamwork.

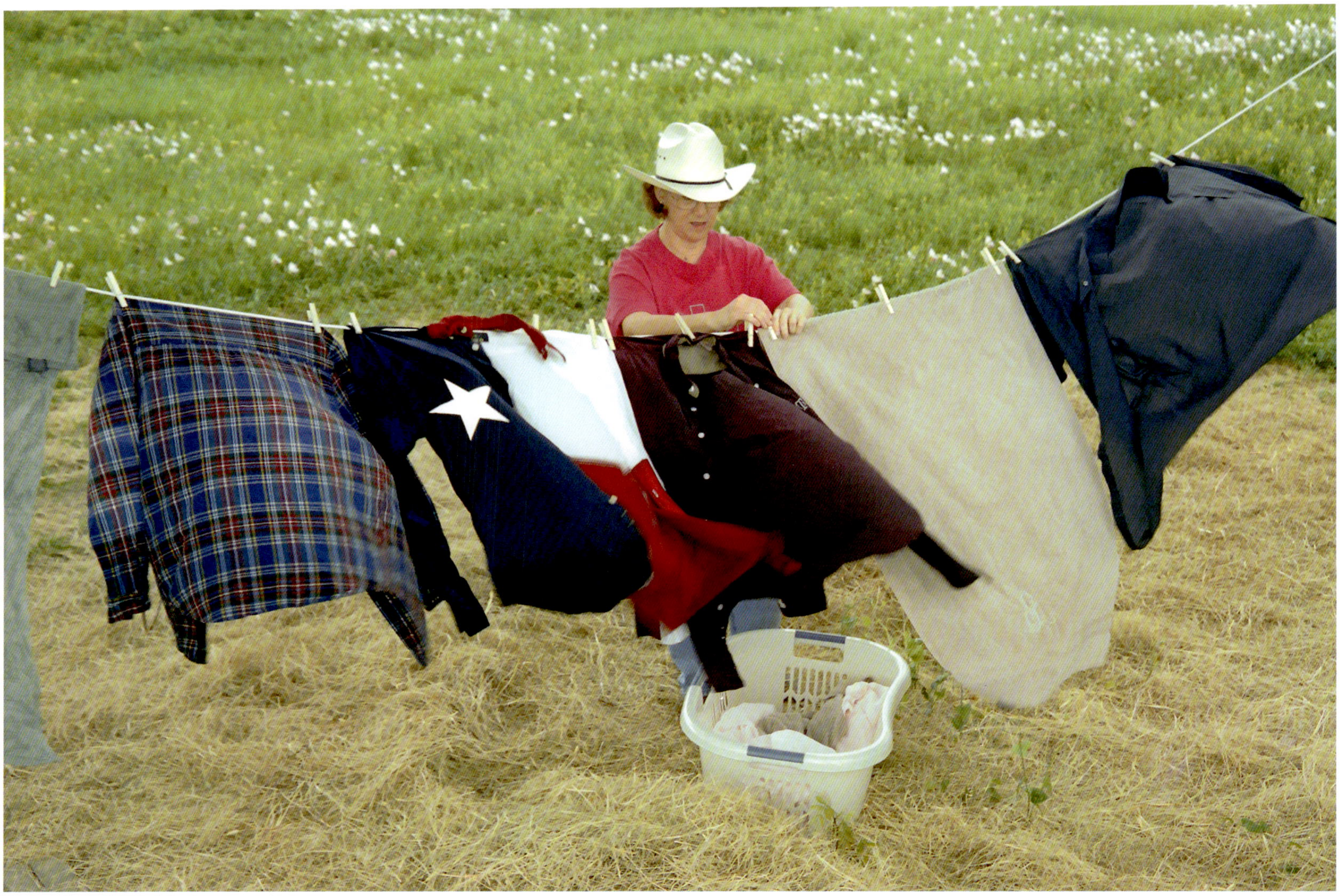

"Clothes Line" (Dorcas Jenkins, Washington County), 2005

Dorcas Jenkins of the Rio Red Ranches in Washington, Texas, takes advantage of a beautiful spring day to hang her laundry, making sure her Lone Star flag shirt is hung with care. Air dry.

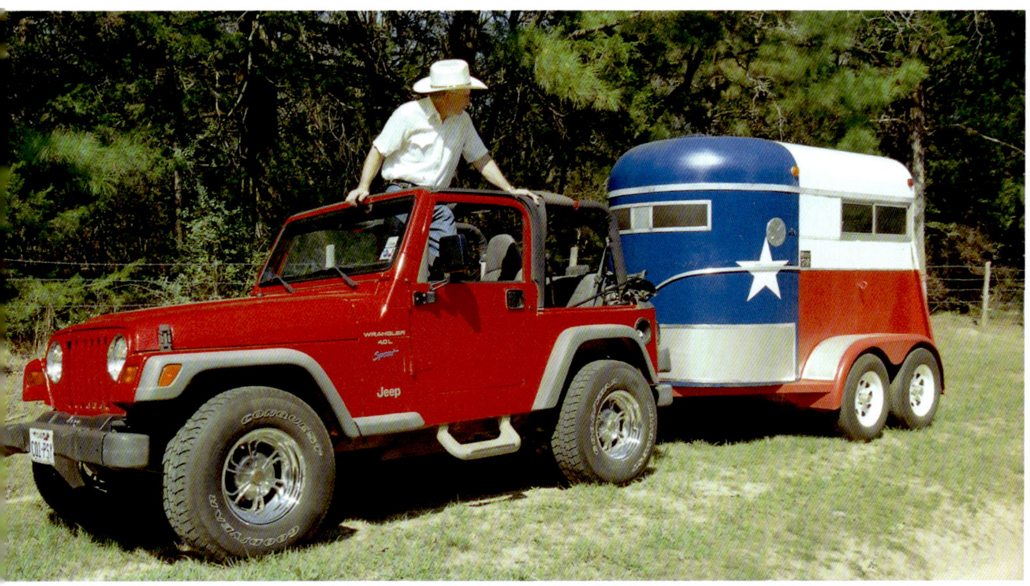

"Happy Trails" (Mike Smith, New Ulm), 2005

Mike Smith of New Ulm checks his trailer on his Lonesome Longhorn Ranch. Mike's wife, Patti, gave him the specifications for the trailer's restoration and painting.

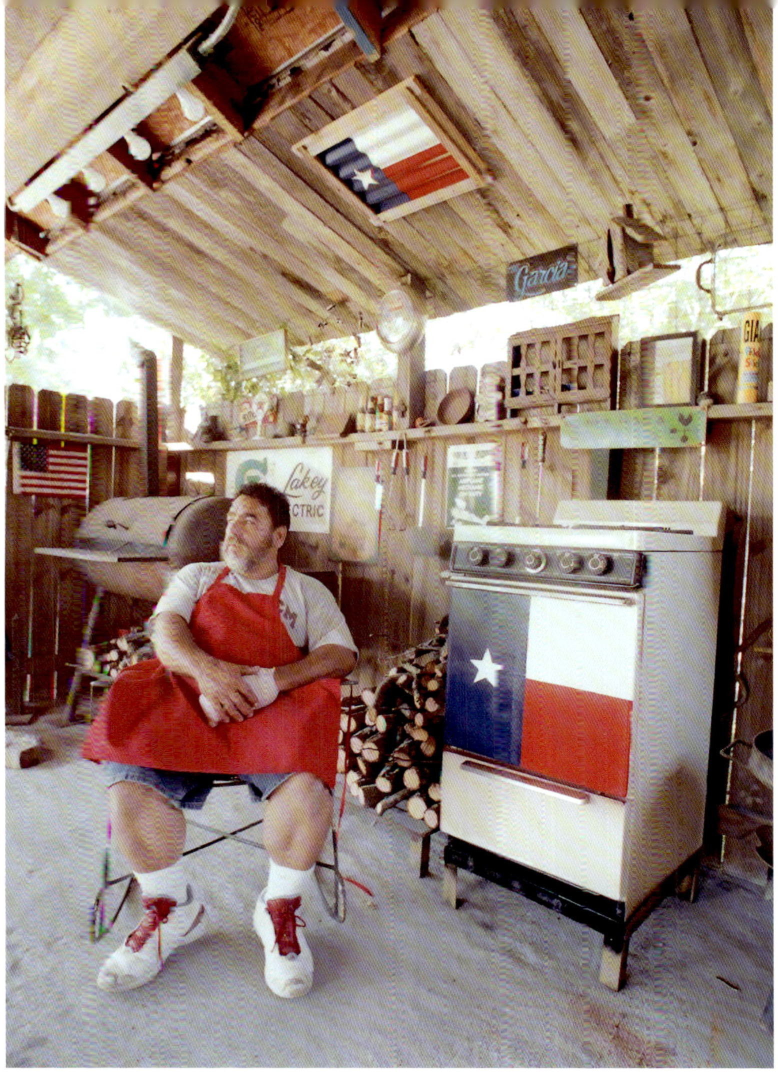

"Range Cook" (Ray Garcia, outside cooking area, Houston), 2005

After cooking all day and cleaning up, Ray Garcia sits in his outside cooking area on the near north side of Houston. Ray built his cook-off area with Lone Star pride in mind. Well done.

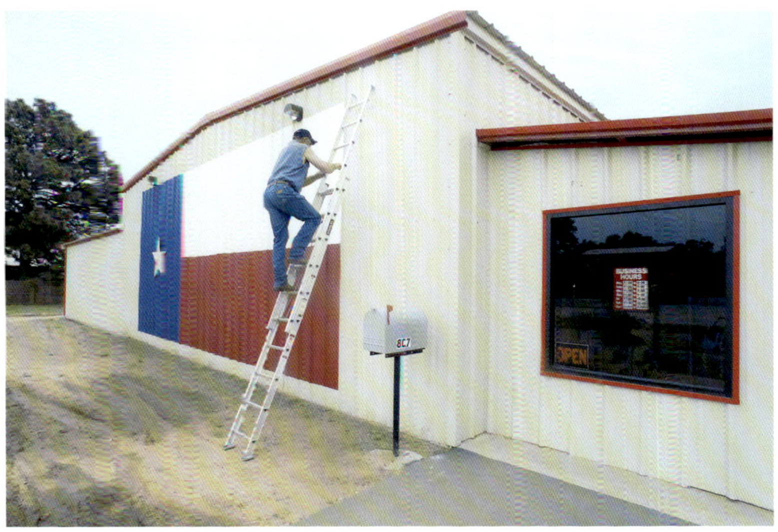

"Up the Ladder" (Morris Grayson Steakhouse, Childress), 2005

Morris Grayson runs Grayson's Steakhouse with his wife, Connie. Working on a ladder, Morris checks and repairs his outside lighting on their Lone Star flag. Daily special.

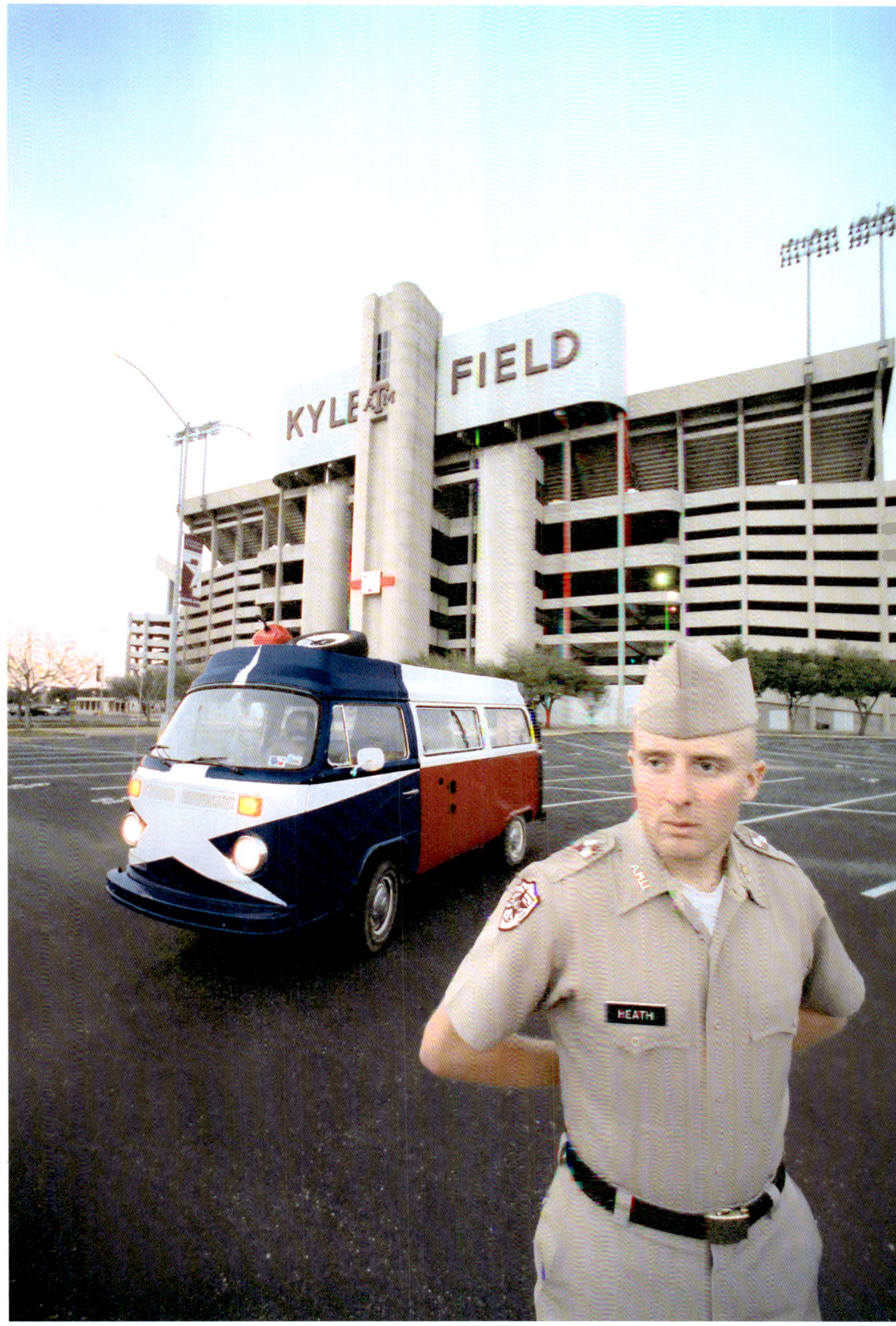

"Cadet" (Sam Heath, Texas A&M University, College Station), 2005

Sam Heath, a member of the corps of cadets at Texas A&M University, stands at parade rest in front of Kyle Field. He and a couple of his buddies painted his Lone Star Volkswagen bus during a weekend. Dress-right-dress

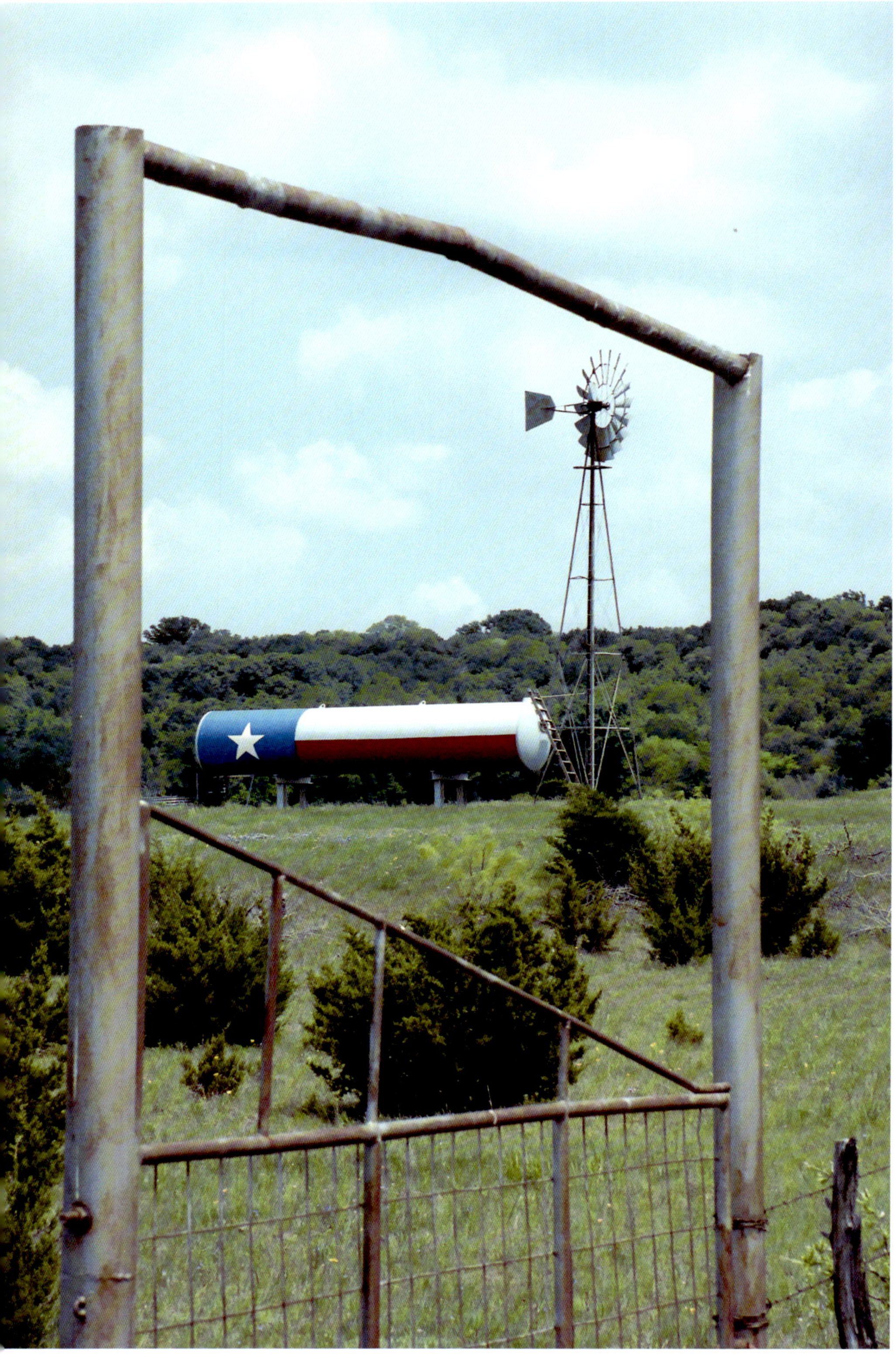

"Water Tank" (Prudence Jones family farm, Lanham), 2005

A Lone Star water tank sits in the field all alone, framed by one of Prudence Jones's farm gates. The Jones family farm is located in Lanham on State Highway 22. Keep up with the Joneses.

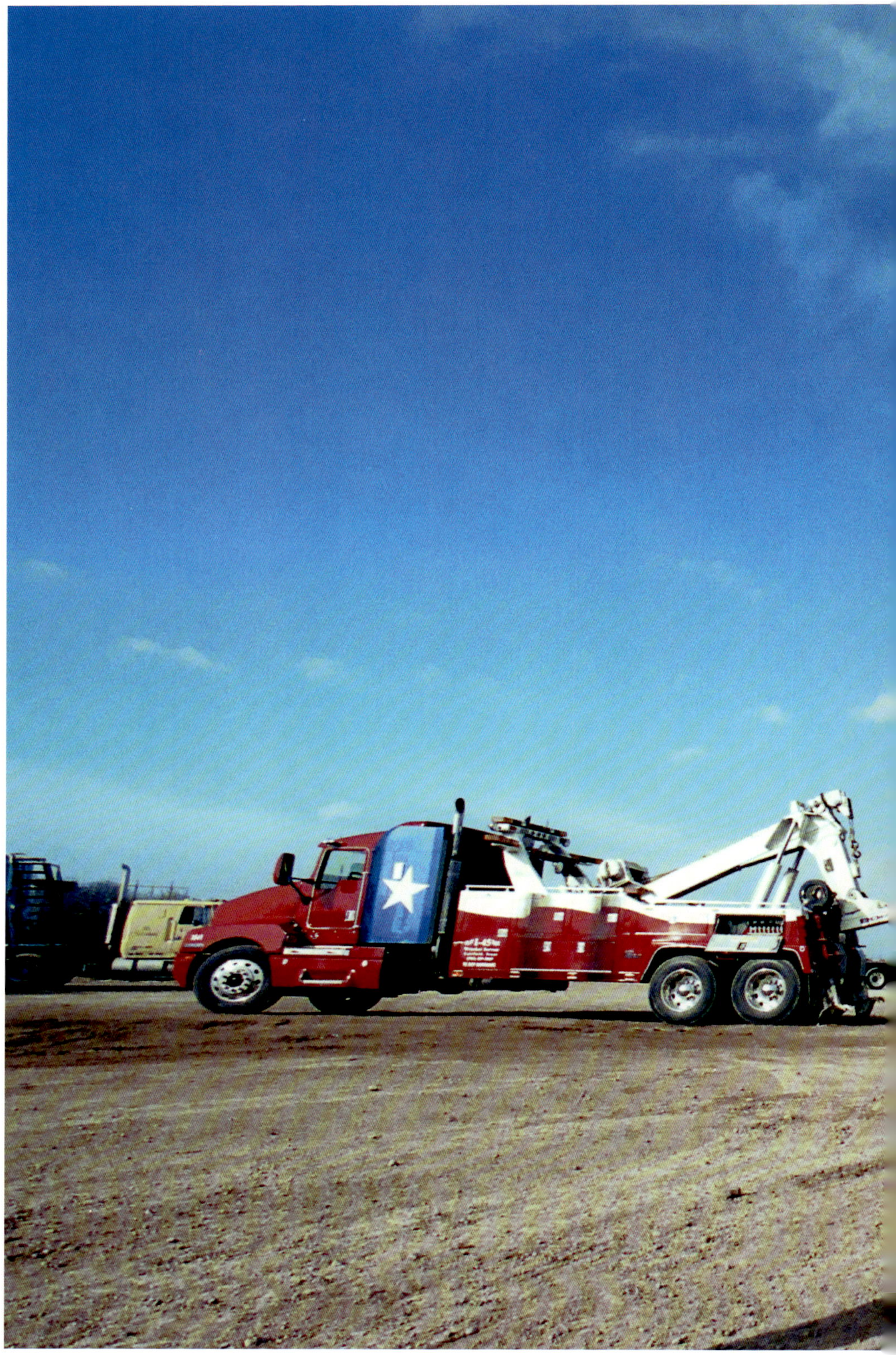

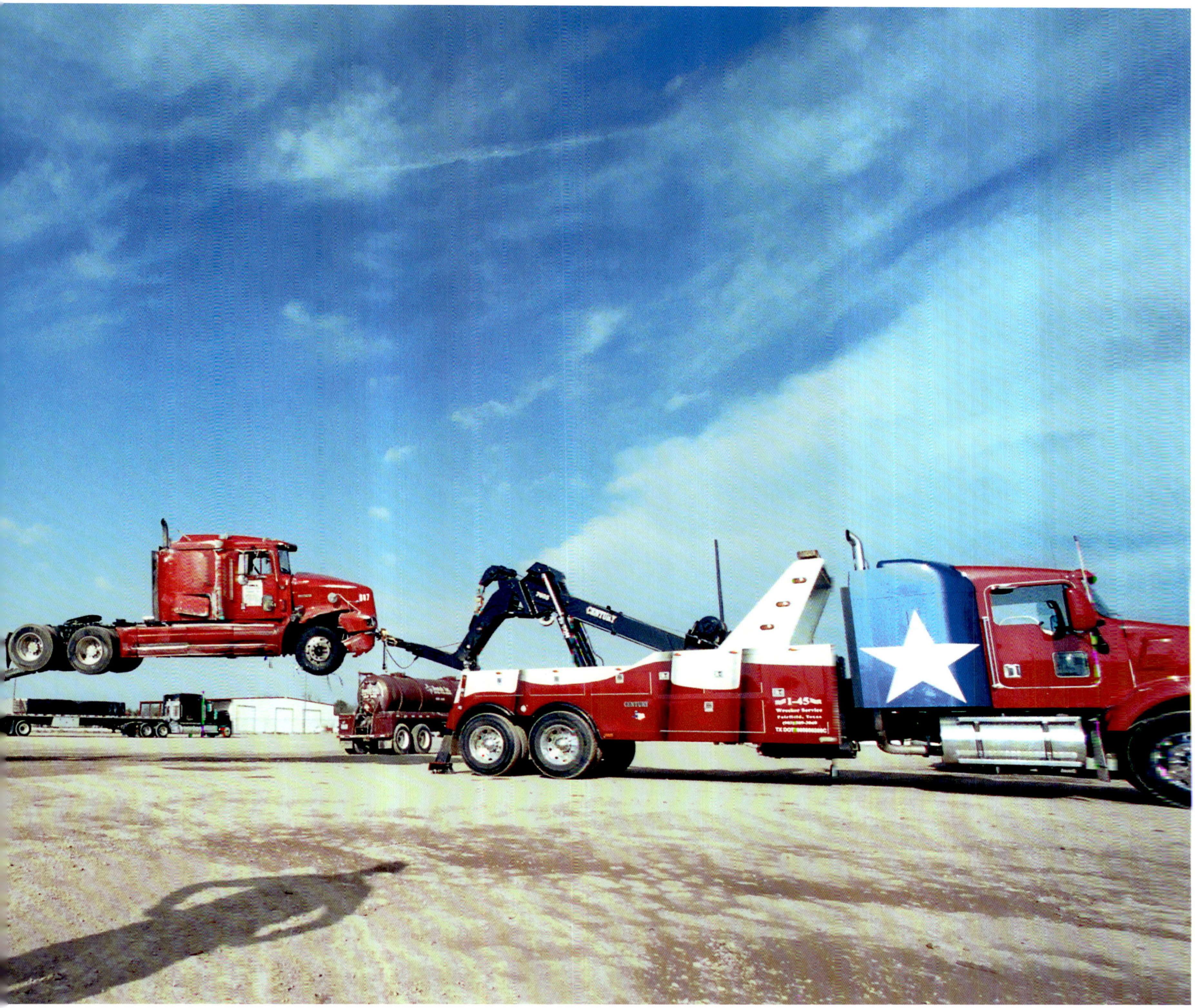

"Long Tall Texan" (I-45 Wrecker Co., Fairfield), 2004

Owner David James's shadow casts a long form, pointing out his two 2000 Kenworth tow trucks. These Lone Star wreckers can handle thirty-five to fifty tons and have come to the aid of many a longhauler passing through Texas. Hook 'em

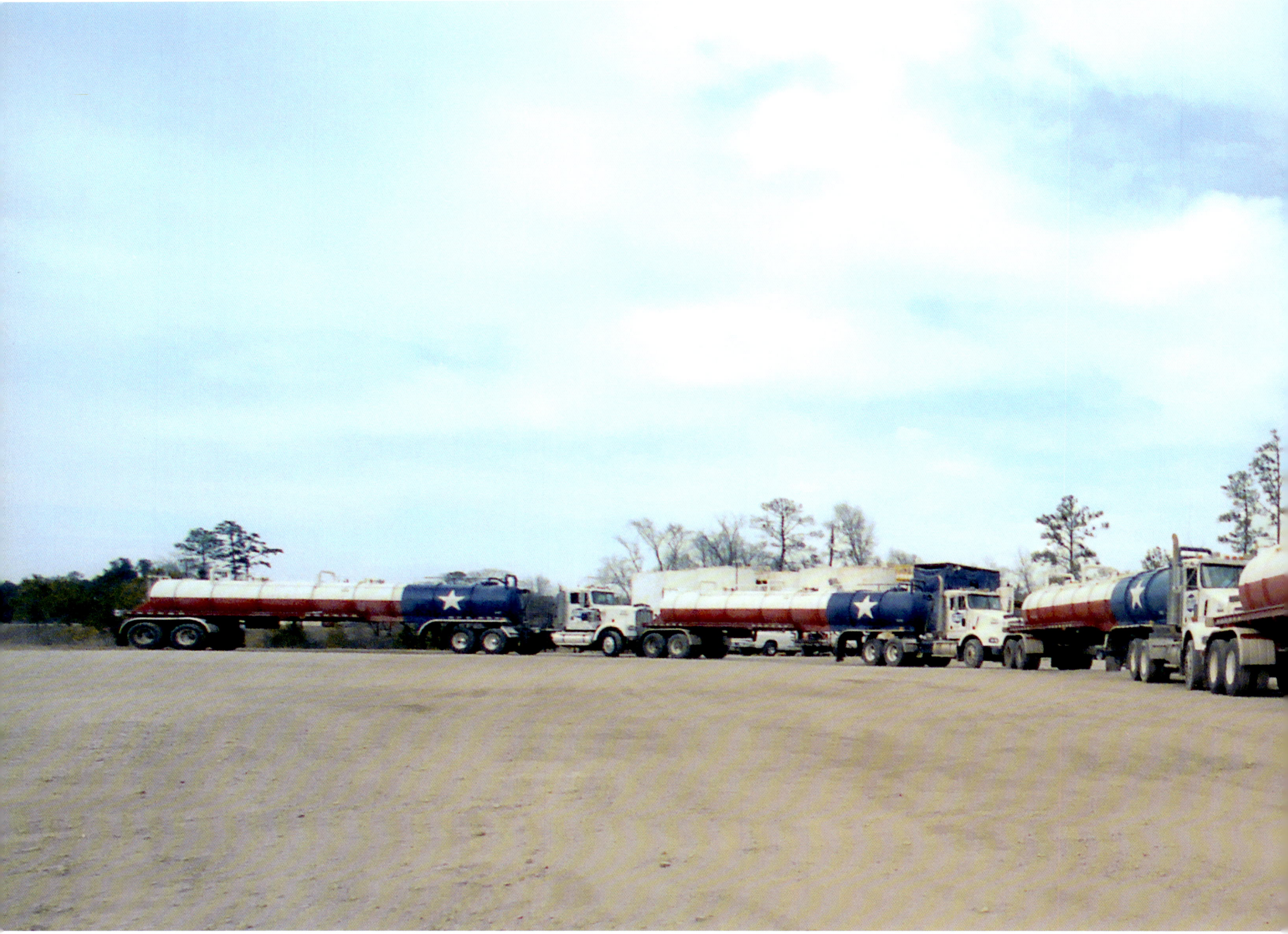

"Tanker Line" (Steve Simpson & Associates, Brookland), 2005

At the start of the day, Lone Star tanker trucks line up at Steve Simpson & Associates, Inc., in Brookland, a small East Texas town. The company specializes in drilling fluids and twenty-four-hour vacuum services. It's a gusher.

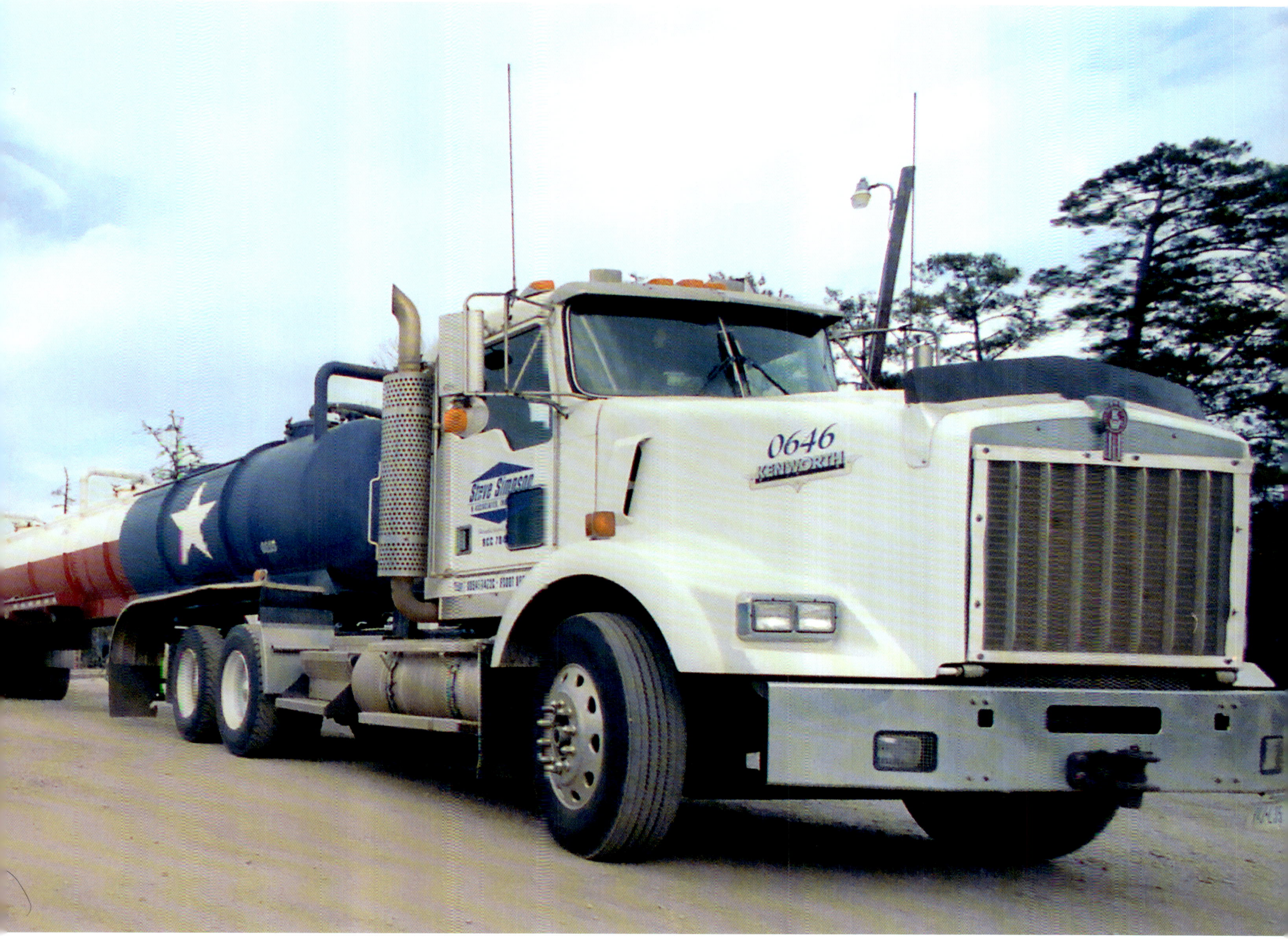
Steve Simpson
0646
KENWORTH

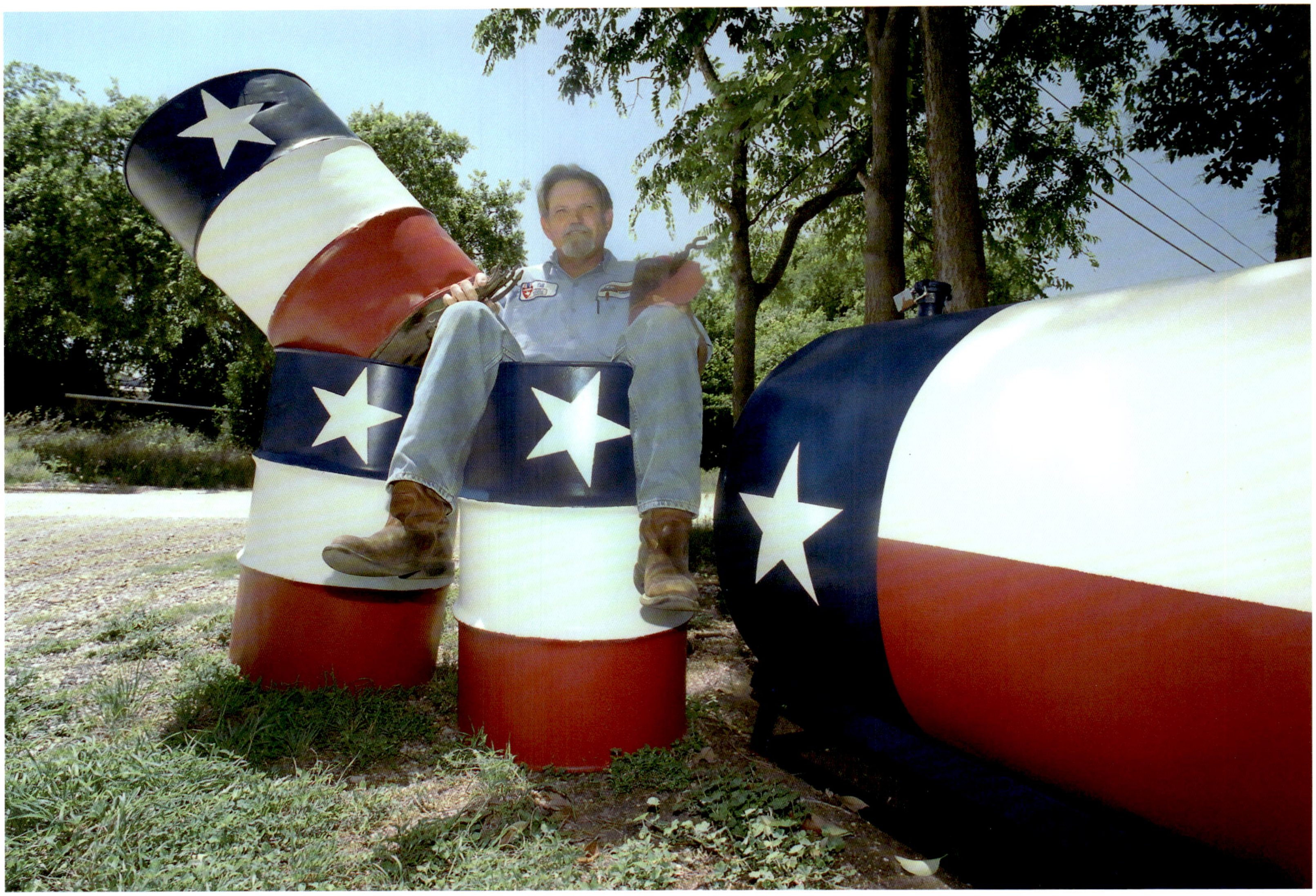

"Over a Barrel" (John's Garage, Kerrville), 2005

Bill Lackey, owner of John's Garage in Kerrville, sits on top of one of his fifty-five-gallon barrels, along with an old-time oil drum used for recycled oil. Bill has run the garage, started by his father, for more than fifty years. Bill painted the barrels himself. Drumming up business.

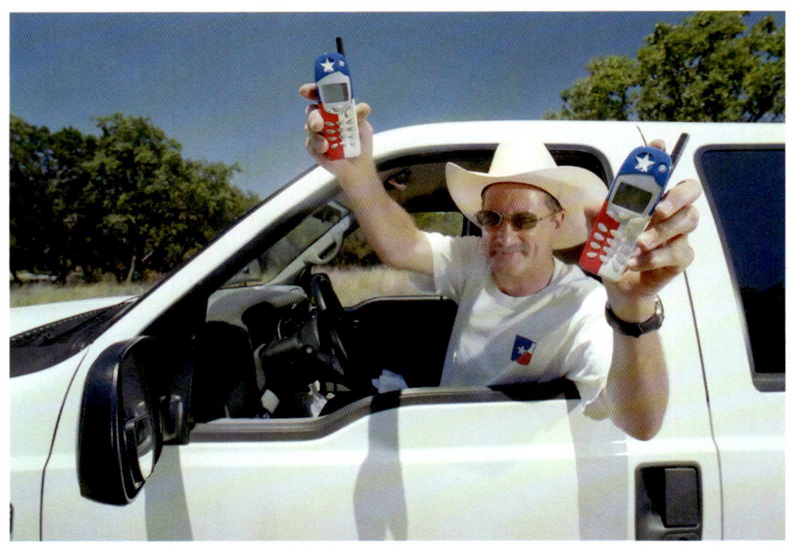

"Phone Home" (Jim Daigle, Kerrville), 2005

In Kerrville, wearing his ever-present western hat, Jim Daigle chats on his Lone Star cell phones.

"Army" (Kerrville), 2007

For artist Becky Beale, there's no mistaking the theme of "Army" the Armadillo. Army's permanent home is the office of Dist. 53 State Rep. Harvey Hilderbran. No road kill here.

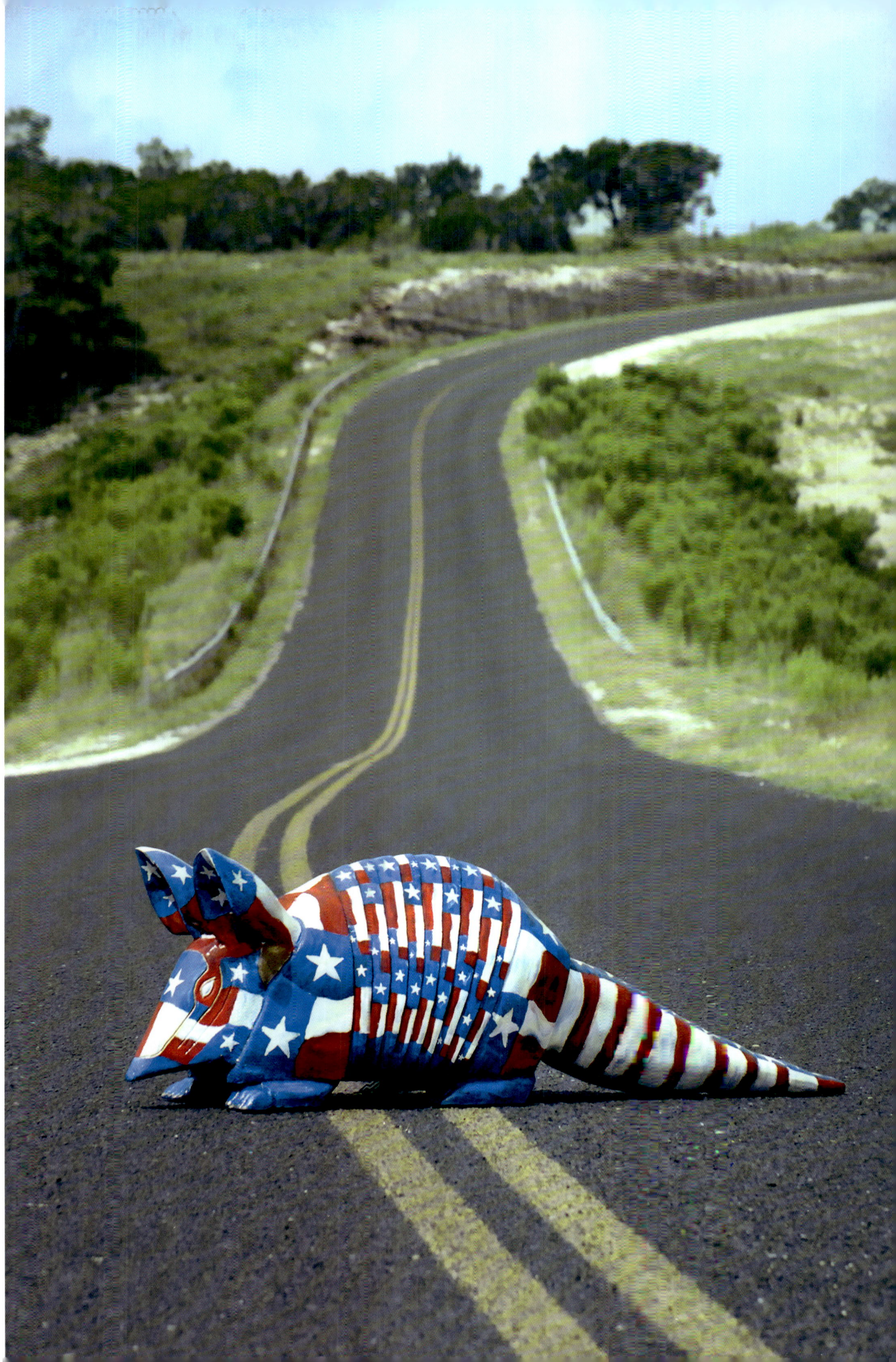

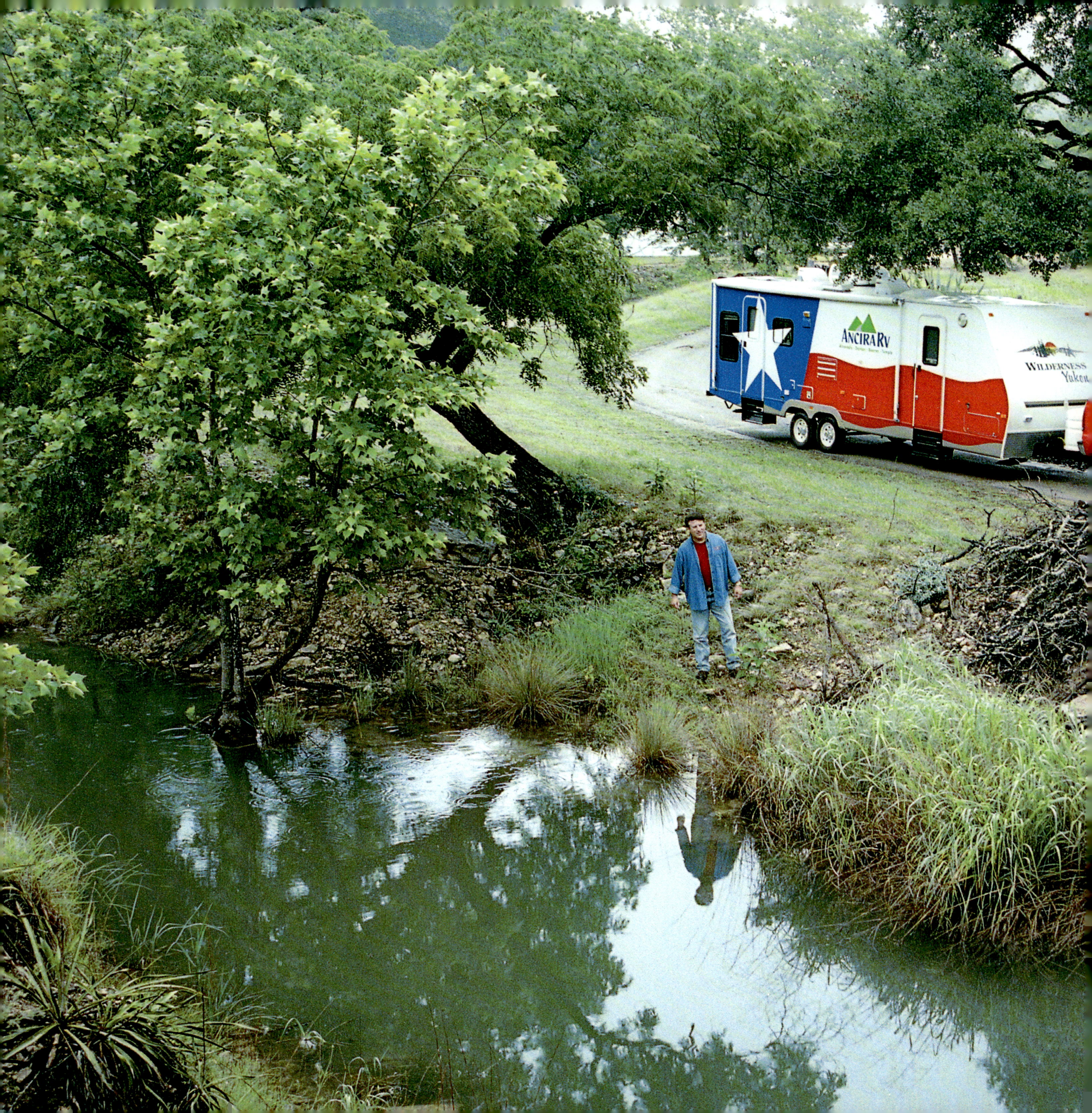
ANCIRA RV
WILDERNESS
Yukon

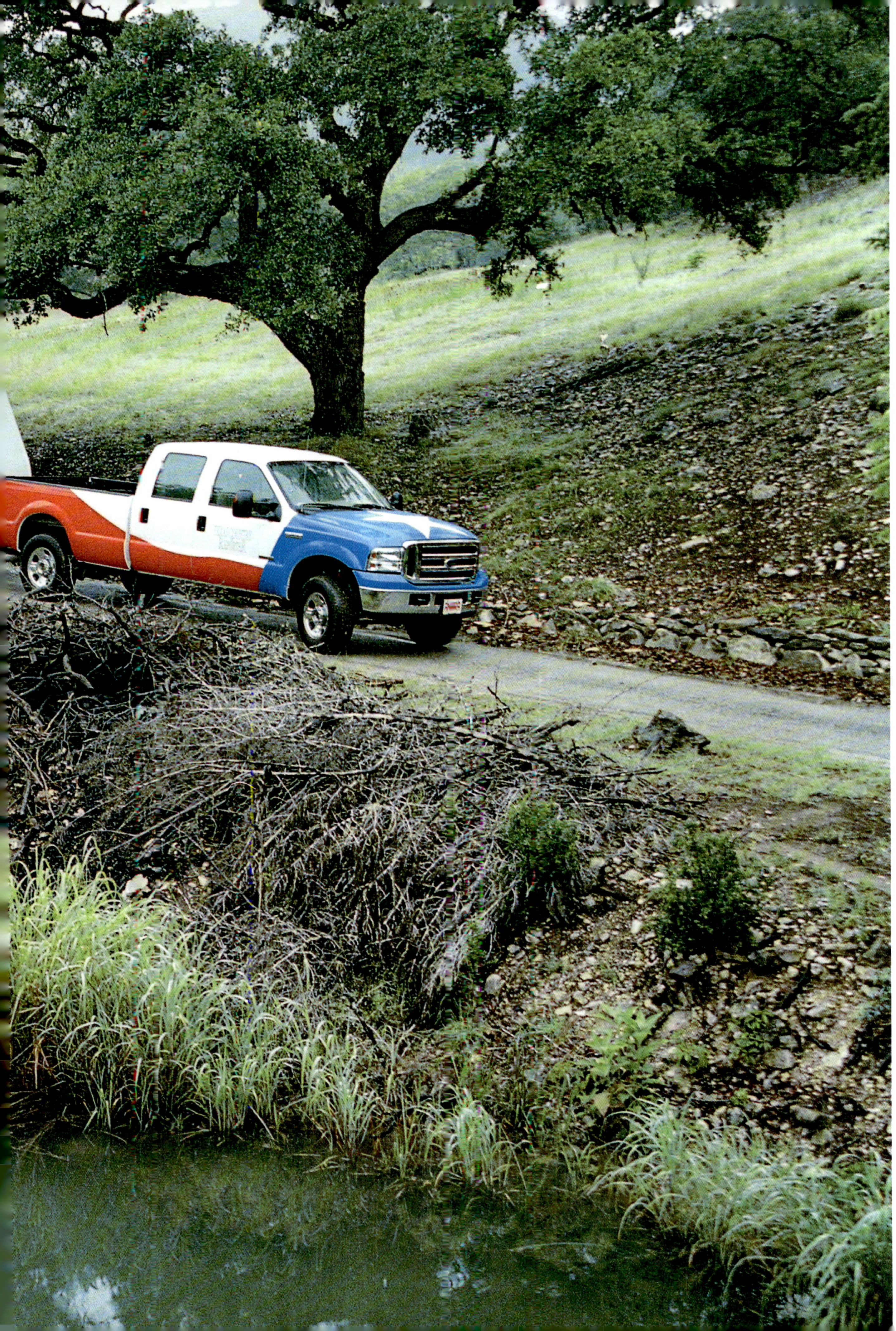

"Newshound" (Texas Country Reporter, *Medina*), 2005

Bob Phillips has been traveling the Lone Star state for more than twenty years, reporting on all the highways and byways. Bob is well known for his top-notch reporting and his vehicles. As seen on TV.

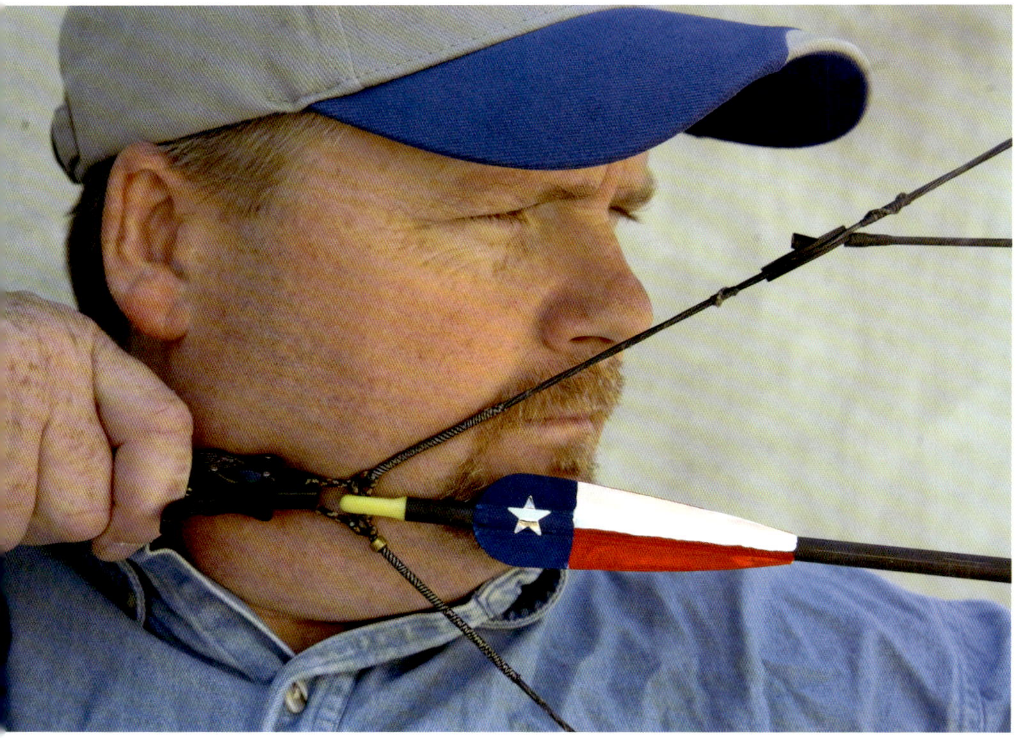

"Take Aim" (Scott Van Klaveren), 2006

Archer Scott Van Klaveren, an avid Texas bow hunter for more than twenty years, lines up his shot using a compound bow. His homemade arrow's fletching sports the Long Star flag. Bull's-eye.

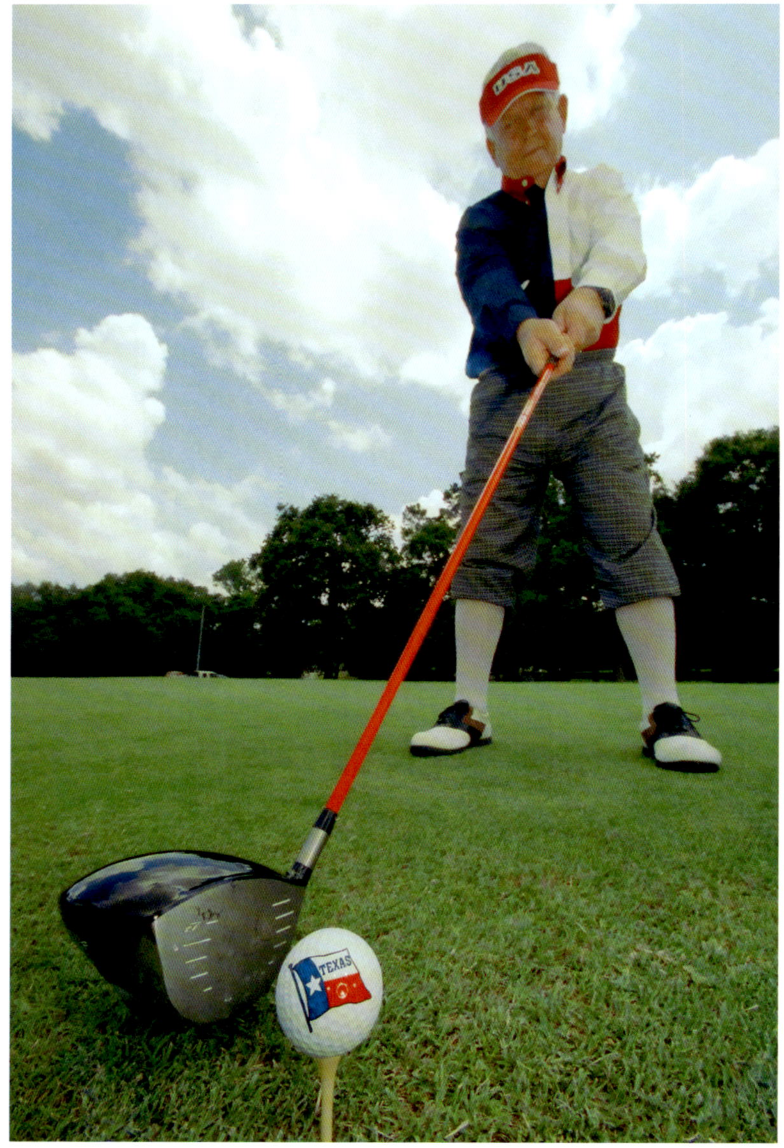

"Fore" (Johnny Storenski, Houston), 2005

Johnny Storenski tees off, dressed to a "T" in his Lone Star outfit. Johnny, the owner of Josephine's Restaurant in Houston, sponsors a golf tournament every year to benefit a charity in the Houston area. Straight down the middle.

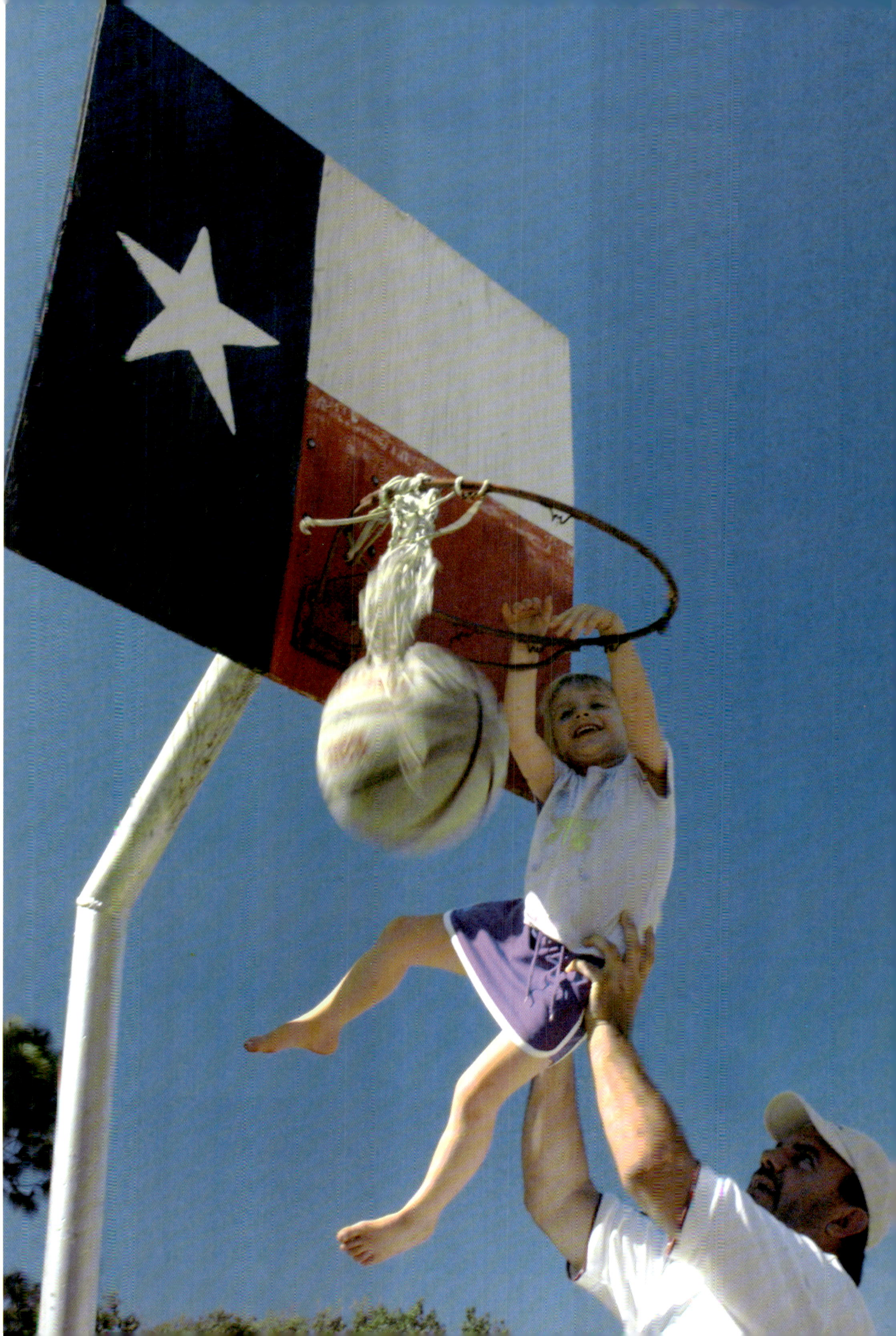

"Slam Dunk" (The Drapela Family, El Campo), 2007

Little slammer Patty Drapela, age 4, of Richmond, slams one down with the help of her father, James, at her grandmother's home in El Campo. The Lone Star backboard was painted by her Aunt Patty. Two points.

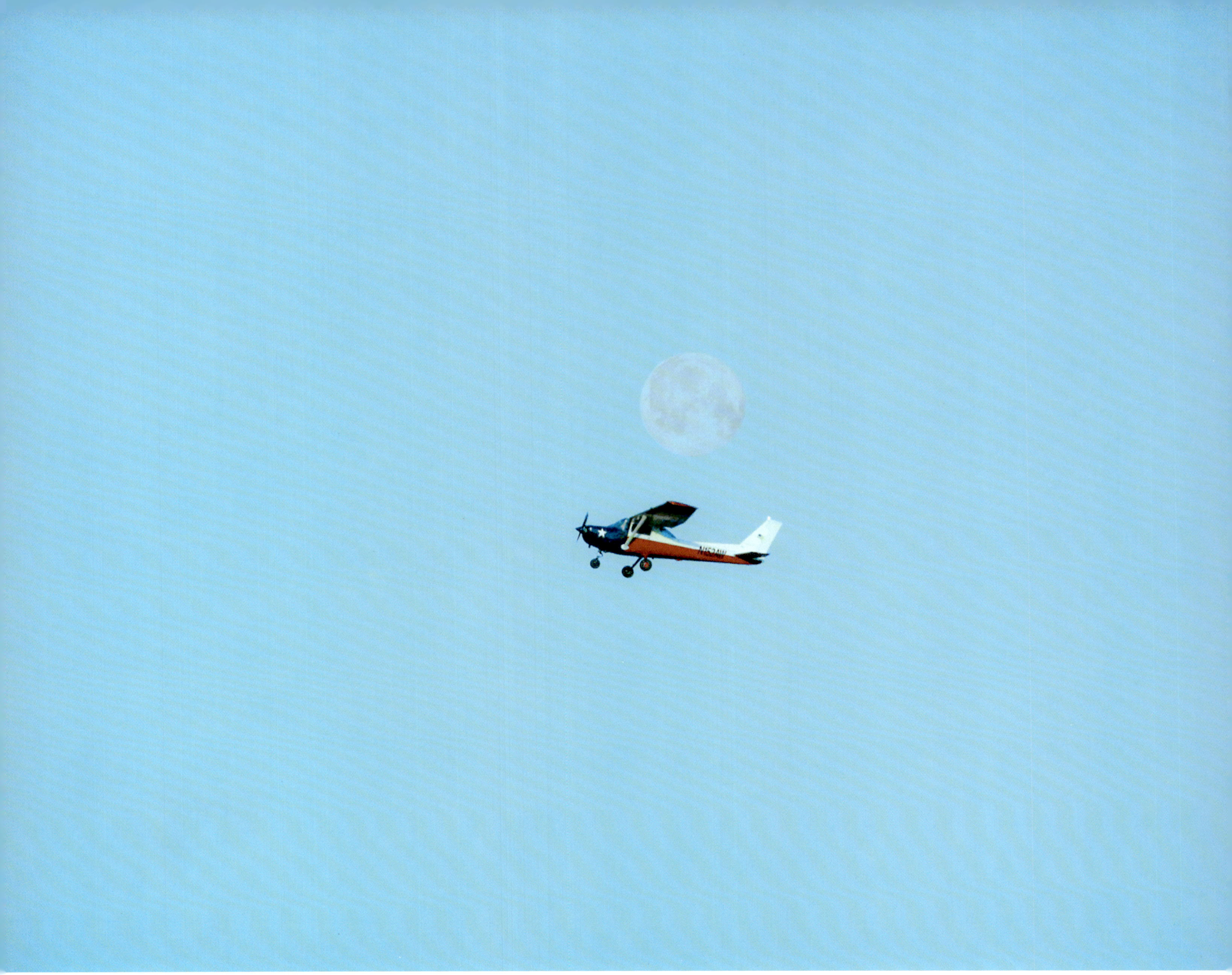

"Harvest Moon" (Anse Windham, Kingsville), 2005

With the wind at his back, Anse Windham glides past a full moon during an early morning flight. Anse is well known throughout the state for his single-engine Lone Star flag airplane. Flying high.

Afterword

TURNING THE LENS ON THE PHOTOGRAPHER

WHILE ON ASSIGNMENT in Cisco, Texas, one day in the year 2002, *Houston Chronicle* photographer E. Joe Deering was trying to find just the right setting for a magazine story. There in that Eastland County town of about four thousand, he noticed a Lone Star flag painted on the side of a building. Not fifteen minutes later a pickup truck drove by with a Texas flag painted on the side of the door. E. Joe thought, "Well, isn't that interesting?"

From Cisco he had to go to Lubbock. "On my way to Lubbock, I passed a barn with the flag painted on its roof, and that's when it hit me: there might be something to this flag thing. Then I started looking for them."

He was not quite sure what he was going to do with the Lone Star pictures, but he decided then that he would start photographing everything "Lone Star" he saw. And so began the project that led to the compiling of this book.

It might seem odd that E. Joe, a native of Michigan, would be the person to chronicle Texans' obsession with their state flag. After graduating from high school in Kalamazoo, E. Joe joined the U.S. Army. After a three-and-a-half-year stint, he returned to Michigan and took entrance exams at Michigan State University. There, a

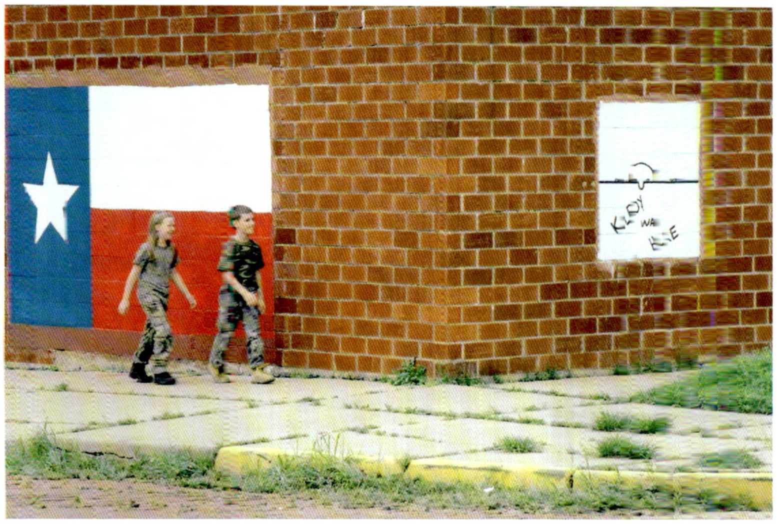

counselor told E. Joe he would be better suited with a major or career that was "creative."

"In the interview after the exam, a counselor told me that there were three areas of intelligence. One was centered on learning, one was practical, and one was creative. He told me to forget about the first two," E. Joe says.

"That was really a turning point in my life. Everybody tried to make me book smart, and I'm not. So I quit trying to be that kind of smart."

E. Joe thought about going into commercial art but was then introduced to photography. He soon found himself enrolled at Brooks Institute in Santa Barbara, California. After he graduated, he got a job with the *Houston Chronicle,* where he spent his entire career.

Even though E. Joe isn't a native Texan, he sounds and acts like one. Having lived most of his life in Texas and traveled all across the state, E. Joe said he finally grasped the underlying reason so many people painted the Lone Star flag: "It's just because they like being in Texas and being a Texan. It's that Texas pride."

Lone Star Gazing

"In my line of work, I'm always looking for story ideas, visual story ideas. I was always looking for stuff like that," he explains. "I never got a chance to photograph that barn or the truck in Cisco, but I sure did start looking for other stuff."

Whenever he was out and about, E. Joe kept an eye peeled for representations of the flag. No matter what town he was visiting, he would always ask about such images at the local visitors' center, Chamber of Commerce office, local diner, or convenience store. One of the first pictures he took was of Vernie and Mary Ford's restaurant in the small Texas Panhandle town of Clarendon. The Clarendon Steakhouse not only boasts hearty meals but also images of the Texas and U.S. flags painted on the side of the building. If that's not enough red, white, and blue, the couple also greets customers at the front door with Lone Star flag welcome mats.

As the number of flag uses started to mount, E. Joe told colleagues and friends about his newfound project. Fellow *Chronicle* photographers Carlos Rios and Kevin Fuji were diligent in reporting flags they spotted. E. Joe's scouts found them as backgrounds on billboards and businesses and on items as small as jewelry and rocks and as big as airplanes and hot air balloons. People would approach E. Joe, saying, "You've probably already got it, but I saw this at . . ." E. Joe wanted to know; he checked everything out.

"Most people are thrilled when I ask to photograph," E. Joes says, "because it's something they did and someone is interested in it. It has really been fun for me."

E. Joe was busy snapping Lone Star pictures without any plan in mind when Catherine McIntosh, an editor at the *Chronicle* caught wind of what he was doing. Planning to use them for a photo spread in the *Texas* magazine the *Chronicle* featured weekly in the Sunday edition, she gave him six months to collect more pictures.

Like any photographer or reporter, E. Joe wanted more time for his project. And, like most editors, his editor gave him none. The result of the assignment was an assortment of photos covering eight pages that appeared on Sunday, October 13, 2002.

The magazine piece led to even more phone calls and e-mails to E. Joe from readers who wanted to tell him about their own uses of the Lone Star flag or others they had seen that they thought he might be interested in photographing.

Lone Stars on Display

The publication was also noticed by Patricia Burchfield, who was at that time the curator at the George Bush Presidential Library and Museum in College Station, who was planning a Texas flag exhibit at the library. Burchfield tucked away the magazine piece. About a year after E. Joe's magazine spread appeared in the *Chronicle,* Burchfield contacted him to ask permission to display some of his pictures at the library in conjunction with the exhibit of restored historic flags.

"She asked if they could use twenty or thirty images for an exhibit," E. Joe remembers. "I mentioned to her that it wasn't my call and that I had to check with the powers that be. Of course, the *Chronicle* said, 'yes.'"

The thought of having his photographs displayed at the Bush Museum came as a thrill and honor to E. Joe. "A couple of weeks went by and I got to thinking: I might want to make my own frames. On assignment, I would photograph all these craft shows and bazaars, and I would see people making frames from old wood. I always liked them and thought that's what I'd like to do."

E. Joe approached Burchfield with the idea and, while she didn't say no, she told him she would have to get approval. A few days later, she called back and gave E. Joe the go-ahead.

Now, not only was E. Joe still working full-time and traveling across the state for the *Chronicle,* he was photographing Lone Star images and making frames for them. He started out fashioning them into regular square shapes to fit his pictures, but in typical E. Joe fashion, he decided that just wasn't right.

"I started thinking regular, rectangular frames would be like everybody else's out there. I began incorporating little things to make them look different," E. Joe said. His newly imagined frames became works of art in themselves.

Burchfield called and asked to see some of the frames. E. Joe and his sister, Mary drove to College Station to meet with Burchfield at the library. E. Joe had a half-dozen photos he had framed to show to Burchfield as an example of his work.

"We went into her office and she got sidetracked with a phone call and asked me to set them up. There was a little corner in the room where there was some space. I just set them up there. She had to walk around her desk to look at them.

"She didn't say anything," E. Joe recalls. "She was just looking at them and said, 'Oh my god,' and then walked out of her office. On her way out, she said, 'I'll be right back.'"

E. Joe and his sister stood there, perplexed. E. Joe remembers shrugging his shoulders not knowing what to think. Would the museum say, "Thanks, but no thanks"?

By the time Burchfield returned to her office, it seemed to E. Joe that he and Mary had been standing there for a long time. Following her, a number of museum employees trickled into the office to look at the photos and frames. Soon E. Joe figured out that Burchfield approved of the frames and had only left her office to round up fellow employees to inspect the work.

"Patricia Burchfield turned to me and said, 'Can you come up with seventy-five to a hundred of these?' I said, 'Sure.' That's how it all started."

Burchfield's initial request had been for use of twenty or thirty images; that number had now quadrupled. "The library people were all offering compliments. Then they started asking me questions, wanting some reassurances that I could come up with that many frames," he said. "Being in the museum business, they realized the magnitude of what it was going to take to come up with ideas for the frames; never mind making them. Plus, I had a full-time job."

Getting Framed

E. Joe had one year to make 135 frames and take more photographs to put in them. He already had a list of subjects he wanted to photograph. The frames and photos were to appear in a display at the museum set to open in July 2005.

E. Joe was relentless in hunting down Lone Star subjects and diligently worked at creating his one-of-a-kind frames in his garage workshop. He collected old, weathered wood wherever he saw it. Friends and neighbors also gave him some. At one point, E. Joe stopped and inquired about getting wood from a home that was being torn down. The home was surrounded by a wooden fence. The demolition crew gladly allowed E. Joe to gather the wood from the fence and remove it from the property.

The creativity shown by E. Joe in not only shooting the Lone Star flag photos but in making the unique frames is no surprise to those who know him. Unlike with his photographic subject matter, where he welcomed suggestions from friends and colleagues, E. Joe wanted his frames to be originals. "Don't give an idea for a frame because if you do I'm not going to use it," he would say. "I didn't want people to go to the exhibit and see a frame that wasn't my original idea. I didn't want someone to say, 'that wasn't his idea. I gave him that idea.'"

He may not have wanted ideas for the frames, but E. Joe gladly accepted trinkets, or "do-dads," as he calls them, to incorporate into the frames. "When they walk by the frames at the exhibit, people could say, 'There's my little do-dad.'"

For the speeding patrol car of the Palmer Police Department, E. Joe had made a frame to resemble a jail cell, complete with a lock. The frame for the swing photo in Corrigan in Polk County was hung from two chains, making it look like a swing itself. The wooden drugstore cowboy with a Lone Star ashtray was mounted in a frame that included red wood matches. The small frame showcasing the bumper and Lone Star flag license plate of Houston bootmaker Rick Montana's 1949 Chevy truck was accented with barbed wire. The Lone Star steer picture was framed and accented with a cow bell.

Those first examples set the standard for the hundred-plus other frames E. Joe made, each designed and fitted specifically for the image it would hold. For one of his mailbox photos, E. Joe built the outline of a mailbox with a handle the viewer pulled down to reveal the photo inside. Mimicking many mailboxes out in the country, he included a holder for a newspaper: the *Houston Chronicle,* of course—the April 19, 2005 edition (E. Joe's sixty-second birthday and the day he retired from the *Chronicle*).

A photo of an East Texas barn in Diboll nestled among lush trees was set into a frame that resembled a window. A photo of a barn in Karnack, its doors painted to resemble the flag and boasting a life-size cutout of John Wayne leaning against the building, is in a frame with the initials "J. W." and a lasso on the frame. E. Joe made a "fire ladder" to display two photos showing the Baytown Fire Department fire truck with the Texas flag on the grill.

Artist Pat Glenn, a former Houstonian retired to the Hill Country community of Blanco, has an art studio up on the side of a hill among the lush greenery and wild flowers, where he goes to make what he calls "stuff." The studio is an odd-shaped, two-story structure with a steep sloping roof on half the building. The outside of the two-story section is painted blue with a white star, while the other half is white on top and red below. E. Joe photographed Glenn on the adjoining deck, flying an American and a Texas flag. E. Joe set the studio shot into a frame made with an angle that parallels that of the roof of the art studio itself.

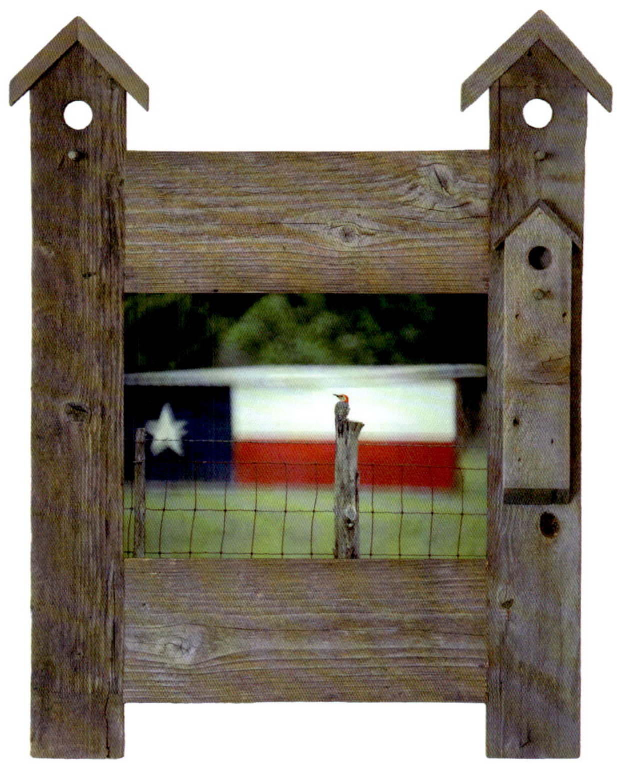

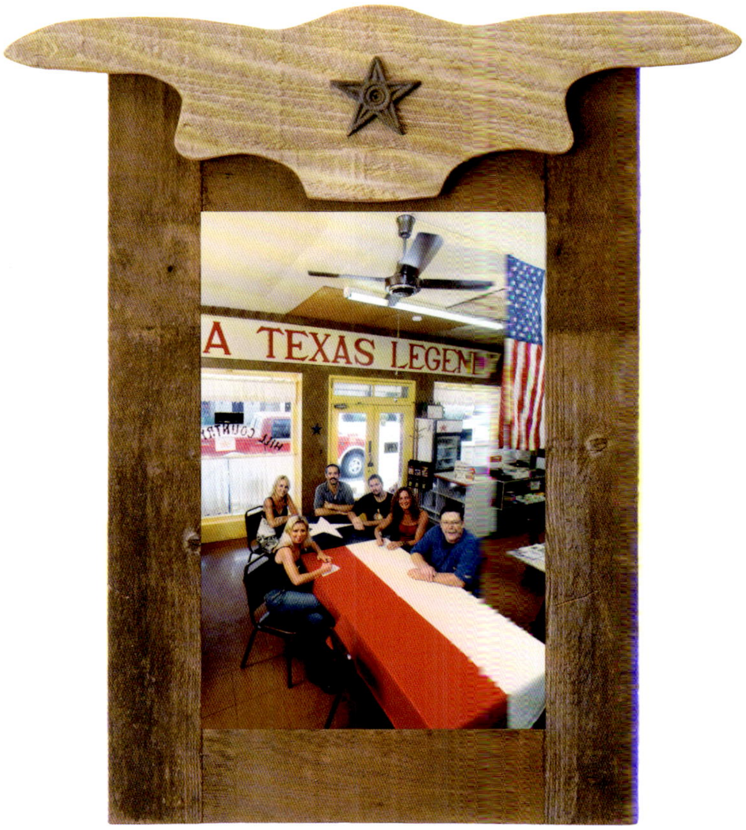

Driving through Dayton in Liberty County, E. Joe had noticed a red, white, and blue item at a muffler shop. Investigating, he found that owner Denny A. D. Talley had taken an old muffler and painted it like the flag. Talley had wrapped the muffler around other old muffler parts to create a muffler Longhorn. E. Joe set Talley's muffler Longhorn into a muffler-shaped frame. Mike and Cleo Castelos, of Fort Stockton, who own the oldest restaurant in the area, are shown holding a stock pot. The frame is shaped like a pot with a spoon and handle on the side.

The framed photos E. Joe took of the many Lone Star windmills are all tied together with rope. "You see so many windmills but every one is different," E. Joe remarked.

The frame for the photo of the Alamo is shaped like the Texas landmark, and E. Joe created a double star frame to showcase the Lone Star Jeep dredging through the water.

A Star is Born

E. Joe recruited a Houston photographer buddy, Mark Burns, to help him print the pictures. When the exhibit opened in 2005, the *Bryan–College Station Eagle* ran a big story on it, and a number of daily and weekly papers around the state wrote about their local icons that were pictured in the show. "It was a packed house," E. Joe said.

Many—maybe half—of the people whose depictions of the flag were exhibited came to the opening. Butter (otherwise known as Rolando De La Garza), the ice sculptor from Houston, was there, and the Lone Star–adorned hang glider and hot air balloon were on display. When members of the staff at Texas A&M University Press visited the exhibit, they shared the enthusiasm of other visitors, and the idea for this book was born.

Index